THE FUTURE OF JEWISH-CHRISTIAN RELATIONS

Edited by

Dr. Norma H. Thompson
Rabbi Bruce K. Cole

Best wishes to
George Alexander
with wonderful memories
of New York University

Norma Thompson
april 5, 1997

International Standard Book Number 0-915744-27-9 (hard cover)
International Standard Book Number 0-915744-28-7 (paperback)
First Printing

© Copyright 1982
Norma H. Thompson

Typesetting
by
Helen C. Cernik

Keystroked
by
Norma M. Crookes

THE FUTURE OF JEWISH-CHRISTIAN RELATIONS

Edited by

Dr. Norma H. Thompson
Rabbi Bruce K. Cole

Published by:

Character Research Press
266 State Street
Schenectady, New York 12305

DEDICATORY PREFACE

This volume on *The Future of Jewish-Christian Relations* is dedicated to

LEE A. BELFORD
Teacher, Leader, Colleague, Friend

on behalf of all those persons in churches, synagogues, universities, seminaries, schools, and agencies whose lives he has touched with a deep sense of commitment, great humility, and wisdom, coupled with a profound sense of humor.

* * * * * *

Lee A. Belford is a native of Savannah, Georgia. After graduating from college and seminary at the University of the South, Sewanee, Tennessee, he served churches in Douglas and Brunswick, Georgia. In 1943 he became a Navy Chaplain. After the war he came to New York for graduate study, receiving his S.T.M. degree from Union Theological Seminary and his Ph.D. degree from Columbia University. He served as Chairman of the Department of Religious Education, New York University, from 1954 to 1974, during which time he was active in Civil Rights and Jewish-Christian Relations. He retired from New York University in August, 1979. His wife, Cora Louise Belford, and his two daughters, Fontaine Belford and Mimi Belford Okino, encouraged his involvement in social causes and provided an atmosphere of Southern graciousness to his activities.

FOREWORD

Throughout history, at least for the past few thousand years anyway, in the name of God and institutional religion, "peace on earth — goodwill to men"[1] has been a most elusive goal. Rather, there has been a history of competition among a variety of Christian religious groups to save everyone's soul from eternal perdition. All too often, the souls the institutional church finds afflicted and in need of saving are the Jews, whose religion in fact lies at the base of the early Christian church. Rather than giving adulation, honor, and respect to its parent, the offspring Christian church chose a course of intimidation, vilification and physical harm directed against the parent, the Jews. This antagonism was reflected in certain passages of Gospel, especially John.

Early church fathers such as John Chrysostom spurred their congregations to action in sermons, often during Holy Week preceding Easter, which gave vent to such hatred of Jews that Jewish communities during that period would lock themselves in their homes for fear of physical harm, or even death, at the hands of vengeful Christian mobs. Jews were accused of Deicide, and were cast in the role of scapegoat. All the ills of society were laid upon the Jews.

This antagonism against Jews culminated in mankind's darkest hour when, in the early 1940's, six million Jews — men, women, and children — were put to death by Nazi Germany merely because these citizens were of a faith different from and despised by the majority.

It was the inescapable reality of the Holocaust burning itself indelibly into the minds of all people that started a process in the institutionalized Christian church which would culminate in the then most dramatic statement about Jews which has changed the course of Christian thinking throughout the world, namely the 1965 Vatican Council II declaration that a) Jews are not guilty of Deicide; and b) that anti-Semitism is unacceptable.

The Vatican declaration set in motion a number of similar statements by national and international church groups which have been collected in an important volume by Helga Croner.[2]

It is against this backdrop that the stage was set for a great leap forward in Christian-Jewish relations in the United States, and it was this "stage-set" that gave the Rev. Dr. Lee A. Belford the momentum and recognition for his work, begun well before Vatican Council II.

Dr. Belford was painfully aware of official Christian attitudes to Jews and consequently Jewish hesitancy to accept the outstretched hands of Christians who truly wanted to dialogue with Jews.

This frustration resulted in Dr. Belford's first book, *An Introduction to Judaism*,[3] written for a Christian audience to pave the way for a beginning of understanding of Jews and Judaism and to begin to show Jews that there were sincere Christians who really wanted to converse with Jews — not to proselytize but to meet as co-equals. His persistence, coupled with his deep and sincere love of all peoples, resulted in his being named as the first chairman of the Committee on Episcopal-Jewish Relations of the Diocese of New York.

It is therefore most appropriate that this book is dedicated to him in recognition for his inspirational leadership. The collection of essays herein were delivered at a symposium in Dr. Belford's honor at New York University upon his retirement.

Bruce K. Cole
New York, New York 1981

NOTES

1. or: "Peace on earth to men of good will."

2. Helga Croner, *Stepping Stones to Further Jewish-Christian Relations.* New York Stimulus Books, 1977.

3. Lee A. Belford, *An Introduction to Judaism.* New York: Association Press, 1961.

TABLE OF CONTENTS

Dedicatory Preface............................... v

Foreword.. vii
  Bruce K. Cole

Introduction..................................... xiii
  Norma H. Thompson

Editors' Foreword................................ xxi
  Norma H. Thompson and Bruce K. Cole

**Part I.   Social Justice from the
            Prophetic Point of View.**.............. 1

Chapter 1. Social Justice from the
            Prophetic Point of View.................. 3
            Robert E. Hood

Chapter 2. Social Justice and the Prophets............ 45
            John J. Kelley

Chapter 3. Social Justice:
            A Developing Concept.................... 65
            John J. Kelley

**Part II.   The Holocaust from the Christian
            Perspective.**.......................... 81

Chapter 4. Some Christian Views of the
            Holocaust............................. 83
            Katharine Hargrove

Chapter 5. After the Holocaust:
            Some Christian Considerations............ 111
            Alice and Roy Eckardt

Chapter 6. Genocide and Resistance:
            Christian Perspectives of the Holocaust...... 127
            Hubert Locke

Part III.   **The Future of Jewish-Christian**
             Relations.   139

Chapter 7.   Future Agenda for Catholic-Jewish
             Relations.   141
             Eugene Fisher

Chapter 8.   New Revelations and New Patterns
             in the Relationship of Judaism
             and Christianity.   159
             Irving Greenberg

Part IV.   **Tensions in Jewish-Christian**
             Relations Arising from
             Mission and Liturgy.   183

Chapter 9.   The Gospel Passion Narratives
             and Jews.   185
             Paul J. Kirsch

Chapter 10. Jesus: Bond or Barrier to
             Jewish-Christian Relations.   205
             Cynthia L. Bronson

Part V.   **Attitudes to be Developed in**
             Education.   211

Chapter 11. Introducing Judaism:
             The First Course and Its Problems.   213
             Jacob Neusner

Chapter 12. An Inconclusive Unscientific
             Postscript.   235
             Paul R. Carlson

Addendum on Matthew 5:17 and Anti-Semitism.   277
             Hays H. Rockwell

INTRODUCTION

At the time of Lee A. Belford's retirement from the faculty of the Program in Religious Education at New York University there seemed no more appropriate way to honor him than to hold a conference on Jewish-Christian Relations and to assemble a book of essays on that subject which would be used as a basis for such a conference. That conference was held in June, 1979, at New York University, and this book is the result of the scholarly essays written on the subject of "The Future of Jewish-Christian Relations," most of which were presented in person at the conference itself. The conference was co-sponsored by the Program in Religious Education, New York University; the Anti-Defamation League of B'nai B'rith, New York Regional Office; and the Episcopal Diocese of New York.

Belford spent many hours during his twenty-seven years of association with New York University working for causes related to social justice and, in particular, to racism and to Jewish-Christian relations. He has said that he felt that being a white Southerner and a Christian imposed a personal responsibility upon him in regard to racial discrimination and anti-Jewish feeling. It was in the South that the greatest injustice toward Blacks occurred. Jews had always suffered at the hands of Christians and even though the Holocaust was not perpetrated by Christians, it occurred in a country that was overwhelmingly Christian by confession and acquiesced to by the majority in much of Christian Europe.

Belford was an early member of the Episcopal Society for Cultural and Racial Unity. He was chosen to be the chaplain of a group of twenty-eight clergy who toured the South in what was referred to as a freedom ride. Most of the clergy were jailed in Jackson, Mississippi. He participated in and enlisted support for the marches in Washington, Selma, and elsewhere. He claims that his most dangerous assignments were as an observer with a Black priest of trouble spots in the South for the National

Council of Churches. One of the purposes of being an observer was to reconcile hostile forces before violence occurred. As a place of retirement he chose a little town in Mississippi where two-thirds of the population is Black.

In reference to Jews, he wrote a booklet called "The Christian and His Jewish Neighbor," which has been widely used as a discussion-action guide. Because most Christians are unfamiliar with postbiblical Judaism, he wrote a book called *Introduction to Judaism* to fill the gap. It was also printed in Germany in German and in England with certain modifications. He has written a number of articles concerned with Christian-Jewish relations. He served for many years as Chairman of the Committee on Jewish Relations of the Episcopal Diocese of New York. His Committee met with a committee from the Anti-Defamation League for discussion, study, and action when needed. The Committee published a guide for use within churches, developed an annual Holocaust commemoration at the Cathedral of St. John the Divine, and encouraged similar commemorations throughout the Diocese. In addition, the Committee helped to ameliorate areas of tension as they arose. He now serves on an advisory committee to the Presiding Bishop of the Episcopal Church.

It is sometimes shocking for church people today to learn that:

> In the Middle Ages, it was not uncommon for Christian mobs to stream from their churches during Holy Week to beat, murder, or otherwise maltreat Jews. A few Jewish communities were actually buried alive in mass graves after their persecutors had listened to sermons accusing the Jews as killers of Christ. The main victims of the Crusades were not pagans, but these supposedly deicidal people whose villages were invaded by Christian warriors journeying to Jerusalem. (Bernhard E. Olson, "In the Church's Closet . . . Anti-Semitism: A Lively Skeleton," *Christian Advocate*, April 22, 1965.)

Yet the same Christians who are shocked by such maltreatment of Jews in the Middle Ages may hear of a swastika being painted on the door of a synagogue in Queens, New York, or of synagogues being vandalized with little thought of the anti-Semitism that exists within their own communities today. These Christians would never think of examining the teachings of their own churches or the curriculum materials used in their church schools for indications that the prejudice against Jews which engenders such actions may have its genesis in the foundational materials of the Christian faith. As a Jewish graduate student, a rabbi, responded to another graduate student, an evangelical Protestant, "As soon as you use the term, Old Testament, our lines of communication are broken. The Torah is not an *old* testament to me."

Studies such as those which Bernhard Olson did on Protestant curriculum materials and those done on Roman Catholic materials by Eugene Fisher and others, as well as the scholarly work on the liturgy, the Church's mission and witness, and the Holocaust are providing a great many new insights as to the nature and roots of prejudice. It is becoming increasingly evident that the roots of anti-Semitism are in the very documents and curriculum materials which the Christian churches are using every week for worship and for teaching. This discovery has raised a call for interpretation of the selections from the Biblical materials used, in order that parishoners may be aware of the historical context in which the documents were written, the populations to which they were addressed, and the purposes of the writers. There is a common belief among many of the writers on Jewish-Christian relations that two thousand years of reading these passages without comment in the churches has provoked continued hatred for the Jews over the centuries, and the negative images are still current today.

Interestingly, this prejudice exists side-by-side with the condemnation of anti-Semitism and racism as such by the churches. *Direct* approval of anti-Semitism is rarely found in the writings of church leaders or the materials produced by denominations, but *indirect* approval creeps in when the materials deal with New Testament theology or religious history. Thus the question of relations between Jews and Christians is much more complicated than just learning to respect one another as human beings. The joint history of the two faiths before the coming of Jesus, the divergent interpretations of the meaning of the life, work, and death of Jesus, the early history of the Christian churches and the gradual separation from Judaism, the continuing history of the Jews — all these contribute to the need for an on-going dialogue involving Biblical scholars, theologians, historians and philosophers, as well as the practitioners in the various agencies related to the two faiths, and the people in the churches and synagogues. The problem calls for the corporate thinking of Christians of all faiths and theological perspectives, as well as Jews representing the various branches of Judaism.

It is to this problem that this book of essays is addressed. It focuses on the future of Jewish-Christian relations, with optimism that the future will be better than the present, that the efforts of scholars and leaders such as those who have contributed to this volume will raise the consciousness of church and synagogue people and that ways can be found to resolve the theological, Biblical, and historical problems. In planning the essays for this book, therefore, we have concentrated on five issues which we consider to be major, although there are other issues which might have been included. In particular, the question of Israel is a source of great tension at the present time, and a section might well have been devoted to the meaning of the existence of Israel in the lives of Jews throughout the world. Some observations on Israel are included, but it is not one of the issues discussed in depth. The five issues include: (1) Social Justice from a Prophetic Point of View; (2) The Holocaust from the Christian Perspective; (3) The Future of Jewish-Christian Relations; (4) Tensions in Jewish-Christian Relations Arising from Mission and Liturgy; and (5) Attitudes Developed in Education.

Both Judaism and Christianity stand within the tradition of the prophets — the prophets of Israel as well as prophetic leaders who have arisen from time to time to point toward a God of justice, but also of mercy. Therefore, it seems appropriate to set this discussion of the relations between Jews and Christians within that prophetic tradition. Although there are distinctive problems in the Jewish-Christian heritage, the basic questions relate to the ways in which human beings treat other human beings. Thus, the question is one of social justice, involving problems of racism, sexism, religious prejudice, economic oppression, and indeed all places where oppression or prejudice exist. The Rev. Robert E. Hood and the Rev. John J. Kelley have provided this foundation of social justice from the prophetic point of view, each from a different perspective.

Within that framework, the issues of Jewish-Christian relations are discussed. First, studies of the Holocaust have been developing among both Jews and Christian within recent years. Services in memory of the six million Jews who died in that infamous event seem mandatory if we are to keep the current and later generations from allowing the horror of those atrocities to fade into the background of history, as if they were no longer important. The numbers of volumes now being published which deny that the Holocaust took place are shocking; they show how easily and quickly human beings can wipe the "unwanted" out of their lives and their histories. It is believed that studies of the Holocaust and commemorative services may help to remind us all that genocide is always a possibility within the human experience, that Jews are having to fight for their very survival today, and that hate and prejudice have not subsided but seem on the increase. The essays on the Holocaust presented in this volume concentrate on Christian perspectives inasmuch as it is crucial that Christians come to terms with the Holocaust and with their own relation to this effort to eliminate a people from the earth. Jews, too, have their problems with helping their young to remember this event as crucial to their own survival, but the problem for Christians seems even more difficult. Therefore, three essays, by Sister Katharine Hargrove, Professors Alice and Roy Eckardt, and Dr. Hubert Locke, present varying perspectives on the Holocaust from the Christian viewpoint.

Second, the section on the future of Jewish-Christian relations attempts to point some directions for movement among the two groups. In previous years, it seemed that what was needed in Jewish-Christian relations, as well as in the relations between various faiths, was for Christians and Jews to come to a position of respect for one another and for the commitments each holds, for an appreciation of the richness of the heritage of each tradition, and for a perspective which sees each other as a human being within the larger family of humankind. But, certainly within the dialogue between these two faiths if not in that between all religious groups, scholars have gradually been coming to the conclusion that more is needed; that there must be changes in the curriculum materials to ferret out those spots which promote prejudice and misunderstanding; that perhaps the Pharisees must be seen in a different perspective from that handed down to Christian people through the centuries; that perhaps theology itself needs to be re-worked, including Christology. For many Christians this movement is confusing and threatening. They ask: Why should Christians have to re-examine their theology, their curriculum materials, their images of such groups as the Pharisees, and their hymns and liturgies? They believe these ideas of the Christian faith come directly from the Bible, and thus from the authority.

These efforts on the part of scholars to examine the basic

materials of Christianity indicate the seriousness of those engaged in the dialogue. Their willingness to look at every possible root for hate and prejudice is commendable. Dr. Irving Greenberg believes the relationship of antagonism between Jews and Christians has its roots in "the dynamics of their growing out of the same covenant and fidelity to their experiences of messianism, fulfilled and unfulfilled." He sees the new revelational events of the present generation as a key to a new relationship between the two groups. Dr. Eugene Fisher calls for "a complete and effective educational strategy" which will replace the negative portrait given to students in the past with a picture based upon greater historical and Biblical accuracy. Such a strategy will examine the understandings which students acquire in their educational experiences of Judaism in New Testament times; it will provide for greater discussion of the relation between the old and new covenants; and it will clarify the roles of the Holocaust and the State of Israel in the life and consciousness of contemporary Jews.

Third, specific focus upon aspects of Christian liturgies and ways in which the mission of Christian churches are perceived is made. Dr. Paul Kirsch sees the reading of the Gospel passion narratives themselves in the liturgies of the Christian Church over many years as a source of tension. After examining each of these narratives, he calls for printed lections to be fitted with brief explanatory prefaces and for longer interpretative prefaces for the clergy as background materials for every lection in the church year in which Jews are described, discussed, or referred to. While this book was in preparation for publication, the Rev. Cynthia L. Bronson addressed the Committee on Jewish Relations of the Episcopal Diocese of New York on the subject: "Jesus: Bond or Barrier to Jewish-Christian Relations." The presentation was so pertinent to the purposes of this volume that it has been included at this point, inasmuch as the way in which Christians and Jews view Jesus is at the heart of the tensions between the two groups.

Fourth, the potential of education at all levels — children, youth, and adults; clergy and laity; elementary, secondary, and higher education; formal and informal education — for alleviating the problems between Jews and Christians is recognized. Many of the attitudes which are assumed by individual Christians and Jews are formed in one or more of these educational settings. Dr. Jacob Neusner addresses this question at a crucial point, the academic study of Judaism in colleges and universities. How

Judaism is presented at this level is seldom considered in the discussions of the relations of Jews with Christians, so Dr. Neusner's presentation of various approaches to this subject provides intellectual stimulation for futher thinking on the academic study of Judaism, as well as other religions. Out of Dr. Paul Carlson's own personal experiences in relating to Jews and Judaism, in what he calls "An Inconclusive Unscientific Postscript," he highlights the possibility that a "new anti-Semitism" has risen in our society, examines the current situation as found in the research related to the attitudes of Christians and Jews, looks at the studies which have attempted to deal with the relationship between education and religion, and projects some possible educational remedies.

Finally, an addendum has been added in the form of a sermon by the Rev. Hays H. Rockwell, in which he, too, states that our times are marked by "a reawakening of the ancient demon of anti-semitism," and he calls prophetically for all Christians to "stand by the Jews," to be "willing to speak up, loud and clear, against every evidence of hostility to Jews." Thus, the volume returns to the prophetic theme advanced in the first chapter, with the hope that the "future" of Jewish-Christian relations may realize the prophetic ideals of justice and mercy.

Norma H. Thompson
New York University
New York, New York

EDITORS' FOREWORD

In addition to the essayists and editors, many persons have contributed to the development of this volume. The idea was conceived in a meeting of the Executive Committee of the Religious Education Fellowship, a student-alumni group related to the Program in Religious Education, New York University. Sister Margaret Ann O'Neill, at that time President of the Religious Education Fellowship, and Donald Russo, Past-President and Executive Committee member, initiated the discussions with the New York Regional Office of the Anti-Defamation League of B'nai B'rith and the Episcopal Diocese of New York. They also read the entire manuscript as part of the editorial process.

The persons represented by all of these agencies and institutions, as well as the editors, are very grateful for the willingness of the essayists to contribute to this work. Their essays have provided the scholarly treatment of the subject of Jewish-Christian relations of which the planners dreamed. The essayists have developed their topics from their own perspectives and patterns of writing. Thus, there has been no attempt to make the styles of handling footnotes conform to one manual or to bring uniformity in the use of sub-headings. The lengths of chapters vary, so it seemed appropriate to add in two short sections not in the original plans as these talks were presented in on-going dialogues and sermons during the preparation of the book for publication.

Norma H. Thompson
Director, Program in Religious
Education
New York University

April 10, 1981

Bruce K. Cole
Director of Interreligious Relations
for New York City
Anti-Defamation League of B'nai B'rith
and Spiritual Leader, East End Temple,
Manhattan

Part I

SOCIAL JUSTICE
FROM THE PROPHETIC POINT OF
VIEW

Chapter 1

SOCIAL JUSTICE
FROM THE PROPHETIC POINT OF VIEW

Robert E. Hood
Associate Professor of Church and Society
General Theological Seminary, New York, New York

The term "social justice" is not an easy concept to define. Most disciplines and professions would lay claim to being concerned with social justice. Indeed, it has become so institutionalized in post World War II American jargon, that the frequency with which it is flashed about endangers both its substance and intended effect. Religious leaders claim that they are stewards of social justice, but so do humanists and atheists. Communist governments make the same claim as do capitalists and industrialists under the rubrics and increasing influence of the corporate responsibility movement.

John Gardner, former Secretary of Education and past President of Common Cause, perhaps summed up the difficulty presented by the ease with which this concept and others are institutionalized and jargonized in our day.

> Twentieth century institutions are caught in a crossfire between uncritical lovers and unloving critics. On the one side, those who loved their institutions tended to smother them in an embrace of death, loving their rigidities more than their promise, shielding them from life-giving criticism. On the other side, there arose a breed of critics without love, skilled in demolition but untutored in the arts by which human institutions are nurtured and strengthened and made to flourish. Between these two, the institutions perish.[1]

In many ways this is the plight of the concept of "social justice" — a fragment of the English language aflame with the enlivened passions of the civil rights movement and anti-Vietnam tribulations but which seems to be on trial in this country currently enthralled in patriotic and ethnic chauvinism. That is, today's societal cross-currents threaten social justice as a concept with the drainage of over-exposure in some ways and obliteration through the process of *obscurum per obscurius* as practiced by such institutions as the present Supreme Court in other ways. Indeed the ever increasing ampelopsis of conservatism in this country suggests a tolerated intolerance and impatience with civil liberties and distributive justice. Yet when this occurs, there is all the more reason for concerned citizens to consider the prophetic tradition with its visions and sign posts and to be even more vigilant and assertive. Therefore, in this lecture delivered in praise of one who has participated in extending social justice to all groups for so many years, I as a theologian interested in the teaching and doing of political theology propose to consider the concept of social justice along the following guide-posts:

Firstly, an examination of the theological foundations of the prophetic tradition in the Old Testament, the foundation stone for both Christians and Jews which provides a point of commonality.

Secondly, an examination of the theological foundations of the prophetic work of Jesus Christ, which provides the authentication for any Christian concern for social justice and establishes that which sets us apart from our Jewish forebears.

Thirdly, an examination of the teaching of a secular prophet concerned with social justice which continues to be a major influence in our day.

Fourthly, an examination of two modern versions of the secularised prophetic tradition which were acutely engaged in the cause for social justice. This aspect is important because here the religious and the secularised prophetic traditions return to each other to form a medley tuned to the cause of liberation.

The term, "social justice," whilst having a long and noble history like the wife of Claudius, is fairly recent as a popular concept. It is not inconceivable that a heightened interest in this concept had seeds planted during the enlightenment and the subsequent French Revolution reaching a high point in the 19th century when Socialism drew attention to the acute unjust and inhuman problems and contingencies accompanying the spreading Industrial Revolution in western Europe and North America. It is not found in the Oxford English Dictionary, although there are several interesting notations about how the word "justice" got into the English language and what it connoted.

Apparently this term *justice* was first adapted from Normandy, it first being noted in the Old English Chronicles of 1137-1154 and connoting "maintenance of right," "a vindication of right by giving reward or punishment." By 1340 the word had come to mean "the quality of being morally righteous" and "the principle of just and fair dealing" as well as the moral attitude of exhibiting just conduct and rectitude. Shakespeare and the Elizabethans understood *justice* in the 16th century to mean an action conforming to a standard or rule of rightfulness, fairness, and propriety. This is very much akin to the biblical and theological understanding of righteousness which no doubt was due to the lack of rigid separation between divine law and the moral underpinnings of much secular law. Certainly there was a variation of this theme in Calvinist Geneva which had a mighty influence on the Puritans in Elizabethan England. Calvin insisted that civil government was one of the primary institutions established by God for maintaining the Christian life in society. As he says in his *Institutes*:

> Wherefore no man can doubt that civil authority is, in the sight of God, not only sacred and lawful, but the most sacred, and by far the most honourable, of all stations in mortal life. This consideration ought to be constantly present to the minds of magistrates, since it is fitted to furnish a strong stimulus to the discharge of duty . . . . What zeal for integrity, prudence, meekness, continence, and innocence, ought to sway those who know that they have been appointed ministers of the divine justice.[2]

Civil authorities are vice regents of God and guardians of the secular expression of divine justice.

With the emergence of the Enlightenment view of the state in the 17th and 18th centuries, the definition of justice began to be transformed as the issue of "rights" became more of a political concern. One began to hear the terms "birthright" and "natural rights." Stanley Benn has pointed out that with the advent of the secular state there was an attending emphasis on certain inalienable and sacred areas. This was to be preserved and protected from governmental and judicial incursion since these rights were deemed necessary for one's proper function as a citizen of the state, and there developed a transcendent component in the understanding of justice.[3]

The Hegelians, particularly T.H. Green and others, introduced the idea of a relationship between justice and morality being a product of an evolving society which looked very much like an Hegelian spiral. The development of public morality or public justice was seen to stem from the unfolding social experience, institutions, and norms of a society. Individual morality, therefore, as well as the justice accrued to individuals did not totally depend on individual rights; rather it was a societal morality and justice provided the communal consciousness that individual morality could be shaped. This idea corresponded very much to Hegel's model for the Prussian state.

But eventually the Anglo-Saxon and American understanding of justice came to be related to human and natural rights. Without tracing the historical development of this very important cornerstone of our political system, may it suffice to mention that the United Nation's Universal Declaration of Human Rights of 1948 extended this basically western Enlightenment idea to an international and cross-cultural level.

> . . . everyone, a member of society has the right to a standard of living adequate for the health and well-being of himself and his family including food, clothing, housing. (Art. XXV)[4]

Prof. Benn comments that the extension of such rights internationally established canons

> . . . by which social, economic, and political arrangements can be criticized. Human rights . . . are politically significant as grounds of protest and justification for reforming policies. They differ from appeals to benevolence and charity in that they invoke ideals like justice and equality.[5]

I suspect that any discussion of social justice, therefore, has to take this kind of mesh between human rights and justice into account, since the concept of human rights clearly suggests that there is a standard which has established basic and minimum societal values needed in order to be a functioning and participating member of any civil or political society. The denial or deprivation of this standard constitutes an affront to humanity and to the community necessary for the nourishment of humanity.

> A man with a right has no reason to be grateful to benefactors, he has grounds for grievance when it is denied. . . . It is on the face of it unjust that some men enjoy luxuries while others are short of necessities, and to call some interests luxuries and others necessities is implicitly to place them in an order of priorities as claims. Upsetting the order then demands to be justified. Human rights are the corollary, then, of the equally modern notion of social justice.[6]

Certainly this is affirmed in a book by George Cabot Lodge of Harvard Business School, *The New American Ideology*. Prof. Lodge suggests that the social value system in America is being altered as this country moves from what he describes as a "Smithian social value system," which, following the dictates of Adam Smith, stressed rugged individualism and absolute property rights as the legitimization of the individual, to a "communitarian social value system," which means that values are defined from the perspective of aims for the whole society rather than on the basis of individual aims. Under an emerging "communitarian social value system" Lodge suggests that "rights of membership" are replacing "property rights" and the Darwinian notion that only the fittest should survive. Such rights as those of survival, adequate income, good health and others are gradually being associated with natural membership and participation as a citizen in American society. And where they do not exist or are weak, the role of government is understood as being the central stimulus for an extension of these rights. One example under this changing social value system might be the shift in the basis for Affirmative Action from simply being a way of redressing unfairness and grievances to particular individuals to being a recognition of the benefit to the entire society when historical injustices for a whole ethnic group are redressed through such a programme.[7]

Several additional preliminary remarks ought to be said regarding the context in which one might derive a working definition of *social justice*. First, we ought to disabuse ourselves of

associating justice only with the law or with orderliness, as in
"Law and order." In the British and American traditions justice
has come to mean something akin to *fairness*: fairness in the
treatment or settling of conflicting claims and competitions according to certain standards, rules, or precedents of equity and
conduct. It includes the Aristotelian idea of impartiality and equal
consideration under certain norms. Prof. John Rawls, author of
one of the standard works on justice, argues that the acting or
doing of justice is a rational decision incumbent upon all individuals by the very nature of their having to engage and encounter others. It is done for the purpose of preserving and
maintaining a community; hence there emerges a reciprocal
condition for fairness and acting "justly."[8] Thus:

> . . . justice, understood as fairness, would not admit to
> the calculation of the advantages of the slaveholder as
> such because his role could not be mutually acknow-
> ledged as part of an acceptable practice by all parties
> involved.[9]

Secondly, even the Enlightenment idea about natural rights
replacing divine authority and, therefore, acceptable as a principle of coherence and equality in civil society would appear to
rest on the idea of a higher form of justice beyond the justice and
laws of the state. Paul Lehmann in his book, *The Transfiguration
of Politics*, points out that even many of the Enlightenment
thinkers assumed that there was a spirit or higher sanction behind the natural laws of the newly emerging democratic and
equalitarian society.[10] Hannah Arendt, who was skeptical of
treating moral ideas as Platonic absolutes even noted in her book,
On Revolution:

> The model in whose image western mankind has con-
> strued the quintessence of all laws, even those whose
> Roman origin was beyond doubt . . . was itself not
> Roman at all; it was Hebrew in origin and represented
> by the Divine Commandments of the Decalogue.[11]

That is, in order for natural law in our secularised democratic
society to be sanctioned as binding on all people, that law has
assumed the sanction of the divine.[12]

Thirdly, for the Christian the word *justice* not only has social
and legal significance, it also above all has theological signifi-

cance. Justice for the Christian has to be seen in light of the judgment of God rendered in the death and resurrection of Jesus Christ. This was a judgment upon sinful man and his world with all its structures and institutions and this judgment had two components. One component was negative, that of a "No" of a gracious God on an ungrateful man, the judgment of a faithful God upon a faithless creature. The source for justice for the Christian cannot be simply classical western philosophy and humanism, as noble as they might be. The norm, indeed the model for first considering justice for the Christian, is God's judgment as Judge. Karl Barth, the noted Swiss theologian, calls this component of God's judgment "His left hand":

> On the left hand it is the case that God judges man and his wrong in all seriousness, that He destroys him genuinely and truly and altogether, that this man has actually to be purged and consumed — a whole burnt offering in the flame of which both he and his sin are burnt up, disappearing in the smoke and saviour, and ceasing to be . . . .[13]

But there is the second component of God's judgment, what some theologians like to call God's great "Nevertheless", that is, Jesus Christ as God's "Yes" to the world who pardons sinful man so that he is reconciled to his Creator. This is the dialectic of the Christian doctrine of justification and, therefore, the fountainhead of what can be considered just. In God's "No" is already God's "Yes"; that is, His grace. That grace is Jesus Christ who rendered sinful man and his world just. Karl Barth calls this God's "right hand":

> I was and still am the former man: man as wrongdoer, whose wrong and whose being in identification with his wrong can only perish and in fact perished when confronted with the righteousness of God, with the life of the One who is majestically and unconditionally in the right . . . . But I am already and will be the latter man: the man whom God has elected and created for Himself . . . the man who is not unrighteous but righteous before God.[14]

It is because man is rendered just through Jesus Christ's act of justification that the doing of *justice* takes on a compulsiveness for the Christian which is fundamental to his being and acting Christian, even when the faith has gone astray from the fact and truth. It is because the act of justification has universal implications that the doing of justice by Christians cannot be merely a private act, as some "born-again" Christians with a renewed allegiance to Victorian morality of individualism like to maintain. As the writer of the letter to the Colossians notes:

> He is the image of the invisible God, the first-born of all creation; for in him all things were created in heaven and on earth, visible and invisible, whether thrones or dominions or principalities or authorities – all things were created through him and for him. He is before all things, and in him all things are held together. (1.15-17)

In this respect, although he gravely misappropriates the New Testament's understanding of justice, Hans Kelsen in his otherwise admirable book, *What is Justice?*, sees the connection between the Christian doctrine of justification as a universal event and the doing of justice when he writes that justice is an ordering of things regulating the behaviour and relations between people.[15]

Finally, a preliminary remark about the context in which I wish to consider the word *social*. Again, Karl Barth puts it well and pungently:

> (Man's) ordination to be in covenant relation with God has its counterpart in the fact that his humanity, the special mode of his being, is by nature and essence a being in fellow-humanity . . . . But this means that He takes man as seriously in his vocation to be in covenant with Him that He calls him to freedom in fellowship, i.e., to freedom in fellowship with others. He calls him to find himself by affirming the other, to know joy by comforting the other, and self-expression by honouring the other . . . . Humanity, the characteristic and essential mode of man's being, is in its root fellow-humanity. Humanity which is not fellow-humanity is inhumanity.[16]

Just as both the Old and New Testaments show God not as a *Deus Solitarius*, but always a God in relationship with man and his world, so man as God's elected partner cannot be complete or fulfilled as *homo solitarius*. Man is preeminently exercising his humanity when he is in intercourse and interaction with fellow human beings.[17] This means that the biblical faith has a most fundamental concern for society as the locus and worldliness as the process for practicing our humanity, for this is the place where God has declared Himself Emmanuel, *Deus pro nobis.*

Thus as I use *social* and as it is synonymous with *society*, I am considering the term to connote a collective system of institutions and organizations, systems and norms, mores and traditions which play a determinative role in socializing members into that given collective. These components help shape and influence individual consciousness, but individual consciousness also helps shape and influence the components of socialization. Therefore, to be *social* in the theological sense means to be in relationship with fellow-humanity which includes not only a concern for values, systems, and norms, but also in engagement with values, systems, and norms. This engagement nourishes one's humanity, which may mean change or it may mean conservation. It is *homo solidarius.*

Likewise, in trying to devise a working definition for *justice*, my primary source is scripture, at least in terms of the prophetic tradition, for it is through this source that Christians and Jews are historically and humanly irrefutably linked. The Hebrew word for *justice*, usually understood in terms of *righteousness*, has a semitic root which comes from the word *tsdq*, meaning "the state corresponding to a norm, a norm which remains to be defined in each particular case."[18] It is conformity to a norm which is neither punitive, judicatory, nor distributive, but rather an evidence of a fidelity or faithfulness that determines action, thinking, and deliberation.[19]

Similarly, this conformity to a norm of right applies to the inward condition of an individual which in turn is reflected in his external actions. When God chastises Israel for her faithlessness, calling her a harlot and a whore, he compares her to Samaria and Sodom which were more righteous or just because they had committed lesser sins (Ezek. 15.48-52).[20]

Finally, justice or righteousness is understood in the Old Testament as the key component in human relationships and dealings between people. "A person is righteous because he acts justly; he does not act justly because he is righteous."[21] This was especially true for the people of the covenant - *B'nai B'rith* - for the Sinai covenant was initiated by God and entered into freely by Israel. It established a chosenness and guardianship for the Israelites, but it also placed claims and responsibilities on ancient Israel: "If you will obey my voice and keep my covenant, you shall be my own possession among all people . . . (Ex. 19.5)." And in Deut. 6 we find what some biblical scholars call the *Credo* of ancient Israel which reminded Israel both of the relationship between Yahweh and herself and also of the obligations and claims placed upon Israel as Yahweh's partner, unequal though she was:

> And the Lord commanded us to do all these statutes, to fear the Lord our God, for our good always, that he might preserve us alive, as at this day. And it will be righteous for me, if we are careful to do all these commandments before the Lord our God, as he commanded us. (Deut. 6.24-25)

From all of this one can suggest that the doing of right or the just in the Old Testament could be variable depending on the circumstances. This is parallel to what has been called "contextual ethics." Paul Lehmann, sometime Professor of Christian Ethics at Union Theological Seminary, distinguishes between "absolutist ethics" and "contextual ethics." "Absolutist ethics" is the application of a "standard of conduct which can be and must be applied to all people in all situations in exactly the same way."[22] "Contextual ethics" means the doing of the right or the just is affected by the circumstances and the relationships of the context or situation depending on the complexity of the particular situation. As we shall see, the Old Testament prophets insist that righteousness and justice are practices modeled on God's relationship with His people rather than absolutes. There is no sense of the Greek ideal in either the Old or the New Testament when it comes to practicing righteousness. Even the enormous preachments of the rejection of Israel found in Amos reveal this relationship. During his several visions, Amos pleads with Yahweh against His judgment and Yahweh relents. (Amos 7.3,6)

What is meant by the "prophetic point of view" or the "prophetic tradition"? This term has been very often abused, especially in this country with its many apocalyptic oriented sects which have used this term in a predominantly futuristic and predicting sense. The Swedish biblical scholar, J. Lindblom, points out that *pro* in the Greek term *propheten* does not mean *fore*telling, but rather *forth*telling. That is, prophets are understood to have something to proclaim forthwith, urgently, which is all the more compelling because it has been transmitted to them through a very personal intense experience with God. This proclamation usually has to do with the situation at hand. Therefore, the prophet is by compulsion and by his special calling a public person, a social being, for, as Lindblom points out, he cannot keep his message to himself.[23]

The prophetic tradition centered preeminently around the auditory, that is, hearing, the oral tradition. The prophet was not a pedagogue or a philosopher or even a teacher; he was a preacher. One might draw parallels between the prophetic tradition in ancient Israel and the role played by preachers in the Civil Rights Movement such as Martin Luther King, Jr. and Malcolm X and in the anti-Vietnam Peace Movement such as William Sloane Coffin. The German allows one to understand the root connection between God's call to the prophet and his calling to Israel. It is because of *der Ruf Gottes* that the prophet's *Berufung* (calling or vocation) drives him *auszurufen* (to proclaim, to call out).

According to Old Testament scholars, this inspiration of the prophets resembled ecstasy of other ancient Near East traditions and cultures, but not in the popular sense of *unio mystica*. The Old Testament prophet is compelled to share the transmitted word of God with others. He dare not withdraw unto himself. I Sam. 10 ff. apparently provides us with the first reference about prophetic beginnings in Israel; otherwise there is little information about how this tradition began in Israel. Saul had frequent contact with ecstatic prophets, so much that he too experienced their ecstasy (I Sam. 10.10). Indeed in I Sam. 19.22-4 he is in such a state of frenzy that he takes off all his clothes and collapses. There was also some foretelling and clairvoyance associated with these early ecstatic prophets, which may be a possible source of the popular idea that to prophesy means to predict the future.[24]

The ecstasy or ecstatic experience however was only a sign of the gifts of *'is 'elohim*—"A man of God." Moses (Deut. 33.1) as well as David (II Chron. 8.14) and Elijah (I Kings 17.18; II Kings 1.10) are all called "man of God." This authenticated and authorized the man to speak of God's revelation to His people. It could be a word of good tidings (II K. 8.1 f.) or it could be a discomforting and unpleasant tiding (I K. 17.17 f.).[25]

But with these early prophets as with the so-called "classical" 8th century prophets, the one event which authenticated both their being and their message was the conviction that they had been called and sent by God. The call meant possession - possession by God. Jeremiah of all the prophets tried to resist the call time and time again. He even called God deceitful because of his discontentment with the heavy responsibility incumbent upon him as a called prophet of God (15.18b). But God reminded him that almost primordially at the time of conception, he had been chosen to be a prophet: "Before I formed you in the womb, I knew you, and before you were born, I set you apart" (Jer. 1.5). Amos was called whilst attending his sheep and cattle (Am. 7.12 ff.). This is thus the first main characteristic of the prophetic tradition — the conviction that one has wrestled with God Almighty and has been summoned by Him as a peculiar witness to His divine presence and revelation in particular human situations.

A second common characteristic of the prophetic tradition is the nature of the word they are called to proclaim — God's word. It was the word of God which gripped and possessed them and which had to be uttered to a faithless nation abandoning the claims of covenant with God.

> The divine word and the divine saying are the most characteristic terms for expressing the content of a prophetic revelation. To have received Yahweh's word is the same as to have received a revelation. The divine word is the mysterious knowledge, the inner explicable certainty, the wonderful insight into divine and human affairs which a prophet receives in the hours of inspiration.[26]

There are some references to "seeing" (II K. 8.10,13; I Sam. 3.21) but ancient Israel as most modern peoples like the Arabs were profoundly a *hearing* people. Therefore, the prophets did not feel they were transmitting their *own* words because the possession by the word of God meant a total identity with God's word. Von Rad points out that the term "word of Yahweh" (God) appears some 241 times in the Old Testament and of these at least 221 (92%) are connected with a prophetic oracle. Thus in the oral tradition of ancient Israel this term had a very significant place. It is also significant that throughout the Old Testament there is always a definite article before "word of God," to wit, "*the* word of God." It is never called "*a* word of Yahweh." Thus the word of God needs no supplementation or implementation by other words.[27]

One ought also to remind oneself that God's word in ancient Israel was considered not only a word of judgment and exhortation, but also a creative and effective word. We notice this at once in Genesis: "And God said, 'Let there be light,' and there was light." (1.3) It was through the divine word that creation thus came to be. Ps. 33.9 records:

For he spoke, and it came to be;
He commanded, and it stood forth.

The word of Yahweh even could restore life to lifeless objects as
witnessed in the valley of the dry bones by Ezekiel (Ezek. 37). And
even the devil was aware of the efficacy and creative power of the
word of God, for during the forty days when Jesus was in the
wilderness, the devil tempted him by saying "If thou be the Son of
God, *command* this stone that it be made bread." (Lk. 4.3)

But the word was neither temporally nor nationally limited. It
was understood to have universal dimensions. Isaiah insists not
only that all of mankind listen and obey the word of God but that
all of the heavens and earth also obey: "Hear, O heavens, and give
ear, O earth, for the Lord has spoken." (1.2) There is a kind of
biblical imperialism claimed on behalf of the word through the
insistence of the prophets that though uttered in a particular
situation, it has universal significance beyond the borders of the
ancient kingdoms of Israel and Judah. Jeremiah invokes all nations of the earth to pay heed to the word of Yahweh. (6.18 f)

One suspects that so few in our day can identify with the power
of the spoken word because so much of the language has been
lost or trivialized through the instant dribbles of television and
the almost immoral and abusive misuse of the language through
the advertising industry, not to mention the lost art of letter-
writing. We have been lulled into a muddleness and inattention
regarding the word, written or spoken, through the comfort
provided by the whirling dervishes of clichēs, jargon, euphem-
isms, and slang, not to mention trendy attempts to ethnicize the
language in certain parts of this country. But the Old Testament
prophets persist like the unceasing *nevermore* in Edgar Allan
Poe's poem, *The Raven*. Nor does the objectivity of that word
depend on its subjective receptivity by the audience. Ezekiel is
commanded to carry out the word whether the people listen or
not. (3.10f)

A third communality of the prophetic tradition is that it was an
example of what Kierkegaard called "the scandal of particularity."
That is, whilst they spoke to a particular, contextual situation,
God's truth leapt over those temporal boundaries and had universal significance beyond Israel. Whilst the prophets often were
advocates for the "old-time religion," (I K. 18.18; 21), they also
spoke to political situations, insisting on change (I K. 22; Jer. 22.1
ff.), dealt in foreign affairs (Isa. 7.37), addressed military situations
(Isa. 39.15 ff.), as well as the exploitation of one special class by

another; that is, the word of God in the prophetic tradition is a free word bound neither by a people or a nation. At the end of Amos, God threatens to reject Israel, noting that just as He delivered Israel from bondage, so He also delivered other peoples. Israel has no special claims on God or His word:

"Are you not like the Ethiopians to me,
O people of Israel," says the Lord.
"Did I not bring up Israel from the land
of Egypt,
and the Philistines from Caphter
and the Syrians from Kir?" (9.7)

Ought this not possibly to be remembered when antisemitism is displayed by one semitic people toward another semitic people and not just be thought of as something perpetuated by Christians upon Jews?

What are some of the hallmarks of this theonomic ethics displaying and containing both God's "No" and God's "Yes", His judgment *against* society and His grace *for* society?[28] Here we shall restrict our attention to glimpses of society in the 8th century B.C., which was the point of reference for so many of the prophets during the classical formation of this tradition.

Israel and Judah were independent kingdoms by the middle of the 8th century. In fact, they were as large as the entire empire of Solomon in the 10th century B.C. Trade and prosperity flourished. The fact that they were at peace also helped stabilize the economic and political picture. There was a great deal of Red Sea trade as well as a revival of the copper trade along the Arabah. From excavations in Samaria we know that other industries flourished such as weaving and dyeing at Debir.[29] In Amos we learn that the construction industry was thriving (3.15; 5.11).

The houses of the upper classes were elaborately furnished (3.14), outfitted with very comfortable cushioned couches and lounging arrangements (6.4), which was quite an advancement for Israel, a nomadic people. They had their servants and slaves, and wine flowed abundantly. There were summer homes and winter homes, many of which were adorned with valuable ivory (2.15). Amos also tells us that because of the economic organization of the society, the small farmer with his marginal existence was very dependent on loan sharks who were liable to foreclose on his land and evict him and his family at the slightest calamity, such as drought, or crop failure (4.6-9). Indeed, as Prof. Denner

reminds us, the prophets are the most important clue for understanding the social structure and society of ancient Israel and
Judah.[30]

Much of the internal life of the 8th century B.C. was determined
and directed by the upper classes of the city-states of Jerusalem
and Samaria which centered around the monarchy and by the
civil servants and court attendants. Historically this was due to
David deciding, after his victory, to incorporate the disenfran-
chised Canaanite aristocracy into his empire both because of
their administrative and military expertise as well as their sophistication. (II Sam. 24.7; I K. 4.7-19)[31] One must not forget that Israel
was a nomadic people.[32] This meant that a part of the Canaanite
upper class customs came to be concentrated in Jerusalem, the
capital of the southern kingdom of Judah, which was the central
place for the top civil servants who made appointments for the
rest of the country. Hence there was a *de facto* confluence of the
political, administrative, and economic groups in these two
cities.[33]

The economic security of the civil servants, which included
judges as well as administrative managers, was closely linked
with the monarchy. In Canaanite practice, much of which deliberately influenced the practices of this formerly unsophisticated
people, the top civil servants were provided with land from the
king's lands, often resulting in dispossession of the poor and
eviction of farmers who might be farming these lands. The more
one acquired, the more one wanted.[34] Am. 5.11 indicates that
tribute was demanded of the farmer by the owner, although this
could also be the tithe which could be collected by the officers of
the monarch.[35] Both Amos (8.4-6) and Isaiah (5.8) complain of the
affluent enriching themselves through agricultural and land-
purchase monopolies. The judicial civil servants also used various legal and judicial procedure for making money which included blackmailing poor people. (Am. 5.l7; 10.11)[36]

This corruption also affected the religious life. Even though
the religious places and shrines were well-attended (Am. 4.4 f.;
5.21-24), they were not practicing the faith of Yahweh. The foreign
Canaanite fertility rites were used in the religious places (Hos.
1.3; 4.6-14) and the priests were charging fees solely for the sake
of enriching themselves (Am. 7.12; Mi. 3.5). John Bright, the noted
Old Testament scholar, comments:

> The state of Israel, externally strong, prosperous, and
> confident of the future, was inwardly rotten and sick

past curing. The uneasy feeling was abroad, voiced by
Amos and Hosea but surely shared by others, that
Israel was done for . . . . Israel had, in fact, begun to die.
It was thanks primarily to the prophets that, as the
northern state went to grace, to be followed more
tardily by her southern sister, Israel's faith received a
new access of life.[37]

One could say that the chief components of social justice for
the 8th century prophets in ancient Israel were as follows: First,
the cause and plight of the poor, the disinherited, the dispossessed, and the underdog are to be a fundamental and unending
engagement for the chosen peoples of the covenant, both Christians and Jews. Permit me to put it in more provocative but more
contemporary language as Karl Barth once put it regarding the
never-ceasing social ethic of Christians:

> The Church is witness of the fact that the Son of man
> came to seek and save the lost. And this implies that —
> casting all false impartiality aside — the Church must
> concentrate first on the lower and lowest levels of
> human society. The poor, the socially and economically
> weak and threatened, will always be the object of its
> primary and particular concern, and it will always
> insist on the State's special responsibility for these
> weaker members of society.[38]

There is no neutrality or "balanced" view amongst the prophets
when it comes to this point. Indeed Amos would seem to be
saying at points that the doing of social justice has its real authentication in helping the helpless and oppressed.[39]

Secondly, the biblical prophetic tradition saw an intimate
relationship between the corruption of societal and interpersonal
relations and the corruption of religious and ethnic responsibilities, which, for them, really meant a corruption of our humanity.
The Old Testamemt prophetic tradition understood one's faith
to have an essential corporate and communal component for it
both to be faithful to the covenant of the Fathers and to be authentic. One Christian theologian drew parallels to a similar
relationship existing in the west during the Cold War period:

> . . . so long as there is in the west "freedom" to start
> economic crises, "freedom" to throw grain into the sea,

even though people were hungering in (Russia), so long
should we as Christians refuse to speak an uncondi-
tional "No" to the east. We accuse it of its inhuman
methods not without some justification. But we do not
forget that they can accuse us of an inhumanity, namely,
an inhumanity shown in our deathly respect for material values which in a fundamental way corrupts our
thinking and acting.[40]

Thirdly, this tradition understood God's word to include the
transcendent in its standing apart from other words and yet embracing other words and worlds. Hans Wolff in his very helpful
Die Stunde des Amos calls this "shock speech."[41] Amos called the
comfortable elegant women of the wealthy classes:

cows of Basham . . . who oppress the poor, who crush
the needy, who say to their husbands, "Bring that we
may drink." (Am. 4.1)

Basham was located in the northeastern part of Jordan, east of
the Sea of Galilee, and was noted for its excellent grazing land and
outstanding herds. They understood all morality, political as well
as social, economic as well as religious to come under the judgment and supervision of God. One ought not to confuse morality
with a political programme or ideology. There was no prophetic
programme for governing the civil society comparable to the
claims of the European so-called "Christian Democratic" parties.[42] There was no prophetic religious economics. But neither
would the prophets have understood any disinclination to be
engaged in judgment on these matters because of a rigid separation between the realm of "moral and spiritual values" and that
of political and economic institutions. It is therefore significant
that several of the prophets saw a connection between *mispat*
(justice) and *sedagah* (righteousness). Perhaps the best remembered citation of this parallel between these two attributes is
Amos' horrendous:

I hate, I despise your feasts,
    and I take no delight in your solemn assemblies. . . .
But let justice roll down like waters,
    and righteousness like an ever-flowing stream. (5.21,24)[43]

It was because the people of Israel were acting unjustly that they
were judged unrighteous, according to Amos. Thus, as he says in

that deafening passage which suggests that even if they tried to do justice, they could not because of their sinfulness,

> "They do not know how to do what is right," says the Lord,
> "Those who store up (the products of) violence and robbery in their strongholds."[44]

Fourthly, God's "No" is understood in the context of His "Yes", His grace. That is, to say God is to point toward His "Yes" to man established and affirmed in the Sinai covenant. Likewise, to say God is to point toward His "No" to man disestablished and enslaved by sin. But the prophets stress that in the "No" of judgment is already hidden the "Yes" of reconciliation. "My people are bent on turning away from me," laments God in Hosea, "so that they are appointed to the yoke, and one shall remove it." But then God weeps and reveals His grace:

> How can I give you up, O Ephraim!
> How can I hand you over, O Israel!
> How can I make you like Admah!
> How can I trust you like Zehoi-im! . . .
> For I am God and not man,
>   the Holy One in your midst,
> and I will not come to destroy. (11.7-8, 9b)

We must now move to a second part of the prophetic tradition as it is understood in Christian theology. Here the model moves from men to the God/man called Jesus Christ. In particular one must pay attention to the Reformation doctrine by John Calvin, namely, the prophetic office of Christ, a doctrine rediscovered by the Protestant Reformers just as the doctrine of justification was rescued and rediscovered during that period. John 6.14 links the office of prophet to the person and work of Jesus Christ. Jesus has just provided for the feeding of the five thousand from the five barley loaves and two fish given by a lad in the crowd. After gathering up the left-overs, there are some twelve baskets of scraps. The people seeing this exclaimed: "This is indeed the prophet who is to come into the world."

Exegetically, C. K. Barnett claims that the people may have been thinking of Moses when they gave this title to Jesus.[45] He had provided his people with miraculous food as had Moses in the wilderness. Theologically, the prophetic work of Jesus together with the other titles of "priest" and "king" were mentioned by

Eusebius of Caesarea in the 4th century.[46] It was also mentioned by Aquinas, although he did not develop the idea.[47] But the primary source for this idea is John Calvin. When Calvin published the first edition of his *Institutes* in 1536 he spoke only of the two offices of Christ: priest and king.[48] But three years later in the edition of 1539 he speaks of the prophetic office together with the priestly and kingly offices, although he had not yet begun to speak of the three-fold office. However, in his Cathechisms of 1543 and 1545 he spoke freely of Christ as "King, Priest of Sacrifice, and Prophet."[49] Calvin saw Jesus Christ as the fulfillment of Old Testament prophecy because:

> Christ does not convey another's word - He is the word.
> He is not given a revelation - He is the revelation,
> the self-revealing one.[50]

It was through Calvin's teaching on the *munus Christi propheticum* that Lutheran theology picked up the strand, although the Lutheran, Andreas Osiander (1498-1552) had written about the three-fold office before Calvin, but without any wide-yielding influence amongst the Lutherans apparently.[51]

It is as the fulfillment of the prophetic tradition that Christians understand Jesus Christ to be the transformer of the tradition. There are certain interconnections between the ancient tradition and the prophetic work of Christ which ought to be mentioned. First, both take place within history. This means that the contextual situation is important for the doing of the prophetic work. This is not a Greek doctrine of timelessness, which is foreign to both testaments. This is a Hebrew doctrine about God's taking time and temporality with utmost seriousness. Otherwise, one always runs the risk of imposing absolutes and principles on situations regardless of the context or temporality.

> What makes the prophets prophets, each in his own time and situation, is the fact that they perceive these declarations and to the best of their ability must hear and proclaim them. But primarily and quite independently of their particular commission and its execution, of their existence and activity as prophets, it is the fact that this history makes such declarations.[52]

Secondly, the two traditions are related through the claim for universality. Whilst God made a covenant with a particular people and therein established the norm for justice and righteousness in human relations as well as in human/divine relations, the claims of that covenant did not exhaust itself with the relationship. Israel is both a particular vehicle and the prototype vehicle for summoning all peoples to a similar relationship with God. (Isa. 43.8 ff.; 55.5)[53]

Thirdly, both traditions speak of God's being at work now in temporal affairs:

> Even including its inner vacillations and the contradiction exposed by the prophets, in its totality and interconnection it is Gospel, good news. We must not miss the *cantus firmus* of this positive continuum above the dialectic of the prophets. It is not entirely silenced even in them.[54]

That is, both proclaim God's judgment and wrath in the light of the glad tidings of His grace.

Yet there is a distinction between Jesus Christ as prophet and the Old Testament prophetic traditions. First, Jesus Christ is not prophet in addition to His work as Lord and Savior. He Himself is the Word which shapes the spoken prophecy conveyed by the Old Testament prophets and is the substance of that proclamation. He can pronounce the word much more authoritatively and demand obedience because He Himself is that Word.[55]

Secondly, Jesus Christ as prophet does not speak as a witness to the covenant relation between God and His people and the subsequent antagonism between them. As reconciler, He is *the* fulfillment of that covenant and has overcome the antagonisms. The prophets could never claim this as "mouthpieces" for God. To use a Tillichian phrase, Jesus Christ is "the eternal now."[56]

Finally, whilst the Old Testament prophets interceded for their fellowmen, they could not remove the contradiction between God and man. But Jesus Christ is both Yahweh and the sinful Israelite, both the Lord who became a servant and the servant who became Lord.

> It is not a new or different covenant which is established and proclaimed in the history of Jesus Christ. It is the one covenant in a new reality which is only now fulfilled in this form ... because it is only now immediately and directly comformable to this basis, content, and goal

as the reality of the Messiah Jesus latent in what came before, in the history of Israel and its prophecy. It is He, who, as the electing God and the elected man in one person, is the basis, content, and the goal of the covenant of God with man. It is He who is the one Prophet of this covenant.[57]

This prophetic office of Christ can be linked particularly to possessions and private property, as the term private property is popularly understood in our culture with its legacy of John Locke and his defense of it. The noted New Testament scholar, Werner Kummel, rightly points out that in the New Testament there is no statement about the nature of rights of private property which can be considered mandatory for all Christians. But he is incorrect when he attempts to press this point as a legitimacy of the claim that there is no apprehension about property in the New Testament or about its character and effect on acting justly on behalf of the neighbor.[58] The most adamant admonitions about the dangers possessions and private property pose for the doing of justice can be found in St. Luke's Gospel, although not here alone. Jesus reminds his followers that "no one can serve two masters . . . . You cannot serve both God and mammon" (Lk. 16.13; cf Matt. 5.24).

Hengel in his book, *Property and Riches in the Early Church*, comments that the word "mammon" is neither a Hebrew nor a Greek word or even a hellenized semitic word. It is of Aramaic-Phoenician etymology and means "possessions" or "property."[59] It is used in a negative sense here and elsewhere in the New Testament. Conceivably the Early Church did not translate it because the name itself transmitted idolatry: service of mammon to the neglect of service of God was demonic and idolatrous. Clement of Alexandria (? - ca 215) in his *Quis dives* interprets the word to mean that which is fundamentally characteristic of private property itself, namely, *adikia* or "unrighteousness."[60] It is under the rubric of mammon that Jesus tells the parable of the property owner and Lazarus which is found in St. Luke's and St. Matthew's Gospels, after which He reminds us not to be anxious about food, housing, and clothing. That is, possessions and private property have seductive qualities often when it comes to acting and doing justly toward the dispossessed and outcasts of society. In an interesting reversal of roles, Jesus promises rewards for the landless, the dispossessed, and the poor:

> Blessed are you poor, for yours in the kingdom of God.
> Blessed are you that hunger now, for you shall be satisfied.
> Blessed are you that weep now, for you shall laugh. (Lk. 6.20-22)

In the same passage he admonishes the affluent:

> Woe to you that are rich, for you have received your
>   consolation.
> Woe to you that are full now, for you shall hunger.
> Woe to you that laugh now, for you shall mourn and weep.
> (Lk. 5.24-25)

Another factor mentioned is that possessions and property can delude us in thinking that we are acting justly when in fact we may simply be acting charitably. This is illustrated in the story of the well-to-do young man who asked Jesus what he ought to do to inherit eternal life. After establishing that the young man had indeed been doing the "religious" things of the Law — not killing, honoring his parents, not stealing — He then reveals that incredible dialectic and reversal which often shakes the very foundations of our being: "Sell all that you have and distribute it to the poor," Jesus advised the affluent young chap, ". . . and come and follow me." This is the radical cost of discipleship. The conclusion of this story is really the telling part: the young man upon hearing this turned away from Jesus and went away despondent and despairing, "for he was very rich." (Lk. 18.23) And it is at the departure of the rich young man that Jesus makes his famous comment:

> For it is easier for a camel to go through the eye of a
> needle than for a rich man to enter the kingdom of
> God. Lk. 18.25

Furthermore, it is not without significance that all three gospels preserve this last bit of the story, thus indicating that this was an important moral which was handed down orally in the various Christian traditions. (Cf Mt. 19.24; Mk. 10.25)

What then is to be the role of possessions and private property and how ought Christians to regard them? There is hardly any doubt in my mind after examining the texts of the gospels that the fundamental role of possessions and private property is their use for the furtherance of social and communal aims. This is not a programme for some kind of nationalization. But Jesus makes it clear again and again that the problem with possessions and riches is that the "I" all too often replaces the "thou" both in the interior life of the owner and in his external behavior and action. In Lk. 8.11 ff. Jesus tells the story of the seeds sowed by the sower and notes in v 14:

> And for what fell among the thorns, they are those who hear, but as they go on their way, they are choked by the cares and riches and pleasures of life, and their fruit does not mature.

This parable is also retained in all three synoptic gospels.

This point might also be illustrated in the story of the Good Samaritan. Jesus relates how the Samaritan used his possessions for errands of mercy to care for even one's foe and enemy, who also falls under the relationship of "neighbor." Prof. Hengel correctly makes the point that Jesus is not interested in theories about the rightness or wrongness of possessions in themselves or about the origins of private property:

> Jesus attacks Mammon with the utmost severity where it has captured men's hearts, because this gives it demonic character by which it blinds men's eyes to God's will — in concrete terms, to their neighbour's needs . . . . This radical criticism of riches may be rejected as hopeless enthusiasm, like the demand to renounce force and love one's enemies, but particularly today, when there is so much talk of a "definite utopia," one might well ask whether not only Christianity but the whole of mankind does not need the goal which Jesus' message provides. Such different figures as Leo Tolstoi, Albert Schweitzer, Mahatma Gandhi, Toyohito Kagawa and Martin Luther King may be cited as examples.[61]

With the enlightenment came the profanization of the dogmatic, which was the Western Church's primary means of intellectual control. With the Enlightenment were sown the seeds for the secularization of the prophetic tradition. Perhaps the most telling and long-lasting example of this was Marxism, a faith which has spread beyond the western boundaries of its 19th century evangelism, a faith which understood social justice to be a *modus operandi* for a socio-economic system which

continues to change and present a very feasible alternative to a
number of people in the modern world, particularly Third and
Fourth World countries, not to mention Eastern Europe and the
variants found in western European countries with Social Democratic parties. It is primarily as a social system with particular
social and political aims that the alternative economic organization of Marxism and socialism are to be understood, I think.

Karl Marx (1818-1883) and Friedrich Engels (1820-1895) sought
through empirical analysis of anthropology and social relations
to answer two questions: 1) With all the new wealth and spread
of affluence in industrializing countries, such as England,
Western Europe, and North America, why are there so many
poor and underprivileged people? 2) What are the consequences
of the driving force for technology and the technologizing of the
means of production for the achievement of communal goods,
services, and justice for the greater number of people, most
especially the disinherited masses of industrial society?

Marx and Engels understood themselves primarily as secular
advocates for the poor, and thus one can aptly include them
within the prophetic tradition. It was this self-consciousness
which moved them to seek out and understand the relationship
between the physical conditions and methods of production
and the formation of human institutions and relationships. Thus
Marx and Engels must be liberated from the textbook myth that
they are primarily economic determinists. As Engels wrote in a
letter to Starkenburg in 1894:

> What we understand by economic conditions which
> we regard as the determining basis of the history of
> society are the methods by which human beings in
> a given society produce their means of living and
> exchange the products amongst themselves . . . .
> According to our conception this technique also de-
> termines the methods of exchange and the division of
> products . . . and the division into classes also and
> hence the relationships of lordship and servitude and
> with them the state, politics, law, etc.[62]

There were predecessors to Marxism, who are often called
Utopian Socialists because they tended to base their insights
about the relationship between the economic institutions and
injustices of a society more on religious or philosophical ideas of
brotherhood than on empirical analysis: Henri Count Saint-Simon

(1760-1825), Charles Fourier (1722-1837), Felicite de Lamennais (1782-1854), Robert Owen (1771-1858). But it was Marx and Engels who used empirical means for getting at why the poor seemed to be getting poorer and the rich richer in spite of the material promises of capitalistic forms of economic organization. One ought not to forget that 19th century society affirmed more or less the social posture of the Christian church in western European countries, namely, that the poor would receive their rewards at the *eschaton*. Oscar Wilde caught the gist of the 19th century's attitude toward the poor which was more or less sanctioned by Christians through their indifference and social class blindnesses. Writing in an essay entitled, "The Soul of Man under Socialism," he quipped:

> . . . sometimes the poor are praised for being thrifty.
> But to recommend thrift to the poor is both grotesque
> and insulting. It is like advising a man who is starving
> to eat less.[63]

Karl Marx, though born a Jew, was baptized and reared as a Christian. Engels was also a Christian. It was therefore two disillusioned Christians who examined the intimacy between the social actions of the Christian churches on behalf of social justice and industrial exploitation. It was with some justified disheartedness that Marx wrote in the *Deutsch-Brusseler Zeitung* in 1847:

> The social principles of Christianity proclaim the
> necessity for a ruling class and a subject class . . . . The
> social principles of Christianity declare that heaven is
> the place where all injustices will be duly rectified,
> and therefore, these principles justify the continuation
> of such injustices on earth. The social principles of
> Christianity explain every outrage perpetrated by the
> oppressors on the oppressed either as a rightful
> punishment for original sin, or something of that sort,
> or a trial visited by the Lord in His infinite wisdom
> upon his redeemed. The social principles encourage
> dullness, lack of self-respect, submissiveness, self-
> abasement, in short, all of the characteristics of the
> proletariat.[64]

There are three main points which can be mentioned as Marx's reply to his first query about the causes for the poor in wealthy capitalist societies. First, the most important factors in the formation and development of human society historically have been the production and reproduction of the means for existing and surviving. That is, as Engels says in his *Origin of the Family*, the stuff of history is materialism which has to be understood in two ways. On the one hand, this means the production of tools needed for surviving like food, clothing, shelter and the things necessary for improving that production. On the other hand, this means the reproduction of human beings or the race itself for the continuation of society. The way in which a society goes about perpetuating these two horns of its materialism has been largely shaped by the various economic stages of development.[65]

One ought to note at this point that *materialism* is not used here in the sense that the French Encyclopedists used this term, which is the basis of our understanding of the term. *Materialism* as Marx and Engels use it would seem to mean the affect and shaping of social organizations and institutions as well as human social relations by the industrialization of the means of production. It is on the basis of this idea that Marx describes "religious feeling" as a social product rather than as a transcendent component. Therefore, it is of crucial structural importance in understanding social justice for the Marxist that the economic organization and systems of a society be intimately connected to the social, political, and ethical aims and institutions of that society.

Secondly, poverty is a structural component necessary for the functioning of a capitalist industrial society since the means of production and survival are either owned or controlled by a small group with capital. This private ownership of capital is not restricted to individuals; it can also include institutional control and ownership, such as banks, insurance companies, oil monopolies and cartels, companies, etc. It can also include that odious institution of slavery, which, whilst not originating in capitalist countries, was refined and used for the furthering of the economic aims of those countries.[66] As Engels notes in his analysis of the relationship between capitalist countries which speak of themselves as civilized:

> Civilization opens with a new advance in the division of labor. At the lowest stage of barbarism men produced only directly for their own needs . . . . (Civilization) creates a class which no longer concerns itself with

> production, but only with the exchange of the pro-
> ducts – the *merchants* . . . . Now for the first time a
> class appears which, without in any way participating
> in production, captures the direction of production
> as a whole and economically subjugates the pro-
> ducers . . . .[67]

One indeed may ask whether the various welfare programs in this country are not in fact deliberately designed systems intended to maintain a large number of economic cripples who cannot be absorbed into the production schemes either by private industry or the government.

The historian, A. J. P. Taylor, aptly captured the flavor of Marx regarding the disinherited in industrialized capitalist countries when he wrote:

> Perhaps Marx's greatest political legacy was practical,
> and not in the field of theory at all . . . . This legacy was
> his insistence on working-class independence in polit-
> ical affairs, with a clear working-class programme and
> working-class leaders . . . . (Marx's International Work-
> ing Men's Association) demonstrated his principle that
> the emancipation of the working class must be the
> work of the working-class themselves . . . .[68]

This has been the guiding light of the early trade union movements in most capitalist countries with the exception of the United States, where the trade union movement opted for fitting into the political and economic ideologies already provided. Nowhere does one find the stringent anti-Communism amongst the international trade union movement as is found in this country. It is possibly Marx as a secular prophet who provides the poor and working classes with a means of rescuing themselves from what Hegel called "the insignificance of finitude."

Thirdly, it is the dissolution of the classes and the structures perpetuating and supporting the gaps between the various social classes that Marx thinks would be a key toward social justice for the greater number of people in a society. Even a reformed capitalist society cannot remove these basic differing class self-interests and antagonisms. Thus change in social relations can and will take place when there is a change in the ownership and social aims of the means of production in a society.[69]

The last category under which I wish to consider this theme

of social justice and the prophetic point of view is the role of blacks in this country, where, as has been hinted at previously, both the hearing of the word as an effective power (Old Testament prophetic tradition) and the drive to alter structures so that social relations could be altered (secularized prophetic tradition) would seem to come together. These people, heirs of that "strange institution," have moved historically in this country as a people holding on to the proclaimed word, albeit from Christian preachers or street preachers. They have been the invisible prophets.

In a haunting essay comparing the status of the black in the South with that of his brother and sister in the North, James Baldwin strikes out with the lament, "Nobody knows my name." He points out that neither the South which always claimed that it "knew" its Negroes, nor the North which claimed that it freed the Negro, really knows his name.[70] It is the ambiguity of the North which continues to render the black an "invisible man" (Ellison). There is something profoundly deep in the passion for wanting to have a name, a lament which has particularly characterized the black's pilgrimage since his forced exile from Africa. There is also something profoundly biblical in the black's despair with this invisibility in this country.

The noted Old Testament scholar, J. Pedersen, in his classic study of ancient Israel, points out that:

> . . . the soul in its entirety, with all its blessing and honour, finds expression in the name, *shem* . . . . To know the name of a man is the same as to know his essence. The pious know the name of their God (Ps 9.11; 91.14), i.e., they know how he is . . . . He whose name one knows fully, one loves. Yahweh knew the name of Moses, in that he had chosen him, and Moses found grace in his sight. (Ex. 33.17)[71]

But at the same time the extermination of the name was experienced as annihilation. After Saul had been in the clutches of David and fearing for the dynasty and the future of his family, he burst into tears and said to David: "Swear therefore unto me by Yahweh . . . that you will not destroy my name out of my father's house." (I Sam. 24.21)

One of the more sensitive commentators on the black experience of being unknown as well as invisible was W.E.B. DuBois. He noted very poignantly in his book, *The Souls of Black Folk*:

After the Egyptian and Indian, the Greek and Roman,
the Teuton and the Mongolian, the Negro is a sort of
seventh son, born with a veil, and gifted with second-
sight in this American world – a world which yields
him no true self-consciousness, but only lets himself
see himself through the revelation of the other world.
It is a peculiar sensation, this double-consciousness,
this sense of always looking at one's self through the
eyes of others, of measuring one's soul by the tape of
a world that looks on in amused contempt and pity.[72]

Many events and heroes could be examined in the journey
toward restoring the black's name, but in terms of a prophetic
point of view, I should like to submit only two periods. One is
the Harlem Renaissance of the 1920's, especially looking at one
of the forthtellers of the Black Power rebellion of the 60's and
70's, namely, Marcus Garvey. The other is the 1960's when the
locus of the prophetic tradition shifted deliberately from the
industrially underdeveloped and agrarian South to the badlands
of the industrialized North, particularly looking briefly at the
role of that urban prophet, Malcolm X.

The Harlem Renaissance was an epoch which produced
enormous creative and imaginative enterprises by blacks in
New York. Nourished by a rising black middle class literati and
growing self-consciousness about wanting a name, authors,
poets, dancers, musicians, actors, painters, and politicians
exploded with efforts of ethnic liberation. It was an epoch
embracing both the American black and the West Indian culture
in spite of many strains and tensions often existing between
these two groups thrown together in the ghettoes of the North-
east. James Weldon Johnson, Claude McKay, Countee Cullen,
Langston Hughes, Jean Toomer, Jessie Fauset are but a few
strands in this black medley.

Prof. Nathan Huggins in his study of the Harlem Renaissance
points out that World War I really gave birth to the "New Negro."[73]
Several events had occurred. One was the organization of the
Pan-African Congress in 1919 by W.E.B DuBois and others. This
Congress and subsequent ones had a vision of what could be
called "black ecumenicity" between Africa and her American
legatees in the Diaspora. It sought to focus international attention
on the African colonies and to raise consciousness amongst
American blacks about African links. This consciousness-raising
ought to also be seen in the context of nationalism in Europe

which had been released both by the break-up of the Austro-Hungarian Empire and by the establishment of several new countries by various ethnic groups.

Another event was the return of New York's 15th Infantry Regiment from the war and its triumphant victory parade down Fifth Avenue in February, 1919. The regiment consisted of Negro volunteers who went to fight for the United States in Europe, only to be assigned to the French Army as the 369th Regiment because of prejudice and the refusal of the U.S. Army to command black combat troops.[74] It was, incidentally, this same segregated regiment which went to fight so admirably in Korea and also was mentioned in various dispatches, only to be dissolved by the U.S. Army after the policy for integration in the armed forces was announced at the end of the Korean War.

Indeed Alain Locke, a black professor at Howard University, wrote a book entitled *The New Negro* in which he claimed that the Old Negro was merely a fiction of white minds assisted by blacks because the blacks discovered that conforming to stereotypes paid off. So, wrote Locke:

> . . . for generations in the mind of America, the Negro
> has been more of a formula than a human being.[75]

It is also curious and possibly more than a coincidence that during this period many whites began to discover Negroes as a literary possibility, albeit in stereotyped and often flagrantly racist form: Van Vechten's *Nigger Heaven*, O'Neill's *Emperor Jones*, E. E. Cummings' *The Enormous*, DuBose Hayward's *Porgy*, Sherwood Anderson's *Dark Laughter*.

Yet there was an accompanying political theme of a longing for Africa because of the lingering pained insecurity of blacks in this country. The man who heard this lament and who proclaimed a word to bind up this lament was one Marcus Garvey, born in Jamaica in 1887 and died in London in 1940. Garvey was in many ways the more militant leader of the legacy actually left by Edward Blyden (1832-1912), also West Indian and an early advocate of international blackness.[76] Fired up by Booker Washington's *Up From Slavery*, Garvey came to New York in 1916 and established his Universal Negro Improvement Association which he had actually originally formed in Jamaica two years previously.

He proclaimed a new evangelism which insisted that only the black himself could liberate himself. His dramatic cry, "Up, you mighty race," fed an undernourished emotional appetite as did the pageantry and color attached to his large rallies and parades through Harlem. He founded a newspaper, *Negro World,* which was alone amongst black newspapers in refusing to accept advertisements for preparations claiming to straighten kinky hair or bleach the skin. One of the black nationalist groups which came out of and outlived the Garvey movement was the African Orthodox Church, which was founded in New York City and still survives in Harlem.[77] This church taught about the blackness of Christ and the Blessed Virgin somewhat ahead of the later apostles of black theology. Whilst most of his business enterprises failed, Garvey was very bent on providing the Negro with vehicles for economic independence and liberation.

He supplied a needed pride and positive self-image for American Negroes far beyond Harlem. His U.N.I.A. was established in several other states as well as in England and the Caribbean. Garvey provided both hope and courage in the face of lynchings and continued rejection of blacks by whites. But he was also concerned to improve the daily lives of blacks in this country by instilling them with racial confidence so that they would move toward self-help and self-reliance. This was demonstrated at the Sixth International Convention of the Negro Peoples of the World which he organized and presided over in Kingston, Jamaica in August, 1929. At the gathering amongst other themes discussed and deliberated were representation at the League of Nations on behalf of Pan-Africanism, social and educational centers for isolated Negro communities, particularly in rural areas, health and nutrition instruction.[78] It was during Garvey's time that the first large-scale production of Negro dolls reached the market.[79] John Hope Franklin commented on the effect of Garveyism and his appeal for racial pride:

> Its significance lies in the fact that it was the first and only real mass movement among Negroes in the history of the United States and that it indicates the extent to which Negroes entertained doubts concerning the hope for first-class citizenship in the only fatherland of which they knew.[80]

The contribution of Garvey was finally recognized and institutionalized by the Jamaican House of Representatives in 1952 when it passed a resolution recommending that Garvey's birthday be observed as a public holiday.[81] This was done, significantly enough, ten years before that colony gained its independence from Britain.

The link between Garvey and the black who was known variously as Malcolm Little, Malcolm X, and El-Hajj Malik El-Shabazz was established through Malcolm X's father, a Garveyite and Baptist minister. Noticeably, the link between this vigorous urban street preacher and prophet and the biblical prophetic tradition was also his father. In his *Autobiography* Malcolm X tells the story of how his pregnant mother was threatened by the Ku Klux Klan, not in the South but in Omaha, Nebraska, because of his father's activities on behalf of Garvey's U.N.I.A. The Klansmen reminded her that it was "the good Christian white people" who were bitter about his father's activities amongst the so-called decent Negroes of Omaha.[82] Eventually in 1929 the whites burned his family's house in Omaha whilst the family was inside. The family moved on to Michigan, but his father continued his activities on behalf of Garveyism also in Michigan, taking young Malcolm to meetings of the U.N.I.A. in Lansing.[83] It was in 1931 that his father died, believed to have been a victim of a lynching, afterwards put across streetcar tracks and almost cut in half. It was the truncated stump of a strong father seen by young six-year-old Malcolm Little. He noted the vigor with which his father held on to life even in this condition:

> He lived two and a half hours in that condition. Negroes then were stronger than they are now, especially Georgia Negroes. Negroes born in Georgia had to be strong simply to survive.[84]

This was the Malcolm Little phase which included his imprisonment and his voyages as a hustler on the streets of Detroit and Harlem. It was during his time in prison that he became acquainted with the teachings of the Honourable Elijah Mohammed and the Black Muslims. He corresponded with Elijah Mohammed, Messenger of Allah, and after his release from prison, he joined the Muslims and changed his name to Malcolm X as both a symbol and a conviction that with Islam the Black man in America can be born anew. In some thoughts about Negro History Week, Malcolm X expressed the reason for establishing one's new birth and identity as a follower of Islam:

> Just as a tree without roots is dead, a people without history or cultural roots also becomes a dead people. And when you look at us, those of us who are called

> Negro, we're called that because we are like dead peo-
> ple. We have nothing to identify ourselves as part of
> the human family . . . . Formerly we could be identified
> by the names we wore when we came here. When we
> were first brought here, we had different names . . . .
> But once our names were taken and our language was
> taken and our identity destroyed and our roots were
> cut off with no history, we became like a stump, some-
> thing dead . . . . Anybody could step on us, trample
> upon us, or burn us . . . .[85]

After tutelage in various Muslim mosques in America, in 1954
he was sent to be the chief minister of the Black Muslim movement in Harlem where he ripened, matured, and took on the
mantle of a religious prophet for urban blacks to urban whites
for the cause of social justice. His constant theme was separation
and black self-reliance – self-reliance spiritually, religiously,
economically. Once accused of wanting the same thing as the
racists and segregationists, Malcolm distinguished between *segregation* and *separation* as the Muslims understood them:

> *Segregation* is when your life and liberty are controlled,
> regulated by *someone else* . . . . Segregation is that
> which is forced upon inferiors by superiors. But *sep-
> aration* is that which is done voluntarily, by two equals –
> for the good of both![86]

It was yet another name change which directed Malcolm X
toward yet another appraisal of the role of social justice in the
racial situation: El-hajj Malik El-Shabazz, a name which reflected
the "Damascus Road conversion" which he underwent during a
pilgrimage to Mecca. At a press interview in Cairo in 1964
Malcolm X was asked what impressed him most about the Hajj
to Mecca. He replied: "The *brotherhood!* The people of all races,
colors, from all over the world coming together as *one*. It has
proved to me the power of the One God."[87]

The interracial, intercultural nature of the Islamic culture
and faith as he witnessed it at Mecca never ceased to fill Malcolm
X with awe. As he noted in a diary which he had kept during the
journey:

> There were tens of thousands of pilgrims, from all
> over the world. They were of all colors, from blue-eyed

blonds to black-skinned Africans. But we were all participating in the same ritual, displaying a spirit of unity
and brotherhood that my experience in America had
led me to believe never could exist between the white
and the non-white.[88]

All of this was part of what he called a "rearrangement of my
thought-patterns."[89] But he also sought to link this to a need for
international black solidarity. To this end in 1964 he founded the
Organization of African Unity which was patterned after the
Organization of African Unity in the motherland.[90] As Prof. John
Clarke rightly detects, Malcolm X understood that negotiations
and unity were actually significant when both partners were
equal. Thus for there to be black/white unity, there had first to
be black unity.[91] This was a political and cultural link with Africa
which was Marcus Garvey's vision left unrealized. It was also
after the Hajj that he began to hold meetings in Harlem's
Audubon Ballroom for non-Muslims, hoping to establish a covenant of unity amongst blacks.[92] On Sunday, 21st February, 1965,
at one of the gatherings he held in the Audubon Ballroom in
Harlem, Malcolm X, as he continued to be popularly known,
was assassinated.

The Rev. Wyatt Tee Walker, a friend and associate of Martin
Luther King, Jr., and advocate of the path of non-violence in the
struggle for social justice, gave a comparison of King and
Malcolm X. He suggested that Malcolm X brought forth a new
kind of assertiveness amongst American blacks which was necessary and important in establishing being and presence as
blacks:

The non-violent movement in the South broke the
shackles from many chained minds in the North
through its raw courage alone . . . . The new-found
assertiveness of the Negro in the North went off in as
many different directions as the personalities through
whom it was filtered . . . . Vicariously through (Malcolm
X), some Negro men got up off their knees for the first
time in their lives and touched their manhood as if it
were a new Christmas toy.[93]

Having come to the end of our various unveilings of the prophetic tradition, how might one in summary fashion speak of
social justice and the prophetic point of view. One finds favoring

language in Brueggemann's book, *The Prophetic Imagination,* which might offer some clues. Brueggemann insists that whilst our affluence allows us to overlook others' pain or to rationalize our way around it, and whilst our taking oppression for granted permits us to dismiss the cries and messages of the injured and marginal as agitators or crazies, and whilst we are convinced that everything is accessible and solvable, thus reducing all spiritual problems to matters of psychology or psychiatry, nevertheless the prophetic point of view has an important role.[94]

The prophetic role has constantly been one of criticizing, which is one of its more important functions as it attempts to measure the morality in the affairs of men by the judgment given by a greater authority with the intention of moving men to just actions. Prophetic criticizing should provide an element of the transcendent in ethical decisions; otherwise the danger is that ethics and actions will be grounded solely in the morass of pragmaticism and expediency. When this occurs, it is more than likely that we will find ourselves again being spoken to by Amos: "They do not know how to do the right." This is not necessarily the action of reprimand, although this also belongs to the prophetic tradition. The prophetic engages in "the language of grief, the rhetoric that engages the community in mourning for a funeral they do not want to admit. It is indeed their own funeral."[95]

But the prophetic point of view also includes what Brueggemann calls "prophetic energizing," that is, activating people to cut through the language — "a language that engages the community in new discernments and celebrations just when it had nearly given up and had nothing to celebrate."[96] Marcus Garvey understood this very well with his cry, "Up, you mighty race," as did the prophet Micah when he said many centuries ago:

> He has showed you, O man, what is good;
>   and what does the Lord require of you
> but to do justice, and to love kindness,
>   and to walk humbly with your God. (6.8)

Notes

1. *Time* Magazine, June 14, 1968.

2. *Institutes of the Christian Religion*, Bk IV, Chap. XX, pars. 4-8. Cited in Waldo Beach and H. Richard Niebuhr. *Christian Ethics*. New York: Roland Press, 1973, p. 292.

3. "Rights," *Encyclopedia of Philosophy*, Vol. 7 & 8. New York: Macmillan, 1967, 195-199.

4. *Ibid.*, p. 198.

5. *Ibid.*

6. *Ibid.*, p. 199.

7. Cited in *Social Value Systems Analysis*. Center for Ethics and Social Policy. Berkeley, 1978, p. 8-9.

8. *Encyclopedia of Philosophy*, Vol. 3 & 4, p. 298.

9. *Ibid.*, p. 300.

10. *Transfiguration of Politics*, New York; Harper and Row, 1975, p. 252-254.

11. *Ibid.*, p. 225.

12. Cited in Lehman, *ibid.*, p. 256.

13. *Church Dogmatics*, IV/1. Edinburgh: T & T Clark, 1956, p. 542.

14. *Ibid.*, p. 544.

15. *Loc. Cit.* Berkeley: University of California Press, 1957, p. 1-4.

16. *Church Dogmatics*, III/4, p. 116-117.

17. *Ibid.*, p. 117.

18. Edmond Jacob, *Theology of the Old Testament*. A.W. Heathcote and P. J. Allcock, Trans. New York: Harper and Brothers, 1958, p. 94.

19. *Ibid.*, p. 94. Cf. Lev. 19.36; Deut. 33.19; Ps. 23.3.

20. *Ibid.*, p. 95.

21. *Ibid.*

22. *Ethics in a Christian Context.* New York: Harper and Row, 1963, p. 125.

23. *Prophecy in Ancient Israel.* Oxford: Basil Blackwell, 1973, p. 1.

24. Lindblom points out other examples of this foretelling, such as I K. 14; 1 K. 17.1; II K. 1.2 ff.; II K. 8.1; II K. 4.27. *Ibid.*, p. 49-50.

25. *Ibid.*, p. 60-61.

26. *Ibid.*, p. 55.

27. Gerhard von Rad, *The Message of the Prophets.* London: SCM Press, 1968, p. 66-67.

28. Lindblom defines "theonomic ethics" as being characteristic of prophetic ethics. "Behind all that they apprehended as right and good, they set Yahweh as Authority and Guardian. Every offense. . . was at the same time an offense against Yahweh's holy will." *Op. Cit.*, p. 346.

29. John Bright, *A History of Israel.* Philadelphia: Westminster Press, 1959, p. 240.

30. H. Donner, "Die soziale Botschaft der Propheten im Lichte der Gesselschaftsordnung in Israel," *Oriens Antiquus.* II. 1963, p. 229.

31. *Ibid.*, p. 230.

32. See a very illuminating treatment of Israel's nomadic roots in Roland de Vaux. *Ancient Israel*, I. New York: McGraw-Hill, 1965, p. 3-15.

33. Donner, *Op. Cit.*, p. 231.

34. *Ibid.*, p. 234.

35. *Ibid.*, p. 235.

36. *Ibid.*, p. 236.

37. Bright, *Op. Cit.*, p. 248. *A number of writings dealing with the poor in scripture and the Christian tradition have appeared, including: Richard Batey, *Jesus and the Poor.* New York: Harper and Row, 1972; Rachel Hosmer, *Attitudes to Poverty in Christian Thought.* (Unpublished S.T.M. Thesis, General Theological Seminary, 1976); Peter B. Miscall, *Concept of the Poor in the Old Testament.* (Unpublished Ph.D. Disser-

tation, Harvard University, 1972); Milton Schwantes, *Das Recht der Armen*, Frankfurt, 1977.

38. This essay, "Christian Community and Civil Community," is found in Karl Barth's *Community, State and Church*. G.R. Howe, Trans. Gloucester, Mass: Peter Smith, 1968, p. 173.

39. The most frequently cited theme in Amos is concern for the poor and needy. Wolff points out that he mentions the "helpless" (dal) (2.7; 4.1; 5.11; 8.6); the "poor" (*'ebyon*) (2.6; 4.1; 5.12; 8.4; 6); the "oppressed" (*'ani*) (2.7; 8.4). In 2.6 and 5.12 he parallels the righteous and the needy. Hans Walter Wolff *Amos the Prophet*. Foster R. McCurley, trans. Philadelphia: Fortress Press, 1971.

40. Karl Barth, "Die Kirche zwischen Ost und West," *Der Goetze Wackelt*. Berlin: Kathe vogt Verlag, 1961, p. 137.

41. *Op. Cit.* Munich: Chr Kaiser Verlag, 1969, p. 65.

42. See Hans Maier's *Revolution und Kirche: Zur Frühgeschichte der Christlichen Demokratie*. Munich: Deutscher Taschenbuch Verlag, 1973, p. 9-67, 248-268 for a very good treatment of the history and ideology of the European Christian Democratic parties and their relationship to the state. *Revolution and Church* is the title of the English edition.

43. Wolff maintains that Amos uses this pair of words as a measuring rod for Israel's carrying out of justice and right. *Amos the Prophet*, pp. 59, 64.

44. Terrien - this is a word used only, again, by Isaiah, but is not a word of the convenant tradition in pre-exilic times. It is also found in the wisdom tradition. "Amos and Wisdom," *Israel's Prophetic Heritage*. New York: Harper & Bros., 1962, 112-113. Cf. Wolff. *Ibid.*, p. 56-57.

45. *The Gospel According to St. John.* London SPCK, 1958, p. 230.

46. Cited in Karl Barth, *Church Dogmatics*, IV/3.1, p. 13.

47. S. theol., III, ques 22, art. 1, ad 3. Cited in Barth, *Ibid.*

48. John F. Jansen, *Calvin's Doctrine of the Work of Christ*. London: James Clarke & Co., 1956, p., 39-40.

49. *Ibid.*, p. 42.

50. *Ibid.*, p. 101.

51. "Moreover, we must understand this of His office; that He is Christ, King, and High Priest. For as Christ means anointed, and only Prophets, kings, and priests were anointed, so one sees that all three offices apply to Him: the prophetic office, for He only is our teacher and master (Matt. 23.8) . . . . Cited in Jansen, *ibid.*, p. 37.

52. *Church Dogmatics*, IV/3.1, p. 55.

53. *Ibid.*, p. 56.

54. *Ibid.*, p. 61.

55. *Ibid.*, p. 49-51. Cf. Jansen, *Op. Cit.*, p. 69-79.

56. Paul Tillich, *The Eternal Now*. New York: Charles Scribner's Sons, 1963, p. 122-123.

57. *Church Dogmatics*, IV/3.1, p. 69.

58. Werner Kümmel, *Conception of Property in the New Testament*. Geneva: World Council of Churches, 1951, p. 1.

59. Martin Hengel, *Property and Riches in the Early Church*. John Bowden, Trans., Philadelphia: Fortress Press, 1974, p. 24.

60. *Ibid.*

61. *Ibid.*, p. 30.

62. Cited from Marx and Engels, *Correspondence*, 516-517 in Carl Landauer, *European Socialism*, 1. Berkeley: University of California Press, 1959, p. 144. Landauer also argues against the labeling of Marx as a historical materialist. *Loc. Cit.*, p. 143-145.

63. Cited in Alvin Redman, ed., *The Wit and Humor of Oscar Wilde*. New York: Dover, 1959, p. 185. Cf. *The Works of Oscar Wilde*. London: Spring Books, 1963, p. 915-936.

64. Cited in Paul Oestreicher, *The Christian-Marxist Dialogue*. New York: Macmillan, 1969, p. 35.

65. Frederick Engels, *The Origin of the Family, Private Property, and the State*. New York: International Publishers, 1972, p. 71-72.

66. For an analysis of the relationship between the economic aims of slave-handling countries and the actual slave trade, see Eric Williams, *Capitalism and Slavery*. New York: G.P. Putnam's Sons, 1966.

67. Engels, *Op. Cit.*, p. 224-225.

68. Karl Marx and Frederich Engels, *The Communist Manifesto*, with an introduction by A.J.P. Taylor. New York: Penguin Books, 1967, p. 40.

69. From Marx's *Poverty of Philosophy*, p. 88. Cited in Landauer, *Op. Cit.*, p. 144.

70. *Nobody Knows My Name.* New York: Dial Press, 1961, p. 98-116.

71. *Israel: Its Life and Culture*, I-II. Copenhagen: P. Branner, 1926, p. 245. Cf. Abba's article in *The Interpreter's Dictionary of the Bible*, III. Nashville: Abingdon, 1962, p. 500-508.

72. *Loc. Cit.* Greenwich: Fawcett Publications, p. 170.

73. Nathan I. Huggins, *Harlem Renaissance.* Oxford University Press, p. 52.

74. *Ibid.*, p. 55-56.

75. Cited in Huggins. *Ibid.*, p. 57.

76. An adequate development of this pioneer in Pan Africanism is given in the biography by Hollis R. Lynch, *Edward Wilmot Blyden: Pan-Negro Patriot.* Oxford University Press, 1967.

77. The religious dimensions of Garveyism are discussed quite fully in a recent book by Randall Burkett, *Garveyism as a Religious Movement: The Institutionalization of a Black Civil Religion.* Metuchen, New Jersey: Scarecrow Press, 1978.

78. Edmund D. Cronon, *Black Moses.* Madison: University of Wisconsin Press, 1964, p. 150-156.

79. *Ibid.*, p. 175.

80. From *Slavery to Freedom*, p. 483, cited in *Black Moses*, p. 215-216.

81. *Ibid.*, p. 218.

82. *The Autobiography of Malcolm X.* New York: Grove Press, 1964, p. 1.

83. *Ibid.*, p. 6-8.

84. *Ibid.*, p. 10.

85. John Henrik Clarke, ed., *Malcolm X: The Man and His Times*, New York: Collier Books, 1969, p. 323-324.

86. *Autobiography*, p. 246.

87. *Ibid.*, p. 338.

88. *Ibid.*, p. 340.

89. *Ibid.*

90. The charter for this organization is found in Clarke, *Op Cit.*, p. 335-342.

91. Introduction by John Henrik Clarke in *Malcolm X: The Man and His Times*, xxii.

92. *Autobiography*, p. 364-382.

93. Clarke, *Op. Cit.*, p. 66-67.

94. Walter Brueggemann, *The Prophetic Imagination*. Philadelphia: Press, 1978, p. 41.

95. *Ibid.*, p. 51.

96. *Ibid.*, p. 69.

Chapter 2

SOCIAL JUSTICE AND THE PROPHETS

John J. Kelley, S.M.
Catholic-Jewish Relations for the Diocese of Brooklyn,
Co-chairman, Rockaway Catholic-Jewish Council

For some time I have been teaching a course on "Jesus as Prophet" to Catholic adults in the Rockaways in New York City. This course must base itself in large measure on the prophets of the Jewish tradition. Another of my interests, a lifelong interest, is Catholic social teaching. Thus, in writing on social justice and the prophetic tradition, I write from these two perspectives.

The term "social justice" is not a biblical term. No biblical prophet ever used it. A modern term, a neologism invented in the nineteenth century, it has become common coin in western civilization.

The prophets had a burning passion for the holiness of their people, for the goodness which, like flowing water, shall be an unfailing stream of justice and good deeds.[1] The anger of the prophets against injustice, especially against injustice inflicted on the poor, the helpless, the defenseless, is identical to the anger of the Lord God of Hosts. This terrible anger is directed against all who inflict such violence, especially those who have been called to *zedekah*, the justice of holiness (Amos 8:4-6). Due to neglect of the prophetic tradition, until rather recently Catholics have not felt at home with these concepts and these inspired writings.

In teaching the prophets it becomes clear that the terms "justice" and "social justice" fall somehow within both the Jewish and the Catholic traditions. What is less clear is that there are great differences in our understandings of the words themselves.

Our assumptions need to be challenged.

Several assumptions might easily be made by anyone approaching this question. I identify three. The first assumption: the writings of and the spirit of the prophets are the common source of Jewish and Catholic concern for social justice. I believe that this is the assumption made by the esteemed Dr. Abraham Heschel when he wrote (c. 1972):

> . . . when Paul Tillich, Gustave Weigel and myself were invited by the Ford Foundation to speak from the same platform on the religious situation in America, we not only found ourselves in deep accord in disclosing what ails us but above all without prior consultation the three of us confessed that our guides in this critical age are the prophets of Israel, not Aristotle, not Karl Marx, but Amos and Isaia.[2]

A second assumption is that when Catholics and Jews enter into conversation regarding social justice, they may be presumed to be speaking about the same realities. A third and related assumption is that when Catholics and Jews use other terms dealing with social questions, they are using a common language, as for example when the word "religious" is used. When the non-observant Jew says that he is "not religious," however, he means something quite different from what the Christian understands him to mean.

After considerable study and reflection I am changing to the view that all three of these assumptions are erroneous. There are great semantic differences between the traditions. In this essay I shall try to demonstrate how and why this is so, and what ought to be done to improve our dialog and common action.

Why are the traditions so disparate?

Why should two great traditions, each supposedly relating to the same great prophetic figures and the same inspired books of holy writ, have such varying understandings? The question must be asked whether we can bring these great traditions into confluence enough so that we may establish a base for concerted action between them. The hope that common action in the future may be achieved encourages us to resolve these dilemmas.

One major difficulty is that both traditions are in great flux at this moment of history.

The Catholic Church's teaching on social justice has changed radically over the last hundred years. Since the encyclical *On the Condition of the Working Class* in 1891, the stereotype of an "unchanging church" has been thoroughly demolished. In the last thirty years the most fundamental of all the changes has been her own change in her perception of herself, interlocked with her own self-awareness of her abiltity to respond to the social issues.

From a posture of distance and even hostility to social movements in the nineteenth century the Church has discovered herself to be in interaction with the events and the new knowledge of the times. Perforce she has entered into reflection on her innermost being and has been progressively drawn into interaction, first with components of her own being, such as the curial structures, and progressively with elements of the larger world, not least of which is the Jewish tradition. This self-awareness was developed in a particular way in the conciliar decree, *The Church in the Modern World.*

In affirming that the Church is in great change, it may be useful to add two observations: first, this change is not something happening to the Church alone. The total cultural context is under great stress, even as the Church, so much so that the Jewish tradition is also in change, interlocked in the enormous cultural changes of our times. For example, the ordination of women is an issue in both communities. This issue faces the same kinds of problems within the Jewish communities as it does within the Christian communities.

Second, the fact that both traditions are in flux does not seem to make it easier to reflect on these changes. In fact, this flux makes it more difficult to generalize about the nature of the changes. It may be helpful to imagine a spectrum of social change, from left to right. In this visual model of social change, both communities are spread unevenly across the spectrum. Specific issues are treated similarly at a given point on the spectrum; for example, to continue on the women's issue, concern for the rights of women can be identified in both communities on the spectrum. The communities show great similarity in this respect. Other issues also show similarity on the spectrum, for example, the concern regarding abortion. Neither community is the monolith that may have been presumed in the past.

Despite these similarities (and despite great love for the scriptures in both communities) it must not be assumed that there are common sources in the scriptures for social and political theology. In particular, it must not be assumed that the Church's interest in social justice is rooted in her knowledge and love of the prophets of Israel. For such has not been the case. The Church's concern and passion for social justice has been almost untouched by the prophetic element, if we may judge by her official statements. For example, in the encyclical on the condition of the working class (1891), Leo XIII gave thirty-nine footnotes; none of these references is to the prophets. In the encyclical on the reconstruction of the social order (1931), Pius XI gives seventy seven references; none of them is of substance with respect to the prophets. And in the most recent encyclical (*Redemptor Hominis*. John Paul II, 1979) there are some 400 references; most of these are references to the New Testament—only one is from a prophet of the Tanach.

So it may be said that while the scriptural dimension has not been lacking from the official writings, Jesus the prophet and indeed all the prophets of Israel have been strangers to these documents.

Thus it may be held that the two traditions have not been able to meet and to learn from each other. Granted that there has been much mutual interaction in the study of scriptures within the last three decades, the traditions remain far apart. The fundamental reason—though not the only reason—is the disparity of parallel traditions. Two powerful locomotives run on parallel tracks, without appropriate interaction.

The interaction has been described as "minimal, restricted to professionals and scholars" (Rabbi Balfour Brickner, May 31, 1977).

Later in these pages we shall examine how the prophetic element is being reborn within the Christian communities.

In this area of social justice the Jewish tradition and the Catholic tradition have hardly begun to realize that, although they have developed some language which is common to both, in fact they have been very far apart. This is clear in a few examples such as tax support for the religious schools, abortion, religious education, etc. We must ask why it has taken so long for the traditions of social concerns to acknowledge the other, and why there has been so much reluctance to come to a convergence in this area of enormous need?

One aspect of the issue, from the viewpoint of the masses of our peoples, is that both constitutencies have been characterized by reluctance to enter into collaborative patterns of action. For instance, the secular issue of the hunger of the world's famine-beset nations should have brought these two giants into inter-action and cooperation. But negative dispositions continue to characterize the masses, and the masses of our people are ignorant of the traditions of the other.

Will there be a confluence of our traditions?

Major steps have been taken to bring the traditions together at the academic level. Local, regional, national and international conferences take place on a regular basis. But the picture remains a very mixed one.

In 1971, I was invited to give a lecture at Temple Israel in Dayton, Ohio, for the Religion in Life Program of the University of Dayton. In that presentation I offered some reflections

> on the contemporary developments of the Christian and Jewish relationship and . . . on the process by which these two religious traditions may be thought of as passing into the "people of God."[3]

In part, the traditions have not come together because they have not developed a common forum in which they could culti-vate common meanings for common terms. Their priorities have had little congruence. There is some evidence to the con-trary; for example the symbolic words of Isaia and Micah in-scribed on the United Nations building where the hope and vision of peace is expressed, that the nations will hammer

> their swords into plough shares,
> their spears into pruning hooks,
> nation will not lift sword against nation,
> there will be no more training for war.
> (Isaia 2:4-5; Micah 4:1-4)

But taken on the large the conversation between these tradi-tions is merely beginning. The reason ultimately is not that they are inimical to each other, but that they are alien to each other. They are not alien in the sense of being substantially at variance, but alien in the sense of having no common language, no com-mon set of symbols, unknown and somehow fearsome to each other.

The two traditions may be contrasted in some measure by their referents.

It may be useful to contrast the traditions. The Jewish tradition of justice may properly be called the Talmudic tradition. The Catholic tradition on the other hand is almost unrelated on social issues and until recently was known as the Natural Law tradition.

Within the Talmudic tradition Jewish scholarship had focused on questions of the Torah and the survival of the Jewish people. Within the Natural Law tradition Catholic scholarship utilized an Hellenic approach and focused on philosophical questions concerning society, person, human rights and social structures. The differences in orientation may be seen clearly in a few examples from a noted Jewish scholar, Samuel Belkin (*In His Image*, 1960). Reflecting on the halachic differences among the Tanaim, the Mishnaic sages, he points up the character of his tradition, contrasting it to speculative, metaphysical or theological work:

> Our Sages' chief concern was finding a system by which man, in his conduct, would apply the basic religious principles laid down in the Torah. Measured against practical Western concepts of social justice, talmudic laws — recorded in the Mishnah, the Tosefta, the halakic midrashim, and the Gemara — appear quite impractical. Indeed approached from a secular and social point of view, many rabbinic laws are difficult to understand or appreciate. This is so, however, only because the underlying principles, and even the rules of procedure of rabbinic law spring from profound religious and theological concepts, and are not based at all on social theories. (p.17)

And later he makes this more explicit:

> In the Roman and Greek order, the "city," "state," or "society" had a value in themselves. The state, as a state, had metaphysical value and the "state," "city" and "social order" are often spoken of as abstract institutions which take priority over the individuals.
>
> In Jewish tradition, however, all such terms are unknown. (p. 117)

Another statement by the same author helps us to understand why there is so little concern for the common good:

> Jewish law . . . is primarily an expression of the Jewish concept of individuality as it affects man's relations with his fellow man, is more concerned with individual morality than with the protection of society. (p. 216)

It may be appropriate to identify the meaning of Natural Law. This is the term used by traditional Catholic social thought to indicate that the categories being used are in fact worked from philosophical bases (rather than theological), from assumptions which can be seen as deduced from reason, but which are compatible with theological truths though they are not in themselves theological by nature.

Thus, the nature of society is considered as a truth of the natural law, known by the light of reason. Understanding of humanity as being a mirror of the divine can be the philosophic, natural law foundation of man's concern for man. Obviously in a dialogic situation it is helpful to the conversation if all the participants can accept the natural law foundation rather than having to argue over the nature and value of society. Concretely, however, at the present time there is less tendency in the Catholic community to speak in these terms.

By contrast, the Talmudic tradition has a totally different methodology. It is understandable then that the two traditions, like ships in the night, went past each other without sharing a signal of common concern.

The prophets have not been present to the conversation on social justice.

As we have mentioned, the literature of the prophets remains unknown to many Catholics. It is the part of scripture where they have a shallow, biased, almost fundamentalist understanding. Possibly the most common Christian error in the reading of the prophets is to read and hear only the messianic texts and to understand these only in a univocal, ahistorical sense.

This is not to say that the best of Catholic scholarship is not at ease with the best of Jewish and Protestant learning. The strength of the professional scholars, accompanied and made possible by an irenic move away from polemic, is rapidly filtering through to the nonprofessional. But being at ease has not yet penetrated the constituencies. At present the being-at-ease is an academic strength, with pastoral applications still only on the horizon. The best that can be said at the popular level is that church members are beginning to speak of themselves as belonging to a "prophetic community." We shall return to this perception later.

Catholic renewal is searching its sources – this means among other things that scholarship must go to the Tanak, the Jewish bible, afresh. The prophets must come alive again. And the meaning of the texts with their implications for social justice must be learned anew if the Catholic community is to play its proper role in the reconstruction of the social order.

Although Catholic social doctrine has developed from the earliest times, received in some measure from the parent Jewish body, the Catholic social doctrine which concerns us here is the product of the last hundred years. This doctrine has been much more Greek than biblical. The modern development of this body of doctrine begins with Leo XIII in 1891, especially with his encyclical *Rerum Novarum*, literally "concerning revolutionary change."

This Catholic position is changing rapidly. Within a world context of renewal of learning, in bible as well as in secular disciplines which relate to understanding of the bible (such as anthropology), the Catholic performance has been little short of spectacular. In biblical studies this renewal dates mainly from 1943, the date of the encyclical *Divino Afflante Spiritu* of Pius XII.

Besides the change in biblical studies and biblical categories, Catholic scholarship has done a monumental shift from Aristotelian categories to contextual, organic, process categories. Indeed in the Church a new vision of man is being born.

In addition, there has been a renaissance of Christian interest in prophecy. This has taken place in two ways. First the scholarly interest in the bible has produced substantial developments in this area. I think of John Bright's study on Jeremiah (1965) and John L. McKenzie's volume on *Second Isaiah* (1968) (Both volumes were published in the Anchor Bible Series), and Joseph Blenkinsopp's book on *Prophecy and Canon* (1977).

Cardinal Roy has commented on the need for such studies:

> . . . there is *a whole field of theological and pastoral research to be studied* (fortunately this task is already being widely undertaken) on the idea of "prophetism."[4]

The second way in which this idea has taken hold is at a more popular level: the charismatic movement has made numbers of Christians consider the gift of prophecy to be a normal gift within the Christian communities. A flurry of paperback books and pamphlets have appeared for more popular consumption. Some of these have serious academic qualifications.[5]

One serious weakness of all the studies that I have been able to examine is their inability to integrate the issues of social justice with the theological and pastoral reflections on prophecy. In fact, the most consistent criticism of the charismatic movement has been its inability to develop a thrust for social action.

There are many discoveries for Christian students of the prophets. As Christians take up the bible anew to study the history, the presence, the ministry and message of the prophets of Israel, they will learn many surprising things. Not least is that as they develop a sense of history, they will find themselves increasingly at home in the company of the *neviim.*

They may be surprised to find that there were historical periods in which the prophets were very active and other periods in which the gift was not operative:

> There was general agreement [in the Jewish community] that prophecy, in its special connotation, ceased with the overthrow of the first Temple [c. 586 BCE] although it lingered with a few during the exile. When the latter prophets, Haggai, Zechariah, and Malachi died, the Holy Spirit departed from Israel.[6]

Another discovery that may upset them is that the prophet is not simply one who foretells the future, a stereotype that is difficult to efface. Among the surprises is that of Moses as the prototype of all the prophets and especially of a great prophet and teacher who is to come (Deut. 18:18-19; 34:10; Numbers 12; Acts 3:22; 7:37).

Another surprise will be learning of the expectations of the Jewish people concerning Elijah and his imminent return (Mal. 3:1-6, 22-24; Sirach 48:10; Matt. 11:14: 17:10-13; Mk. 9:11; Lk. 1:17). Christians will find the teaching of Jesus and the gospels concerning Elijah very striking. They will begin to perceive Jesus as a man within the tradition of the prophets of Israel.

Among the prophetic ideas which they will find exciting and hopeful is the "day of the Lord," great and terrible, with its forecast of judgment, destruction of the wicked (especially the

enemies of Israel) and the promise of lasting peace. Each of the
prophets will have his distinct message: unique, concrete, crisp,
demanding.

For example, the uniqueness of Amos is pointed out:

> Amos was among the first of the prophets to express
> clearly and unhesitatingly the universal concept of
> God, and the doctrine that social justice was an essen-
> tial part of religion.[7]

The prophets will demand a turning (*l'shuv*) from sin, a return
to the covenant of love and faith, a conversion to true justice.
They will demand integrity, a holiness requiring congruence of
faith and deed. They will promise liberation, shading into redemption and salvation.

Among the prophetic ideas they will be struck by the teaching
of *zedekah*, the holiness which vivifies the person living justly in
the presence of the Lord. In biblical language this holiness is
justice, a quality of the good man, the very substance of the divine.

Christian readers will experience the prophetic anger directed
against unfaithful Juda and Israel. They will be moved by the
imagery and the poetry of the prophets in their concern for the
poor, the widows, the oppressed, the imprisoned. They will
marvel at their passion for integrity of life. All of this they will
find exciting, stimulating, hopeful. We must question, however,
whether they will find there the content of social justice with
the connotation that these words have for them.

Among other discoveries that Christians will make is that the
messianic oracles are not nearly so clear as a fundamentalist
mentality may have suggested. Two ambiguities seem to be worth
mentioning, the ambiguity of time and the people of the prophet's
concern.

The first ambiguity is that of time: the prophets have a most
disconcerting way of bringing together several time frames, the
present, the near (foreseeable) future, and the eschaton. While
popular Christian belief tends to interpret the prophetic messianic passages as written of Jesus as the messia without equiv-
ocation, a little study shows that the prophetic texts often speak
more of a situation which is present to the prophet himself in
his own historical circumstance. He speaks (or writes) ambiguously of a near future (think, for example, of Jeremia's prophecy
of seventy years of exile) and of a last time, the utopia of never-
ending peace. Often he is speaking of the immediate situation,

that present to him. These three time frames (the present, the near future, and the eschaton) are often placed over one another in such a way that it becomes impossible to discern one sense of the text to the exclusion of the other two. The serious reader is both excited and exasperated.

A second ambiguity in the prophetic word is the ethnocentric character of the message. By and large the prophetic word from Yahweh is addressed to Israel, or to Juda, or to those Jews living in a specific time and place. It is not simply addressed to all men everywhere, and not even to all believers. It is addressed to the people of God in the limited sense of Israel. For modern man to bring meaning to these texts which apply to contemporary society, or to all men everywhere is to make an accommodation of the texts which their human authors did not intend.

One example which has been a source of confusion may illustrate the principle: the concept of the remnant, the "shear" of Isaia and other prophets, has a spiritual meaning to Christians which it does not have for their Jewish friends. Christian understanding of it is no doubt an extension of the intention which the prophet had when using this term. For Jews the meaning is more ethno-centric, pertaining to God's care for the survival of his people Israel.

A deeper study of the prophets by Christians will be necessary if we are to use them to illuminate the causes of social justice. Hopefully such study may become an interfaith study.

Associated with this interest in prophecy, a radical re-thinking of Christian ministry is going on within Christian communities.

One of the most obvious developments within the Catholic community is its changing attitude toward ministry. Even as the Catholic community finds the numbers of vocations to the priesthood and the traditional ministry falling off, it also finds that there is a deep change in attitude toward ministry itself. The community is seeing itself as a ministering community, a community that worships, that serves, that heals.

There is a new thrust in ministry. In identifying the changes in ministry, Christians look first to the personal example of Jesus. The ministry of the Church is always a manifold participation in the ministry of Jesus. The example of "the man for others" becomes the criterion for all mission. Of course this does not limit the possibilities to those which Jesus himself is recorded as having exercised.

A reexamination of the ministry of Jesus in the light of our changing world brings out in striking fashion the way that Jesus identifies strongly with the two biblical images of prophet and servant: prophet as one who critically evaluates social structures, and servant as one who lives for the service of others. The "suffering servant" image developed in the four songs of Second Isaia is well known. Matthew and Luke each give us a song descriptive of the person and ministry of Jesus. The servant functions of Jesus contained in Christian perception include:

- to bring glad tidings to the poor
- to proclaim liberty to captives
- to free prisoners and to set the downtrodden free
- to give sight to the blind and to heal the brokenhearted
- to announce a time of favor, a year of grace.

For our purposes it is enough to note that all of the expectations of the ministry of the servant focus on concern for the poor and the disadvantaged, specifically the oppressed and the imprisoned. In other of the servant songs, there is stress on the complementary issues of justice and peace, as well as a concern for the "nations"; that is, the peoples not yet within the covenant.

There is no question that there has been a shift of emphasis in the work of Vatican II from Christ the King to Jesus the Servant. But this has been followed after the council by a further change of emphasis from Jesus the Priest to Jesus the Prophet. There is only one reference in *Gaudium et Spes* (No. 43) to the concern of the prophets, and of Jesus as Prophet, for an integration of life and faith. Much of the new stress on Jesus as Prophet has developed since the Council. The prophet in the biblical tradition is basically one filled with the spirit of the Lord who is able to speak the word of the Lord with courage and wisdom. The prophet like Amos or like Nathan (cf. 2 Sam. 2ff) brings the word of justice; he teaches, he heals, and he also alienates. Because of his function of social critic, he may be a lonely figure. The biblical prophets often die for their efforts at justice.

The Church's ministry to the secular has taken a variety of forms over the centuries. The "works of mercy" have been an integral part of the Church's service to suffering people. Under the title of "the corporal works of mercy," and motivated by compassion for the poor, the Church has taken up the work of hospitals, orphanages, and similar services. Under the title "spiritual works," it developed a system of schools, and took interest in comforting the afflicted. This ministry was concrete and pragmatic, as is the imagery of the New Testament story of the last judgment: "Whatsoever you did to . . . these you did to me."

In the new perceptions of our times, however, the Church has become increasingly aware that it is not enough to answer these problems on the personal and individual level. Social structures, such as the socio-economic systems, need to be reformed in favor of the disadvantaged. This is reflected clearly in the witness of Paul VI in his visits to the United Nations, to Latin America, to Africa and to India, as well as in his writings. In the visit of John Paul II to Puebla in 1979 he spoke clearly of his concern for the poor of Latin America and reminded the people of Jesus the Servant.

Much of the destiny of man is worked out in socio-economic systems. If these are unjust they can be described as subject to demonic powers, in need of exorcism.

It is difficult to state briefly the Church's understanding of its role with respect to the secular. The Catholic theory has been that the Church has no special competence to deal directly with the problems of the secular. Such a sweeping assertion does not exclude its right to teach the moral principles which must undergird the solution of all human problems. And positively the theory is expressed indirectly in the statement, "The temporal is properly the sphere of the apostolate of the laity."[8]

The term "prophetic community" has become increasingly popular in Catholic circles. I have the impression that the term has grown out of the renewal subsequent to Vatican II. In the documents of that Council reference is made to the prophets and to a hope for a new integration of faith and deed:

> (*the*) split between the faith which many profess and their daily lives deserves to be counted among the more serious errors of our age. Long since, the prophets of the Old Testament fought vehemently against this scandal and, even more did Jesus Himself in the New Testament threaten it with grave punishment.[9]

On the one hand one may be disturbed that this is the only reference to the prophets and the integration of faith and deed ("social justice" in the Jewish sense of the term). The uniqueness of the reference indicates that there is no case in support of the prophets as an important element in former Catholic understanding of social justice. (This minimal reference to the Neviim is corrected somewhat by reference to the scriptures in *Justice in the World,* (1971).)

But on the other hand, since the Council fathers thought it appropriate to make this allusion and to add a reference from Third Isaia (Isaia 58:1-12), it may be fitting to say something of this relatively late passage. Third Isaia speaks to a people coming out of exile and slavery who long to experience the presence of the Lord and who are called to a holiness of life. This integrity of life expresses itself in concern for the oppressed, the poor, the homeless, the naked. The text reads in part as follows:

> Is not this the sort of fast that pleases me — it is the
> Lord Yahweh who speaks — to break unjust fetters
> and undo the thongs of the yoke,
> to let the oppressed go free,
> and break every yoke,
> to share your bread with the hungry,
> and shelter the homeless poor,
>
> to clothe the man you see to be naked
> and not turn from your own kin?
> Then will your light shine like the dawn
> and your wound be quickly healed over.
>
> Your integrity will go before you
> and the glory of Yahweh behind you.
> Cry, and Yahweh will answer,
> Call and he will say, "I am here."
>
> If you do away with the yoke,
> the clenched fist, the wicked word
> if you give your bread to the hungry,
> and relief to the oppressed,
>
> your light will rise in the darkness,
> and your shadows become like noon.
> Yahweh will always guide you,
> giving you relief in desert places.
>
> He will give strength to your bones
> and you will be like a watered garden,
> like a spring of water
> whose waters never run dry.
>
> You will rebuild the ancient ruins,
> build up on the old foundations,
> You will be called "breach-mender,"
> "Restorer of ruined houses."

This beautiful poetic passage clearly links the works of mercy to the mission of Israel, integrates faith and deed, so that the presence of the Lord Yahweh is felt, and the light and glory (the *shekina*) are seen.

Unfortunately the text clearly confirms the ethno-centric concern in verse 7, "for your own kin." Even though such integrity will make this people a light for others, for the nations and kings (59:3-6), the sequel (60) is ambiguous in that while it shows the nations coming to Jerusalem, the text is slanted toward a material and even chauvinistic domination of the peoples by Israel. Fortunately the servant hymn of chapter 61 corrects to some degree the ethno-centric character of the vision.

The prophetic community has a larger, broader vision than this: it hopes to be a vehicle of Yahweh's word to the world. Inspired by the example of the great prophets of Israel, it is angered by the unjust distribution of the wealth of the world. Hopeful of living in the Lord, it seeks to develop the gift of divine presence in such a way as to be a sign to the poor of God's care for them. Their goal is the integration of faith and deed.

Placed in a certain clear priority of concerns, the prophetic community desires first to live in the presence of the divine; second, within the prophetic tradition to live an integration of faith and deed; third, in living thus to give witness to the masses of mankind; and fourth, thus to be builders of God's peace in this present age.

Such a vision requires an application, an accommodation of the particular vision of Israel to a more extended vision, a universal vision of the message of "the light to the nations."

In the decade following the use of this passage by the Council — that is, during the years 1965 through 1975 — the vision has been gradually extended. For example, some Catholic religious are seeking to integrate the biblical vision. They are using a two-pronged approach. On the one hand they are attempting to simplify their own life styles and to offer witness directly to the poor, sharing life with them to the limit of the possible.

On the other hand, they are willing to enter into confrontation with the giant corporate structures and to challenge them. An excellent example has been given in confronting those corporations which produce condensed milk and which have been promoting the use of formula milk to the disadvantage of indigenous poor.[10] These religious seem free and willing to join forces with prophetic elements from other faith groups. These religious, sometimes called the "parallel church," are growing in their prophetic stance, showing their concern for the poor of today, as well as concern for the ecology and for the powerless who will inherit the ecology which is handed over to future generations.

To a certain extent it may be said that both of their approaches are more symbolic than real, but it must not be forgotten that the prophets used the symbol as a powerful tool.

The ideal of the prophetic community is the servant, drawn from the symbol presented in the hymns of Second Isaia. The hymns of the sixth century prophet of exile give a composite picture of a healing, caring servant who gives sight to the blind and liberates the imprisoned, who brings "true justice to the nations." Each of the songs shows the servant, *Ebed Yahweh*, in roles quite distinct from an imperial or dominating figure. Gifted by the spirit, the servant brings the message of good news for all mankind. This anonymous prophet, more than any other, is becoming the model.

The revised official liturgy of the Church employs the servant songs in her readings for holy week, as well as for other occasions during the year. Perhaps Matthew's Gospel says it best:

> Here is my servant whom I have chosen,
>   my beloved, the favorite of my soul.
>
> I will endow him with my spirit,
>
> he will proclaim true faith to the nations,
> he will not brawl or shout,
> nor will anyone hear his voice in the streets.
>
> He will not break the crushed reed,
>   nor put out the smoldering wick
>
> till he has led the truth to victory:
> in his name the nations will put their hope.

(Matt. 12:18-21; cf. Isaia 42:1, 2, 3a, 4)

Besides the liturgical shift there is also the declared real possibility of joint social action with Jews, in which Christian Catholics find the servant image a strong motivation:

> . . . today witness by Christians is also moving, where possible, by shared activity into the immense field of social work, with its almost unlimited possibilities of collaboration, so that Christians may reveal in their actions the face of Christ the servant.[11]

It should not be necessary to mention that the Jewish community views this imagery with some suspicion, especially when Christians cite these passages for Christological purposes as the Gospels do. Hopefully the symbol of the servant, ambivalent as all symbols are, may be utilized by both communities without polemic. The needs of God's people demand this.

Jewish appreciation of this image might be summed up thus, "I give you not high office—I give you the means to serve!" (Rabbi Sidney B. Hoenig).[12]

The Faith that Does Justice.

The attempt of Catholic thought to integrate contemporary biblical studies with traditional Catholic social thought is dramatized by a recent volume, *The Faith that Does Justice, Examining the Christian Sources for Social Change* (Editor, John Haughey. New York: Paulist, 1977).

Each of the nine essays in this volume is an excellent statement of a particular dilemma in the dialectic of faith and justice. Inadequate though a mere mention may be, I merely refer the reader to three of the essays which deal more explicitly with questions germane to our topic: "Biblical Perspectives on Justice," by Fr. John R. Donahue; "Modern Catholic Teaching Concerning Justice," and "A Prophetic Church and the Catholic Sacramental Imagination," both by Fr. David Hollenbach.

To complete these remarks on the differences between Jewish and Catholic perceptions of social issues it may be useful to comment briefly on the authoritative referents of the two traditions, Talmud based on Torah versus papal documents based on natural law.

Whereas contemporary Catholic social thought has developed in large measure through the personal concern of the popes, from Leo XIII through the present, the Jewish tradition had a totally different authority and referent.

Jewish writers and thinkers have gone characteristically to the Talmud, a body of commentary on Torah and the scriptures. This body of literature had not yet been edited when Jesus made reference to "the law and the prophets." But it was available to him as to other Jews through the oral tradition of the rabbis.

Unfortunately the Talmud had been virtually inaccessible to Christian writers in the past, much more than the Christian scripture has been inaccessible to the Jewish community.

The concern of the Talmud, it seems to me as an outsider, has been primarily to develop a body of wisdom for the life of the Jewish community in itself. This concern has not been for the relations of the community to a dominant society, except inso-far as the issue of survival was concerned. Civic and social issues have not been its forte.

And so while it is true to say that the Catholic community and the Jewish community resemble each other in that both treasure the element of tradition to complete the presence and under-standing of the scriptures, the very sense of tradition is quite different in the two communities.

With respect to social issues, in the past the Catholic com-munity focus was on natural law as servant of the truth, but servant to a triumphalist Christian community. In the Jewish community the focus was equally inner directed, to serve the community's life and survival. Social issues have been more the concern of Reform Jews who identify with the prophets, and for secular Jews, less for Conservative and Orthodox Jews.

Three conclusions seem to impose themselves. First, it is clear that Catholic teaching on social justice has been less indebted to the prophets of Israel than might have been pre-sumed, more indebted to the scholastic tradition, that is, to natural law and the philosophic tradition, less to a biblical tradi-tion. This had been the situation until the last decade. I develop some differences of Catholic social thought in the essay imme-diately following.

Second, with the renewal of biblical studies in the Catholic community and with new openness on the part of scholarship on all sides, Catholic renewal is moving rapidly toward a greater appreciation of the prophets of Israel, among whom it would number Jesus as prophet and servant.

Third, the integration of faith and deed, theory and praxis, is being taken up by the Catholic community in new and creative ways, especially in new forms of ministry. In doing so it is deeply indebted to the prophetic tradition, especially to the concrete-ness of the prophets.

Finally, the Jewish tradition and the Catholic tradition in social issues do not seem to have any basic incompatibility even though they represent different value systems. They offer much prom-ise for the future as they enter into concerned and sympathetic interaction.

Notes

1. Cf. The prophet Amos 5:21-24. All citations are from *The Jerusalem Bible.*

The Tanach uses two words for justice, *mishpat* and *tzedekah.* I accept Dr. Abraham Heschel's statement that "it is exceedingly difficult to establish the exact difference in meaning" between them, and I appreciate his clarifications (*The Prophets*, I, pp. 200-201). In particular, I welcome his reflection that *tzedekah* goes beyond strict, literal justice to righteousness or holiness.

Fr. John R. Donahue, S.J., explores this same distinction in "Biblical Perspectives on Justice," in *The Faith That Does Justice*, pp. 68 seq.

In this article I intend to include both terms.

2. "No Religion Is an Island," in *Disputation and Dialogue* (F. E. Talmage, Editor), p. 349.

3. *The Relation of Christians and Jews.* University of Dayton Press, 1971, p. 1.

4. "Reflections on *Pacem in Terris*" (1973) available in *The Gospel of Peace and Justice*, p. 563. Italics in the original.

5. Among these may be included:
Walter Brueggeman, *The Prophetic Imagination*, 1978.
F. Washington Jarvis, *Prophets, Poets, Priests and Kings*, 1974.
Barbara Jurgensen, *The Prophets Speak Again*, 1977.
George Maloney, *Listen, Prophets!* c. 1977.
Brennan Manning, *Prophets and Lovers*. In Search of the Holy Spirit, 1976.
George T. Montague, *The Spirit and His Gifts*. The Biblical Background of Spirit-Baptism, Tongue-Speaking and Prophecy, 1974.
Walter Wifall, *Israel's Prophets: Envoys of the King*, 1974.

6. Sanh. 11a, quoted by A. Cohen, *Everyman's Talmud* (1948), p. 124.

7. Sidney B. Koenig and Samuel H. Rosenberg, *A Guide to the Prophets* (1942), p. 49.

8. *Call to Action* (1971), No. 48. These paragraphs (223) have been lifted in substance from my brochure, *The Church in the Town* (Gaba Pastoral Papers, No. 53, 1977), p. 28.

9. *Gaudium et Spes*, No. 43.

10. This effort was begun in 1975 by the Precious Blood Sisters in Dayton, Ohio. Since that time some fourteen Protestant Churches and more than 150 religious orders and Catholic bodies have coordinated their efforts in project "Infant Formula" through the Interfaith Center on Corporate Responsibility, 475 Riverside Drive, New York, New York 10027.

11. Tomassos Federici, "The Mission and Witness of the Church: Catholic Jewish Relations Today," *Origins* (Oct. 19, 1978) 8:18, pp. 273-286.

12. This sentence is from a letter of my friend, Rabbi Sidney B. Hoenig, an outstanding Orthodox scholar. He did me the service of critically reviewing my progress on this paper. Unfortunately, Rabbi Hoenig died suddenly in December, 1979, while this publication was in process.

Chapter 3

SOCIAL JUSTICE: A DEVELOPING CONCEPT

John J. Kelley, S.M.

In my essay on "Social Justice and the Prophetic Tradition," I have shown how disparate the two traditions, Catholic and Jewish, are with respect to social justice, emphasizing their different origins and authorities. In the present essay I should like to explore the concept of social justice within the Catholic community, showing how the Catholic tradition has made quite different developments than the Protestant and Jewish communities.

It is a surprising development of our times that the neologism, "social justice," should have been invented only in the nineteenth century and yet should have received wide acceptance in the world community. It is equally surprising that the Catholic understanding had developed — in a vacuum, as it were — almost void of the prophetic inspiration which has made the term acceptable to Jews and Protestants.

One might discern three phases in the modern Catholic tradition of concern for social justice. The first was in the late nineteenth century when attention was focused on the need of the working man to form unions; this necessarily involved implicitly the concepts of freedom and empowerment. The second phase took place in the first half of this century; it turned about the reconstruction of a new and more just economic order, especially through the restructuring of industry. The third and contemporary phase is the building of peace through the development of peoples, and is currently being expressed in concern for human rights.

It has happened that there are pieces of Catholic theory which remain relatively unknown to the other traditions. One purpose of this essay is to identify these. I shall include some reflections

65

on related aspects of Catholic theory on justice such as social charity, subsidiarity, etc., as these are virtually unknown outside professional Catholic circles.

The continuing development of Catholic understanding is reflected in the evolution of pertinent questions such as the quest for world peace, the emphasis on development, and the current stress on human rights, each of which has been the subject of at least one papal message.[1]

The Neologism, "Social Justice," Is a Power Tool.

To some persons it may seem a matter of indifference whether new words are developed for dealing with new perceptions. But this is a grave error. Words are a most important aspect of the great conversation. Terms which are common need not have common connotations. New terms which are developed express new insights and these in turn give new power to each of the members of the conversation.

Sometimes the semantic confusion exists within one and the same community. I think of the sorry experience of the 1930's with Father Charles Coughlin and his use of the term, social justice. Although almost fifty years have passed, the use of the common term, social justice, does not ensure a common understanding. It is with regret that we look back on the events of that period and understand that there was no agreed-on meaning within the Catholic community.

Today this neologism is becoming a power tool to enable us to develop common language. It is necessary, then, to reflect on how much or how little common meaning is present in the term. Certainly the use of the tool indicates an uneven development in the three traditions.

Protestants and Jews Use the Term Social Justice Differently Than Catholics.

I cannot write with authority concerning the use of the term outside of the Catholic tradition, that is, within Judaism and Protestantism.

In the nineteenth century in the Protestant community Washington Gladden and Walter Rauschenbusch developed what came to be called the "social gospel," the liberal Protestant position on social questions such as unionism. Rauschenbusch, in fact, was popularizing his positions at the same time that Leo XIII was developing the encyclical on the conditions of the working class. Their work was similar to the movement of trains on parallel tracks – the environment was the same, the concerns the same, but the trains neither acted in concert nor did they admit the possibility that they might arrive at the same conclusions.

The first reference which I have come upon in Jewish litera- ture indicates that in the Central Conference of American Rabbis the term was well established by 1915. An article by Abraham Cronbach,[2] "Judaism and Social Justice, Historically Considered," treats the question. Unfortunately, for our purpose, the treat- ment is rather a biblical-Talmudic approach than an historical consideration.

In 1923 Isidore Singer, prolific Jewish writer, authored a pam- phlet entitled *Social Justice.* This work was enlarged and reprinted in 1924. In it the author, who had been managing editor of *The Jewish Encyclopedia* from 1901 to 1905, urged that the churches and synagogues should lead "in the realization of the social and peace gospel of the Hebrew prophets."

Although the Union of American Hebrew Congregations twice developed special commissions (Commission on Social Justice, reports of 1918 and 1928), Jewish encyclopedia articles on justice are silent on social justice, indicating that this dimension remains a minority concern in the Jewish community.

Abraham Heschel's work, *The Prophets*, includes treatment of their concern for justice (Chapter 11, "Justice"); his work was done about 1960. He used the term, social justice, but once in that work and then only deprecatingly, "Is this all the prophets came to teach us – social justice? Are there no other demands to be made, no other goals to be attained?" (p. 207)

From the Protestant side we might refer to the great biblical scholar, Gerhard von Rad, and his fine work on the prophets. He says they had nothing to say to the social question and claims that concern for the secular universe about the prophets is lacking in their writings.[3]

The Use and the Meaning of the Term Social Justice is Expanding.

A brief review of the use of the term, social justice, on the Catholic side may be useful. I shall mention four moments in the history to dramatize the point.

The first Catholic use of the term, according to one researcher, took place in 1845 by an Italian, A. Tapparelli.[4] Over the next fifty

years there is a slow but growing use of the term by knowledgeable Catholics. One example of this was Archbishop Ireland who
used the term in 1893.[5] Not present in the encyclical of 1891, the
term appeared first in papal documents in 1904.

Much later in the context of a world economic crisis, substantial contributions were made by Pius XI in the thirties when he
used the term repeatedly to describe the demands of the common good for the reconstruction of the social order. We have
mentioned that these insights seem to have been made without
any special awareness of the Jewish prophets.

More recently the Vatican documents on peace on earth (1963)
and the development of peoples (1967) have sharpened the focus
on social problems, although the actual use of the words, social
justice, is infrequent. The term is used only once in the Council
documents (*Gaudium et Spes*, no. 90), three times by Paul VI in
Populorum Progressio. It was very significant that early in this
work he recalled the establishment of the Commission on Justice and Peace in 1967 and cited its statement of purpose:

> . . . to arouse the entire People of God to acquire a full
> awareness of the function entrusted to it in these times
> so that on the one hand the development of the poorer
> peoples be promoted, and social justice among nations
> be fostered, and on the other hand that assistance be
> given to less-developed nations that by this aid they be
> enabled to provide for their own development.[6]

Our point in these paragraphs is that the term social justice
is not only a neologism, but the use and meaning of the term
continues to spread. It is appropriate to look at the particulars
of the development in some detail.

The Act of Social Justice is to Organize for the Common Good.

It has been argued, convincingly it seems to me, that the
Aristotelian concept of legal justice, a concept taught by Thomas
Aquinas as a particular virtue under the cardinal virtue of justice,
has been given new meaning in the development of theory by
Pius XI. The pontiff not only reaffirmed the centrality of justice
in man's patterns of virtuous behavior, but he also contributed
two major points to the theory of the reconstruction of the social
order.

a. The first of these is that he gave precision to the under-standing of social justice as a specific virtue. He taught that justice requires of man that he organize for the common good. Social justice demands that man cooperate in the organization of the social structure in which he lives. This is a different appreciation of the demands of social justice than that of the biblical tradition.

The specific act of social justice as taught by Pius, according to one authority, is to organize and to reform for the common good.[7]

b. The second aspect of this teaching of Pius XI which was new was the theory of social institutions. For perhaps the first time in Christian ethics the position was clearly put forth that institutions, considered as moral persons, could be perceived as good or bad, and thus could be seen as worthy of support or in need of reform. The value of structures was thus firmly established, as well as the obligations of individual members of those structures.

Pius' teaching could thus be applied to institutional or structural problems such as Fascism or Nazism, though in fact in the 1931 encyclical he was writing about the reform of the wage scale within industry. In 1937 he did address both of the latter problems, using the same terminology of social justice.

Subsequent popes would apply this doctrine of institutions and their reform to a variety of economic and developmental problems, such as disarmament, international trade, multinational corporations, etc. John XXIII would point out the structural defect in our failure to develop an international institution adequate to deal with world problems. He expressed the need for world government which would be regulated by the principle of subsidiarity - we shall discuss this later. It is only realistic to point out that papal teachings on social justice were neither universally acclaimed nor universally implemented. Similar to the prophets of old, John's teachings often fell on deaf ears and his hopes were ignored by the masses. It goes without saying that his explicitation of theory is almost unknown in secular and non-Catholic institutions. The most successful of all of his proposals was that of peace on earth, but even this had little success in bringing Catholics into the peace movement.

Another New Aspect of Social Justice is "Social Charity."

A Catholic specification which has firm foundation in the encyclicals but which is virtually unknown in interfaith collaboration is the concept of social charity. Introduced as a new term — by Pius XI in 1923, another neologism — social charity is the application of the principle of charity from the personal level to the social order. Charity is the love of a fellowman because the person is made to the image and likeness of God. This charity must now be applied to family and to social structures. By social charity one is required to love the family and the social structures precisely because they are thought of as "person." The social structure reflects the creative beauty of God.

In Christian thought there is an added specifically Christian dimension: the family is thought of as an image of God in his pluralism of persons within the unity of the Godhead. While Jewish thought cannot be expected to embrace this Christian perception, Jews may be expected to know and to understand how this appeals to Christian conscience.

The Catholic In-House Dialog Continues

In *Justice in the World* (1971) the bishops declared that the work of justice is a "constitutive part of the ministry of the Church" (Intro.). The point made was that while the Vatican Council had demanded of the Church that she confront the problems of the world with greater honesty, the new position indicated that the work, the mission or purpose of the Church could not be limited to a sacramental or vertical function. The statement represented a breakthrough in the theology of mission, a new declaration of the temporal purpose of the Church. The term social justice is again used sparingly, only once at the end of the document (no. 62).

In this Synod the bishops inched forward the concern and the dialog and in a particular way began a new integration of the scriptures with the work of justice in the world. Explicit references to justice in the scripture were made in this synodal statement: to the Word (2, 67, 69), to the Jewish scriptures (30), to the New Testament (33, 57) and to the prophetic (47):

> Although . . . it is difficult to draw a line between what
> is needed for right use and what is demanded by pro-

phetic witness, . . . our faith demands of us a certain
sparingness in use, and the church is obliged to live
and to administer its own goods in such a way that the
gospel is proclaimed to the poor.

The development of Catholic social doctrine has thus itself
been an in-house kind of dialog or trialog between Catholic
specialists in social sciences, the teaching authority of the church
and the responsive community of the faithful. The conversation
has been an uneven phenomenon. It would be good, however,
to keep these developments within their historical context: the
principles of sociology and anthropology have developed only
since the middle of the nineteenth century.

Although Catholic social studies developed within the same
time frame as Jewish and Protestant studies, there were two
differences. The first was that the renaissance of Catholic studies
of history, liturgy and theology were closely linked to a renewal
of Thomistic philosophy and scholastic tradition. This was
unique to the Church, thus a special strength but also a special
limitation.

The second was that Catholic biblical studies, though energetically pursued by a small group from 1890 onward, were always
a large step or two behind Protestant and Jewish developments.
It was not until 1943, with the release of *Divino Afflante Spiritu*
by Pius XII, that the way was opened to Catholic biblical scholarship to move ahead with full vigor, not merely in parallel with
their Protestant and Jewish counterparts, but in every respect
learning and collaborating with them. This date also explains a
change of attitude towards the prophets of Israel.

In addition to special meaning attached to social justice, other
terms occur in the conversation which have considerably different connotations in the traditions. One example would be
the difference in usage of the term, secularism. As late as
November 1978 at the National Workshop on Christian Jewish
Relations in Los Angeles, Dr. Samuel Sandmel used the term,
secularism, in a sympathetic interpretation of the word. Catholics have tended to distinguish secularism from secularization,
recalling that secularism as a movement has been historically
associated with hostility to faith and religion. The movement
has been identified with George Holyoake.[8]

The other term, secularization, which is now established
within Catholic circles as a positive phenomenon, seems to
have been brought there under the influence of sociologists of

all persuasions. As late as the Synod of 1974 the fathers rejected this term as descriptive of a phenomenon hostile to faith. By 1975, however, Paul VI was able to offer a clear distinction between secularism as hostile to religion, and secularization as a good and worthy social process:

> Secularization is the effort, in itself just and legitimate, and in no way incompatible with faith or religion, to discover in creation, in each thing or each happening in the universe, the laws wich regulate them with a certain autonomy, but with the inner conviction that the Creator has placed these laws there.[9]

This is one more example of a phenomenon peculiar to the Catholic tradition where an authoritative position evolves, having normative influence. Nothing comparable exists in Judaism or Protestantism.

On the negative side it may be said in all frankness that there is a great need to reduce the gap between Catholic theory and Catholic praxis.

Several correctives seem to be developing to cope with this weakness. The first is a greater awareness of the concreteness of the prophets and their message concerning injustice. One can hardly be brought into touch with Amos' diatribes against the swindlers and the money sharks and remain indifferent to the real victims of the exploitation. The writings of the prophets bring a concreteness which has been badly needed.

A second corrective is the theology of liberation. This theology is developing out of the experience of the poverty of the barrios of Latin America. This experience of Latin Americans of structures of injustice triggers motivation in them which empowers them to act.

In closing the historic meeting of the Latin American bishops (CELAM) in February, 1979 the bishops declared:

> If we cast our eyes over Latin America, what spectacle confronts us? It is not necessary to probe deeply. The evident truth is that the gap is constantly increasing between "the many who have little and the few who have much."[10]

So if the gap between Catholic theory and the reality of the world may be narrowing, much remains to be done in this regard. The short fall of human action to perceived needs is an element which will always remain to some extent. But a prophetic anger can and must be brought to bridge this gap. These two prophetic corrections are being made to Catholic understanding of and response to social injustice.

For this to take place fully it will be necessary to bring about a much more effective forum of Catholic and Jewish thought. The element of Jewish presence to Catholic thought and Catholic thought to Jewish life can be of enormous value. The development of such a forum for the exchange of concerns is one of the most hopeful signs of a symbiotic relationship.[11] Fortunately the atmosphere of indifference to the traditions of the other has begun to yield before the enormity of the concerns of mankind. The traditions need each other if they are to function effectively in meeting the problems of our shared humanity. The problems of our humanity do not yield to isolated efforts.[12]

Conclusions to this Section

I have attempted to make several points in this section. As the term social justice is a neologism, dating from the nineteenth century and not to be found in the scriptures, the connotations of this neologism are changing within our several communities. Apparently the term is of more recent vintage in the Jewish and Protestant communities and does not have the same specifics which have developed within the Catholic community.

Several nuances of the Catholic tradition are virtually unknown in the other communities, among these the associated concepts of social charity and subsidiarity, as we shall see in the next section. There are also great differences in the connotations of common terms such as secularism and secularization.

Much remains to develop common thought patterns, common language and common action between the traditions so that common effective strategies may be implemented in the service of the kingdom of God.

In these reflections we have not focused on Jewish concerns such as the state of Israel or the holocaust, nor have we explored Catholic concerns such as tax relief for private schools or the dilemma of abortion. These important issues and others must form the agendas of the future and will do so if the forum exists. Fortunately the forum is emerging.

Freedom and Empowerment: Subsidiarity

Although the theme of liberation runs through the prophets in some measure, it is only in Second Isaia that liberation from oppression and imprisonment becomes prominent in the prophetic writings. One thinks of the condition of the exiles in Babylon in the sixth century before the common era.

In this section I should like to examine the question of liberation, freedom and empowerment as it has been expressed within the Catholic tradition. Specifically I wish to examine the principle of subsidiarity.

A key issue of our times is the exercise of power and in a special way the empowerment and creativity of the laity. A sense of powerlessness is one of the most destructive realities of our contemporary society. Present structures tend to make persons more and more dependent, rather than self-reliant.

Freedom and empowerment in the Catholic community theory are of relatively recent vintage and are expressed in terms of subsidiary function. The principle of subsidiary function develops only within the Catholic tradition.[13]

A new idea has been born in our day, compatible with the biblical and Jewish tradition, but not yet formulated within Protestant or Jewish social philosophy. The name of this idea is "the principle of subsidiarity" or "the principle of subsidiary function."

Subsidiarity is a response to the dilemma of non-freedom, a new concept to enable all our people to come into a more vibrant relationship with their own creativity. The idea has grown within Catholic social thought for fifty years. It reaches a high point in the Declaration on Religious Liberty (*Dignitatis Humanae Personae*) and the Church in the Modern World (*Gaudium et Spec*, no. 86). But due to the limited exchanges of our respective communities in the past, the idea has been left undeveloped in the interfaith dialog.

This concept perceives social structures as being "subsidiary" to the person and to the primary grouping within which the person lives out his human existence. The larger social structures should serve to enable, to empower the person and the smaller unit (such as the family, the congregation, and the neighborhood) to live in greater liberty, that is to say, more humanely.[14] This new image of service, of ministry as a servant, inspired by the songs of Second Isaia, is becoming a liberating symbol of the presence and concern of the people of God to the peoples of the world.

A Biblical Example: Moses Empowers His Aides.

A biblical example from the greatest of the prophets of Israel will help us to understand the positive aspect of this principle in the existential order. A weary Moses does not know what to do with the volume of the problems which are being brought to him. He has too much to do as judge of his people, he wears himself out in hearing the numerous cases that are brought to him and he has no time or energy for other matters. It requires the wisdom of his father-in-law, Jethro, to suggest that he might do well to organize reliable and responsible men who would accept part of this judging function, while he reserves to himself only those cases which they cannot handle. The text is a beautiful example, certainly the most developed in all of scripture, of the practicality of our principle.[15]

By decentralizing the function of judgment, the great prophet Moses enables his followers to assume roles of leadership in the community.

Subsidiarity Supports Political Activity.

This new insight, subsidiarity, is compatible with the need man has for political power. The encyclical, *Call to Action* (1971), of Paul VI treated of the question of political power at considerable length (sections 24-50). I cite one passage which is of particular importance for our topic:

> Political power which is the natural and necessary link for ensuring the cohesion of the social body must have as its aim the achievement of the common good. While respecting liberties of individuals, families and subsidiary groups, it acts in such a way as to create, effectively and for the well-being of all, the conditions required for attaining man's true and complete good, including his spiritual end. It acts within the limits of its competence, which can vary from people to people and from country to country. It always intervenes with care for justice and with devotion to the common good, for which it holds final responsibility. It does not for all that, deprive individuals and intermediary bodies of the field of activity and responsibilitiy which are proper to them and which lead them to collaborate in the attainment of this common good. In fact, "The true aim

of all social activity should be to help individual members of the social body, but never to destroy or absorb them." (Pius XI and John XXIII). According to the vocation proper to it, the political power must know how to stand aside from particular interests in order to view its responsibility with regard to the good of all men, even going beyond national limits. To take politics seriously at its different levels — local, regional, national and worldwide — is to affirm the duty of man, of every man, to recognize the concrete reality and the value of the freedom of choice that is offered to him to seek to bring about both the good of the city and of the nation and of mankind. Politics are a demanding manner — but not the only one of living the Christian commitment to the service of others. Without, of course, solving every problem, it endeavors to apply solutions to the relationships men have with one another . . . . While recognizing the autonomy of the reality of politics, Christians who are invited to take up political activity should try to make their choices consistent with the Gospel, and in the framework of a legitimate plurality, to give both personal and collective witness to the seriousness of their faith by effective and disinterested service of men. (Par. 46)

Subsidiarity then is a principle by which all men are enabled to act at their own proper level to participate in the formation of social, economic and political structures.

Subsidiarity Respects the Tension Between Person and Society.

A fundamental tension of the human condition is that of individual to community, part to whole, member to corpus. Subsidiarity respects this fundamental tension and empowers creative action.

The mood of our times reflects in a very intense way the strain which exists between society and person. A little reflection leads one to understand that there is a natural tension between each part of a living body and the living body itself. Historically this tension has resulted in two tendencies in human society, one toward the collectivity, that is, the whole, a tendency such as is present in totalitarian societies. Such societies tend to minimize the rights of individuals and minority groups.

The second tendency stems from an atomistic view of society which focuses on the individual and inclines to resist the needs of the common good. In our country this latter tendency has sometimes taken the form of a political effort, such as the Libertarian Movement associated with Senator Barry Goldwater in the early sixties. This tendency seems also to mark certain religious bodies and to express itself in separatism.

It is not difficult to identify these trends within the Catholic and the Jewish communities of our day. For example, the atomistic view expresses itself mainly by way of reaction to the turmoil of change in church, synagogue and society. The totalitarian view on the other hand is generally impatient with the response to the great need for renewal, and generally asks for increased governmental action. Both tendencies would seem to eclipse the other. Each is simplistic in its own way.

These two perennial threats are rendered creative only by a theory of society which recognizes them and manages them in a dynamic homeostasis. This dynamic is achieved by use of the principle of subsidiarity, encouraging initiative and self help.

Such a vision of society, of balanced social tensions and the creative potential elicited by the principle of subsidiary function, needs much discussion between Catholics and Jews.

Proper understanding of this principle allows for concrete action. The insight is well expressed in a Chinese proverb on how to help self help:

> To give a man a fish
> is to give him food for the day;
> To teach a man to fish
> is to give him food for all his days.

Conclusions on Freedom and Empowerment.

What conclusions can we come to in these brief considerations on freedom and empowerment, more specifically on the issue of subsidiarity?

As the concept of subsidiarity is unknown in the Jewish community, it seems to me that prophetic demands for social justice in our time should bring the two traditions together to ask how in fact such a new concept can be used to empower the laity and to work justice.

At first blush — especially if one identifies subsidiarity with the principle of decentralization — it would seem that the Jewish community is indeed not in need of this new dynamic. But if we are asking about the empowerment of the people, then there is indeed a great need for the two traditions to come together with prophetic concern for the powerless and to ask, "What must be done at this point in time to empower our people and to thus enable them to act effectively?"

Conclusions

The two traditions of social justice have had different referents in the past, not one common source in the prophets of the bible, as had been commonly assumed. At this moment in time these traditions are both in a period of considerable transition, both looking to new insights from contemporary developments. For example, both traditions must face the issue of women's rights. The role of women in the ministry, for instance, is unresolved in both traditions.

In our exploration of social justice and the prophetic tradition we have discovered relative strengths and weaknesses in the Catholic tradition. In the dialog between the traditions, the relative strengths of the Catholic tradition are the Church's ability to develop authoritative teaching concerning social issues and her freedom to move into convergence with Jewish and Protestant positions when their values are congruent.

The weakness of the Catholic tradition is twofold: first, the tradition has been too aprioristic and lacking in concrete implementation, e.g., in her inability to bring Catholics and others into support of the peace movement.

Second, her position is really not as well known by Catholics as might be assumed in an authoritarian model, and much of this tradition is not at all familiar to Jewish and Protestant brethren. Concepts such as subsidiarity, social charity, common good, etc., need much more conversation and shared action, especially at the grassroots.

Recent developments, taking place even while this paper was being written, give hope that these weaknesses will be overcome by the present leadership.

In January, 1979, Pope John Paul II asked the bishops of the Latin American countries gathered at Puebla, Mexico, "Have the courage of the prophets!" In context he seems to have been pleading for a bold critique of the evils of the social system prevailing in those countries.

As this essay was being written, the Pope released his first encyclical letter *Redemptor Hominis* ("The Redeemer of Man") on March 15. In taking up the Church's mission (par. 18-22) the Pope took up the question of Christ as prophet. Referring to Christ as prophet or to his prophetic office nine times, the pontiff based himself upon a traditional Catholic triptych: Christ is priest, prophet and king.

John Paul develops the notion that by the union of every Christian with Christ, every Christian shares in the prophetic office. This office ("munus") is seen as being principally a teaching office, so that every Christian should share in the catechesis of the Church.

There is no clear reference to prophetic functions of foretelling the future or of social critic, though it would seem that these are not to be excluded from the teaching function.

Out of more than two hundred references, only two are made to a biblical prophet (both are to first Isaia). Neither of these references touches the substance of this paper. He never uses the terminology of "Jesus as prophet."

The Catholic tradition then is rapidly growing in its awareness of the biblical, especially the role of Christ as prophet, related to the prophets of Israel in their passion for social justice. In its renewal and return to sources the Church is turning to a more concrete and biblically inspired understanding of justice as holiness integrated by faith and deed. There is a growing strength in the hope that common values and common language can be bonded to common strategies and aspirations.

Notes

1. John XXIII, *Peace on Earth*, 1963; Paul VI, *The Development of Peoples*, 1967; John Paul II, Christmas message of 1978 and his first encyclical, *Redemptor Hominis* (March 16, 1979).

2. *Central Conference of American Rabbis Yearbook*, XXV, 1915, pp. 414-423.

3. *The Message of the Prophets* (1962, 1967).

4. Leo W. Shields, *The History and Meaning of the Term Social Justice* (1941), quoted by William J. Ferree, *The Act of Social Justice* (1943), p. 83.

5. John A. Ryan, *Social Doctrine in Action,* p. 42.

6. *Populorum Progressio* No. 5. In this encyclical, the word justice is used seven times and social justice is used three times (nos. 5, 44, 59.).

7. Ferree, *op. cit.,* and also *An Introduction to Social Justice* (1943).

8. T. F. McMahon, "Secularism," in *New Catholic Encyclopedia* (1967), 13:36-38.

9. *Evangelization in the Modern World,* no. 55.

10. Reported in *The New York Times,* February 14, 1979.

11. Cf. the recent message of Archbishop Joseph Bernardin, "Cooperation and Conflict: Issues in Catholic Jewish Relations," January 24, 1979, to the National Jewish Community Relations Advisory Council. Published in *Origins* (February 22) 8:36, pp. 567-571.

12. In opening his first encyclical, John Paul II expressed this insight in his call for a "shared investigation of the truth." *Redemptor Hominis.*
Since these lines were written, some serious efforts have begun to bring the traditions into closer relationships. A major conference entitled "Religious Traditions and Social Policy" has been held and the papers presented are being released in one volume by the Notre Dame University Press.

13. Paul VI, "The Council's Guidance for an Age of Freedom," *The Pope Speaks* XIV (Fall, 1969), pp. 92-95.

14. From the viewpoint of an eminent economist, this insight has been expressed in *Small Is Beautiful: Economics as if People Mattered* (E. F. Schumacher, 1973); cf. pages 241-253.
From the viewpoint of the Catholic sociologist, it has been described as *No Larger Than Necessary* (Andrew Greeley, 1977).
From the viewpoint of political theory, it is supported by Berger and Newhaus in *To Empower People: The Role of Mediating Structures in Public Policy* (1977).
Subsidiarity is well documented in Catholic papal documents since 1931. Because it has not been well understood, it deserves to be studied and applied against the current sense of helplessness.

15. Cf. Exodus 18. For an application to religious life, cf. my article, "Subsidiarity, Principle of Renewal for Religious Life," *The Brothers' Newsletter* 19:2 (Summer, 1977), pp. 44-53.

Part II

THE HOLOCAUST FROM THE CHRISTIAN PERSPECTIVE

Chapter 4

SOME CHRISTIAN VIEWS OF THE HOLOCAUST

Katharine Hargrove, R.S.C.J.
Manhattanville College, Purchase, New York

Today's openness of dialogue between Jews and Christians owes much to the Holocaust theologians of both religious traditions. The constant interchange between them, nowhere more evident than in their current discussions of bridge-Christologies, challenges the rest of us to face facts fearlessly. Like them, correlating our findings, we can examine together the inflammatory question of how Christian Doctrine and the preaching of the Gospel led inevitably to the fires of Auschwitz.

Almost from its birth, Christendom has manifested ambivalent feelings toward the Jewish people. For the nation which preserved God's word for all succeeding generations, everlasting gratitude; for God's people who gave Jesus to the world, Christian joy. But for the Jews who "derided Christ" on Calvary, insensate anger; for the Jews who "killed the son of God on the Cross," perpetual persecution. In due course, the anguish of the Jews came to a climax in the Holocaust.

It is ironic in religious history that the only sacrifice which Gentiles could offer in the Temple at Jerusalem was the whole-burnt offering, that is, the holocaust. According to some interpreters, this cultic act was intended to symbolize the offerer's attitude of submission to and dependence on God, the God of the Jews. It is agonizing to know that the flames of the Holocaust in this, our age, illumine a totally different picture.

Whatever the pundits may find to criticize in NBC's production of Gerald Green's film classic, grass-roots Christians here and abroad admit it has forced them to rethink their creeds in response to the unspoken question: "What would I have done?"

"HOLOCAUST," because it comes to us in an art-form with which we are all familiar, gives viewers an immediacy of rapport, a genuine break-through to the Jewish experience. In no sense does this imply that Christians actually undergo the apocalyptic tragedy through which the Jews lived and died. No matter how removed the Christian reaction may be, it is nevertheless capable of begetting a remarkable power of compassion.

Wherever it has been shown, "HOLOCAUST" has introduced to numerous homes, to millions of people, the account of what happened to quite ordinary persons, "just like us," at a moment when Hitler was mobilizing his army to create a Master Race "not just like us." True, the Weiss family is fictional but that does not hinder the fate of its members from speaking to the sadistic evil of the Third Reich. Where colossal data can lessen intensity by sheer weight, "HOLOCAUST" demands attention by detailing the plight of the protagonists. Even though the theme is stark genocide, something which we can never comprehend, we are enabled to have an authentic if restricted knowledge of this most bestial of crimes. We are not merely exposed to an extraordinary way of seeing persons and events; we are, for our weal or our woe, compelled to examine the texture of our Christianity in view of the premeditated murder of an entire people.

"HOLOCAUST," with its inherent tactility, has in its graphic manner assisted us to bring forth within our own minds images of a *sitz-im-leben* which we ourselves could not have created. Caught up in the drama's quick intimacy, we endure subliminally the lives of each member of the Weiss family. The more conversant we are with the details of their situation, the more we are impressed with the author's careful research. Although his subject remains fathomless, it gives us information which helps us to comprehend the hurt, the doubt, the uncertainty of the inmates of the death-camps. Green's own insight into the depravity of the Final Solution, vicarious though it is, can be therapeutic for those of us who stand outside the Jewish nation.

To discover the religious dimensions of the inhuman hostility of Hitler's dream we must seek help from "The Holocaust Theologians," who speak to us from the heart of their Jewishness. If we do not attend to them, it may be well-nigh impossible for us to make the changes called for in our Christian tradition, a tradition which reprehensibly helped to spawn this satanic malignancy. The pressures of this day and age, with renewed threats of genocide, force us to listen ever more reflectively to what these Jewish teachers are trying to communicate to us.

Let us begin by paying heed to Buber's doctrine of "the eclipse of God." He sets forth there his proposition that demonic powers can and sometimes do conceal God's presence from man. As a philosopher, Buber viewed this interference of human action with divine action as a neutralizing of omnipotence. Like a modern Jeremiah, he cried out that while six million Jews had been mercilessly killed the world made no reply to the divine message clearly shown in their martyrdom.

Buber never lived to read Eugene Borowitz' sermon entitled, "Auschwitz and the Death of God." There is the meta-historical perspective he wanted. As if in dialogue with Buber, Borowitz begins by asking:

> The Jews have known God from their history but what shall we say of His Presence in Jewish history in recent years? Where was He when Hitler did what no man should ever do? Why did He not reveal Himself to a supplicating, forsaken people who might have died in triumph if only they could have been certain that they died in His Name?[1]

These are not the soul-searching echoes of an Elie Wiesel or the abrasive acerbity of an afflicted Wdowinski. They bespeak rather the pregnant vigor of a faith maturing into hope because:

> . . . the Jewish people know that history is more than bondage. We came into being as a people in Egypt and pledged ourselves to God at Sinai so that the message of redemption, dim and obscure as it may be in one era and another, will never be forgotten among men. As long as we are in history, faithful to Him, men cannot ignore God.[2]

Rubinstein sounds a completely different note from either Buber or Borowitz. For him, there is no dynamism from a remembered past, no divine voice from the gas chambers. Neither apparently is there any upsurge of a prayer like that with which Borowitz concludes his exhortation: "Forgive us, Lord, for having failed Thee again and again, and grant us courage to testify of Thee in all our ways, Amen."[3] Nonetheless, despite many charges leveled against him as a philosophical negativist, theological maverick, Rubinstein has his own prophetic thrust:

. . . Traditional Jewish theology maintains that God is the ultimate, omnipotent actor in the historical drama. It has interpreted every major catastrophe in Jewish history as God's punishment of a sinful Israel. I fail to see how this position can be maintained without regarding Hitler and the SS as instruments of God's will. The agony of European Jewry cannot be likened to the testing of Job. To see any purpose in the death camps, the traditional believer is forced to regard the most demonic, inhuman explosion in all history as a meaningful expression of God's purposes. The idea is simply too obscene for me to accept.[4]

Like Rubinstein, Arthur Cohen affirms that the old, simplistic belief in Divine Providence sheds no light on the Holocaust. But while Rubinstein concentrates on the inexplicable senselessness of the Final Solution, Cohen seeks in the death camps for some enlightenment, some lesson to be learned in their ruins.

The first discovery he makes is that what began with the Jews can extend to the whole world. Years ago, Max Dimont called our attention to the extraordinary amount of Xyklon B crystals found in Poland after 1945. He then registered the astounding datum that:

. . . there were no more than 3 million Jews left in Europe. The contemplated mass-killing was no longer 1.4 Christians for every Jew. Nazi future plans called for the killing of 10 million non-Germanic people every year.[5]

Pointing to the Jew in the concentration camp as an object-lesson in modern malevolence, Cohen studies his fellow-Jews through Buber's eyes and deduces:

. . . Standing, bound and shackled, in the pillory of mankind, we demonstrate with the bloody body of our people, the unredeemedness of our race. For us, there is no cause of Jesus; only the cause of God exists for us.[6]

Cohen insists with biblical clarity that whereas Gentiles see in the death camps a paradigm of human brutality, for the Jews they are historically, absolutely real.[7] He underscores what we know from the Haggadah, that the past must become present for the Jew: "In every single generation it is a sacred duty for each man to consider himself as personally brought out of Egypt." Throughout the millenia of persecution, no matter what the suffering, at every Pesach the Jew has ratified his own faith in liberty as the God-given right of every human being, whether Jew or Gentile. Ever since God rescued His people from Pharaonic slavery, Ysroel-Mensch has been a blessed spokesman for and to the oppressed. Israel's memory is Israel's message for all of humanity, for all time, a message writ large at the entrance to Yad Vashem: "Remember and do not forget."

Remembrance, from the biblical standpoint, is essential to Israel's vocation. In the Shema, Israel is called to pay attention: "Hear, O Israel, the Lord, thy God, is one God." Hearing, rightly understood, involves pondering, considering. Consequently, it cannot be that the Shema refers only to a passing adjustment to God's Presence. No. Israel must never, no matter what the circumstances, be oblivious to the nearness of her God.

That is why Cohen pleads that "this real presence of all Israel in the death-camps, experiencing the tremendum, enters the liturgy as surely as it entered the narration of Exodus."[8] The religious ritual on the eve of a holy day highlights for him the unity of his people. The prayer that accompanies the lifting of the cup of wine illuminates the chosenness of Israel: "Blessed art Thou, O Lord, our God, King of the universe Who has chosen us from among all nations . . . ." It is from his vision of the Hitlerian hell-holes that he tells us:

> Jew, simple Jew, nominative universal describing and containing all mankind that bears that racial lineament until the third generation of ancestry, became chosen and was universalized. The deathcamps ended forever one argument of history—whether the Jews are a chosen people. They are chosen, unmistakably, extremely, utterly.[9]

This, from his Holocaust perspective, is the eternal significance of the election of Israel.

Prior to the Nazi onslaught, the Law for the Jews had always been set within the framework of that good news, the Hebrew gospel of God's tender care for the sheep of His flock. Sacred history, indeed, so carefully catalogued proofs of Divine Providence that the bona fide Jew seemed to lack any idea of secondary causality. And it was this same God who enabled Jews to maintain their confidence in Him and, defying the savage *Schutz-staffel*, to chant their Shema with dignity as they died.

As a survivor, Emil Fackenheim importunes every human being to confront the future with unswerving trust in the faithfulness of God. Strong in his Jewish belief that God stands by man throughout history, Fackenheim exhorts his co-religionists to consider that:

> Jews are forbidden to hand Hitler posthumous victories. They are commanded to survive as Jews, lest the Jewish people perish. They are commanded to remember the victims of Auschwitz lest their memory perish. They are forbidden to despair of man and of his world, and to escape into either cynicism or other-wordliness, lest they cooperate in delivering the world over to Auschwitz. Finally, they are forbidden to despair of the God of Israel lest Judaism perish.[10]

Even though Jacob Neusner bluntly assumes that "the Judaic theologizers ill-serve the faithful when they claim Auschwitz as a 'turning' as in Rubinstein's case or 'a new beginning' as in Fachenheim's,"[11] it remains necessary for Christians in this decade to come to terms with Auschwitz. For many of us, a popularizer like Gerald Green effectively overrules Neusner's contention by moving us from the abstract to the concrete, from the dispassionately religious to the painfully human. In her book, *How Catholics Look at Jews*, Claire Huchet Bishop achieves the same end when she answers her own question: "Unless we face Auschwitz in Christian teaching, how dare we speak of dialogue, encounters, reconciliation with the Jews?"[12]

Conservative believers are disturbed by this kind of language. Mentally fettered by their ancient stereotype of the Jew as "accursed of God," they panic interiorly at any mention of a topic which they regard as evidence of a racial paranoia. These troubled diehards, according to the booksellers, are to be numbered among those who take as gospel truth the ultimate lie now being propagated, that is, that the Holocaust is an invention of the Jewish imagination, not something that really ever happened. If it did, it was not the only event of its kind in history.

In the not-too-distant past, some of us might have been able to discuss the entire Hitlerian outrage in the clinical language of the academicians. Spokesmen from Academe, in spite of our stupidity, are helping us over this difficulty. A humanist like Lee Belford tells us in the simplest of terms:

> We affirm that all men are involved in guilt for the death of Christ and in the spirit of His love for all mankind. Yet we repeat phrases that have created a spirit of antipathy toward our brothers — those who have a special place in the economy of God.[13]

In his turn, Gregory Baum makes his case:

> It is true that Christian literature . . . in later centuries has elaborated the Gospel to create a weapon for the struggle against Judaism. Christian authors have covered the mystery of Israel with theological embroidery which has contributed to the contempt and abasement of the Jewish people, and these theories have become so much entangled with the Church's teaching that they have formed the mentality of generations, of whole centuries, even to our own day.[14]

Knowing that answers, formerly available to us in our neat apologetic, no longer seem to hold after Vatican II, we reach out to teachers like these who can help us in the search for truth. The more we feel the oppression in the minds of survivors, the more we have to sacrifice some of the immature, wholly unwarranted likenesses of Jesus which used to comfort us. André Schwartz-Bart years ago wrote of "the blond Christ of the cathedrals," a Nordic inspiration obviously. In retrospect, we must at least concede that such a Christ did little to influence German Christians to follow His way of love, His way of the Cross to help His kinsmen according to the flesh. In the future, adherence to such an imaginary Jesus could conceivably lead us to hand over to an arrogant Arafat his anticipated victory in Palestine.

Grass-roots Christians and intellectuals, together becoming familiar with documented facts like those in Hilberg,[15] are on guard to prevent any recurrence of that peculiar malaise of the spirit which is *Judenfeinschaft*. Cosmetic surgery has never been able, will never be able to overcome this self-propagating antagonism toward the Jews. Superficial treatment in this case is dangerous. We must go straight to the source of the malignancy, a source sharply defined by the Jewish historian, Jules Isaac, in his *Teaching of Contempt*. With clinical expertise he there lays bare the origin of the infection:

> No idea has been more destructive and has had more deadly effect on the scattered Jewish minorities living in Christian countries than the pernicious view of them as "the deicide people."[16]

This diagnosis was the result of what Isaac used to refer to as his life's work. It was for him "a sacred mission . . . a fight for wounded Israel . . . for brotherhood against hatred."[17] Ever careful to establish truth as he from his studies conceived it, he underlines in *Jĕsus et Israel* and again in *Génèse de L'Antisémitisme* his belief that, wherever present, the virulent prejudice in Christianity must be attributed not to the Gospel texts but to misleading commentaries on those texts. The essential message of the Gospel he always defended as commanding nothing opposed to the synagogue.

That is why he visited Pope John XXIII after the latter had announced his intention of calling Vatican II. The Pope had already in 1958 removed the wholly unjustifiable phrase about "the unfaithful Jews" from the Good Friday Liturgy. In the course of their lengthy, substantive conversation they agreed: "Nothing would be more futile than to try to separate from Judaism the Gospel that Jesus preached in the synagogues and in the Temple."[18] Naturally, they spoke of the *Teaching of Contempt*. As the author saw it, although there had been a positive response on the part of many individual Catholics, for all practical purposes the Church at large had done nothing. So he asked that the Holy Father empower a special subcommission at the Council to make an in-depth study of Christian anti-Semitism.

From the very outset, there was obvious dissension among the Council Fathers over any declaration to be made about the Jews. Only because of the patient, skillful management of Cardinal Bea were Pope John's operative principles included in the final draft. A hard battle was won when there was given "primary consideration in this document to what human beings have in common and to what promotes fellowship among them."[19]

Eventually, on October 28, 1965 the final version of *The Declaration of the Relationship of the Church to Non-Christian Religions* was adopted. Addressed as it was only to Catholics, despite its limitations, this was at least a step in the right direction. But nowhere is there mention of the crime of "deicide," a feather in the caps of the episcopal opposition. Temperately the position was taken: "Although the Church is the new people of God, the Jews should not be represented as repudiated or accursed by God as if such views followed from the Holy Scriptures."[20]

Nevertheless, the more we read of the behind-the-scenes maneuvering of the Council's *periti*, the more grateful we are that even one sentence was approved. Some of the members objected that a topic like Catholic-Jewish relations had no place on an ecumenical agenda. Others, those from the Eastern Churches, dreaded anything that might endanger the Arab minorities under their jurisdiction. Still others hesitated to adopt any schema that would interfere in any way with what they considered the pastoral profession of the Church. Sad to say, there were also the 245 right-wingers who voted in the negative.

It was not Pope John but his successor, Pope Paul VI, who signed the historic document with his own hand. From the beginning of his pontificate, Pope Paul judiciously pursued his aim of bringing to completion the gigantic task of the synod. To that end, in December 1963 he announced his decision to visit the Holy Land. Jewish observers in Rome took this as a blessed omen. With every conciliar development, they took new hope; credulously, it would seem, when a few months before the end of the Council Pope Paul delivered a Lenten sermon on the passion of Christ. Basing his words on the New Testament, he preached:

> It describes, in fact, the clash between Jesus and the Jewish people. That people, predestined to receive the Messiah, who awaited Him for thousands of years and was completely absorbed in this hope and in this certainty, at the right moment, when, that is, Christ came, spoke and presented Himself, not only did not recognize Him, but fought Him, slandered and injured Him, and in the end, killed Him.

Here undeniably is antisemitism writ large. How reconcile such words from the Sovereign Pontiff with the salvific will of Christ? How explain a sermon like this to a sincere Jew who, appreciating the Jewishness of Jesus, responds that this kind of reasoning very definitely runs counter to the basic rule of Christianity: "Thou shalt love thy neighbor as thyself?"

It takes the ironic, thoughtful reply of a Jew like Richard Lowry to overcome the initial shock of reading it. He comments:

I do not for a moment suppose that Pope Paul uttered these words with malice. But the fact remains that he *did* utter them and that they *were* suggested by his reading of the New Testament, notwithstanding Vatican II and *Nostra Aetate.*[21]

Traumatic though the Pope's pastoral message was for Catholics and Jews alike, there is the redeeming fact that the sermon preceded *Nostra Aetate.* A few short months after this episode, Pope Paul prayerfully did endorse it. All too often we fail to see the results of this ecumenical "conversion" of his. In the ensuing years, history tells of the changes it helped to bring about in various parts of the world. To mention only a few:

Guidelines for Catholic-Jewish Relations
    issued by the U.S. National
    Conference of Catholic Bishops,
    March 1967

Meeting between Jews and Christians in
    Bogota, Colombia, 1968, organized
    by CELAM and Anti-Defamation
    League of B'nai B'rith

Report of Commission on World Mission of
    the Lutheran World Federation,
    Asmara, Ethiopia, 1969

"Pastoral Recommendations" Catholic Church
    in the Netherlands, 1970

North Carolina State Baptist Confederation,
    Charlotte, North Carolina, 1971

General Conference of the United Methodist
    Church, Atlanta, Georgia, 1972

Statement by the French Bishops' Committee
    for Relations with the Jews, 1973

Statement by the Synod of Basle,
    Switzerland, 1974[22]

The permanent test of Pope Paul's adherence to the principles of *Nostra Aetate* was the inauguration in October, 1974 of a special Commission for Religious Relations with the Jews. As early as January, 1975 that same Commission published its "Guidelines and Suggestions for Implementing" the Conciliar Declaration of 1975. Before sketching practical approaches to meaningful Christian-Jewish dialogue, the document recalls that:

> . . . the spiritual bonds and historical links binding the Church to Judaism condemn (as opposed to the very spirit of Christianity) all forms of anti-Semitism and discrimination, which in any case the dignity of the human person alone would suffice to condemn . . . .[23]

Praxis compels correlatively that Christians must

> . . . therefore strive to acquire better knowledge of the basic components of the religious tradition of Judaism: they must strive to learn by what essential traits the Jews define themselves in the light of their own religious experience.[24]

Throughout the Christian world since *NOSTRA AETATE* but more markedly since 1975, increased attention has been paid to every phase of religious education. School texts, prayer books, all kinds of communication are constantly being examined. Of set purpose, Jews and Christians work with one another in this area not only to remove pejorative clichés about the Jews but more importantly to give due prominence to the role of Judaism in salvation history. In view of the broad spectrum envisaged, there is a very important paragraph in the "Guidelines" addressed to those in the field of higher learning:

> Research into problems bearing on Jewish-Christian relations will be encouraged among specialists, particularly in the fields of exegesis, theology, history and sociology . . . . Wherever possible, chairs of studies will be created and collaboration with Jewish scholars encouraged.[25]

John Oesterreicher from the Institute of Judaeo-Christian Studies at Seton Hall University stands as a theologian well-equipped to judge the specialists. One of his critiques entitled,

The Anatomy of Contempt, illustrates his credentials. Calling Rosemary Ruether to task for her *Faith and Fratricide,* he faults her on every score. Mainly censuring her for isolating herself from the rich stream of fraternal inspiration available to her, he decides for himself that "If Dr. Ruether's effort were to succeed, it would abort the Jewish-Christian dialogue."[26] The effort to which he refers is her expressed desire to create a "new theology." That her Christology does not agree with Oesterreicher's is no surprise. That it calls forth a negative judgment from Borowitz who esteems her is quite another matter. When he probes her thought, he has to admit that as he sees it, "God retreats from the foreground of the religious scene"; . . . "he may be mentioned from time to time, (but his) role is relatively passive and inactive compared to humanity."[27]

Such a reduction of religious belief to the category of the social or the historical is null and void for Jews, no less than for Christians. To a Cohen who desires that "the real presence of all Israel . . . enter the liturgy" it is unreasonable. What makes sense for him can be found in the Passover Haggadah where ritually "In every generation each man must regard himself as though he personally went forth from Egypt." As Jewish witness to Divine Providence, "then every post-Holocaust Jew must regard himself as though he personally went into the camps and emerged."[28] This transition from the human to the divine through the celebration of God's action in saving His people is a sign that "Survival itself can be a sanctified response to an inhuman world."[29]

In the spirit of this concept, Christians bring to their Yom HaShoah memorial service their worship, their prayer. Before the commemorative candles are lit, they ponder the words:

> At this sacred time, we pause to remember a tragic era in our history, when light was obscured by darkness, when the forces of evil were arrayed against our brothers and sisters.
>
> . . . Auschwitz, Dachau, Buchenwald, Treblinka, Bergen-Belsen, Theresienstadt — these very names evoke horror and terror.
>
> . . . And yet we recall these names and the barbarous acts associated with them so that the travail of our brothers and sisters may inspire generations yet unborn to learn well the lessons of an evil time. Their

memory must remain forever etched in the conscience of mankind.

. . . we must transform grief into compassion. We must give evidence of our remembering them through acts of kindness and courage.

. . . O Lord, remember Thy martyred children, as we pledge to remember them. And may their memory be for us a challenge and an inspiration.[30]

If Christians are loyal to the promises made in this anamnesis they bear witness in their way to the convenantal relationship between themselves and God. In every age, especially in our own, there are human imbalances, crisis situations, cataclysmic uncertainties. Within the context of law and liturgy we are asked to accept the interpenetration of the heavenly with the earthly. Well may we ask: "What finally is that ultimate and unutterable mystery which engulfs our being, and whence we take our rise, and whither our journey leads us?"[31]

In Jewish-Christian thinking, monotheism has always had to grapple with the paradox of a God who seems to be either imperfect or lacking in authority since the world He created is so full of the vilest evil. Philosophically, we can explain to ourselves that God is completely good and thus can only cause good. In Auschwitz, however, how could a son of the Covenant declare before his captors that "The Life of Torah within the congregation of Israel in the Presence of God — this is what the Jewish ideal makes possible?"

An innovative kind of answer to this disturbing question is coming to us from the Holocaust theologians. They are doing it by introducing us to the wisdom of old, the human gift divinely conferred on a prayerful sage like Akiba. Where Auschwitz is the key-word that permanently conjures up the lurid hatred that is anti-Semitism, they tell us that the "enslaved Shekinah" must bespeak the pathos of God. For too long a time we have heard little or nothing of the God of Israel who shares in the sufferings of His people. It takes a Rabbi Akiba to bring us back to this God. Reverently he approaches his theory of exile:

Were it not expressly written in Scripture, it would be impossible to say it: Israel said to God: Thou hadst redeemed thyself, as though one could conceive such a thing (*asmeka padita*). Likewise you find that whither-

soever Israel was exiled, the Shekinah, as it were, went
into exile with them. When they went into exile in
Egypt, the Shekinah went with them . . . they were
exiled to Edom, the Shekinah went into exile with them
. . . . And when they return in the future, the Shekinah,
as it were, will return with them.[32]

In contradistinction to pantheistic world-views, this God who
somehow "shares" in the destiny of His people has since biblical
times been the sure foundation on which Jewish faith rests.
Moltmann, under the influence of a modern spokesman for
God like Abraham Heschel, adopts the idea in its entirety:

> . . . the God-situation in which Israel discovers itself as
> God's people is different. It is the situation of the
> pathos of God and the sympathy of man. The God-
> situation in which Christians discover themselves as
> Christians is once again different. It is the situation of
> the incarnate, crucified God and the loving man.[33]

The scandal of the Cross in Pauline theology has come down
to us as "to the Jews indeed a stumbling-block and to the Gentiles
foolishness" (1 Cor.1:22f). Jews in the majority of cases have
constantly refused any kind of apotheosis as completely heretical.
But this common belief of Jews and Christians of God entering
somehow into the very heart of human suffering has not been
lost in the Holocaust. And Elie Wiesel, in his story of the youth
slowly struggling to death as his Nazi persecutors watched, hints
at the omnipresent "exposed God." To a man who asks at sight
of the boy, "Where is God now?" another onlooker answers:
"Here he is – he is hanging here on this gallows."[34]

While the Christian doctrine of the Incarnation remains foreign to Judaism, an orthodox Jew like Michael Wyschogrod takes
on the task of trying to explain it to his co-religionists:

> If Judaism cannot accept the Incarnation, it is because
> Jews do not hear that story, because the word of God
> as it is heard in Judaism does not tell them this, and
> because Jewish faith does not witness to it. When the
> Church accepts the Incarnation, it does not do so
> because it somehow discovered that such an event
> should take place, but because it hears that it was the
> free and gracious decision of God, a decision that could

not have been foretold by man. Strangely, enough, viewed in this light, the antagonism between Judaism and Christianity could be, though not dissolved, at least brought into a context within which it is a matter of difference in faith, with regard to the free and sovereign action of the God of Israel.[35]

A biblical historian like Michael Wyschogrod has indefatigably carried on the ecumenical task of restoring unity betwen Synagogue and Church. He makes no false pretense at conciliation. Stable in his own orthodox faith and very knowledgeable about the faith of the Church, he invites all of us to broaden the parameters of the Judaeo-Christian dialogue.

It is interesting to note at this juncture how the Lutheran World Federation meeting at Oslo, Norway in 1975 sounds very much the same note:

> Emphasis should now be placed upon the *dissemination* and *use* of studies and declarations that are our common possession. In the pursuit of this objective, European and American committees are now able to give more effective leadership in the collection, interpretation, and distribution of useful study documents.[36]

The range of this approach can be found in reports from any Jewish-Lutheran-Catholic Colloquium here in the United States. At one such conference held October 29-30, 1980 at the Graymoor Ecumenical Institute, John Koenig set forth some Lutheran reflections on the Jewishness of Jesus. "Right teaching," he declared firmly, "is necessary because (and only because) wrong teaching adds unnecessary burdens to human consciences, erects false barriers between us and God — in other words, imperils the goodness of the Gospel."[37] Here, germinally, is the sincere effort at reform called forth by Jules Isaac.

The rationale for Koenig's paper is the fundamental coincidence of the Jewish people and the gospel. Although he takes his cue from Chapters 9-11 in Paul's Epistle to the Romans, he centers his attention on Chapter fifteen. He argues that here Verse 9 must be translated linguistically, that is, as being accomplished in the past but continuing in the present. Therefore, he posits, "Christ has been and still is" carrying out his servanthood to Israel. This eschatological mission of Christ has a corollary developed by Baker, a fellow Lutheran whom Koenig quotes:

The gospel does not come to Gentiles because of the permanent eclipse of Israel or because Paul denies Israel's particularity. Rather, it comes to the Gentiles as God's ratification of his promises to Israel in Christ. The issue is not particularism versus universalism but universalism within the context of particularism.[38]

Koenig, in conclusion, accentuates his conviction that "... the gospel is not fully the good news unless its Jewishness is acknowledged."[39] His observations, originally presented as a response to Clemens Thoma's latest work, "A Christian Theology of Israel," stand as a solid commentary on the Swiss theologian's singularly challenging study. In this novel attempt at developing the encounter between Jews and Christians we find on every page Thoma's profound knowledge of the development of biblical, talmudic, medieval and modern Jewish thought. As co-editor of the *Freiburg Rundbrief* and consultor on Christian-Jewish relations for the Vatican Secretariat of Christian Unity, he has access to up-to-the-minute information about dialogical contacts throughout the world.

In the Foreword to the book, David Flusser speculates that Thoma's survey of Jewish intellectual history is "... a field not well known to Christian theologians, not even to those who like to pass strict judgment on Israel." That Jewish appraisal brings to mind the paragraph in *Nostra Aetate*:

Since the spiritual patrimony common to Christians and Jews is thus so great, this sacred Synod wishes to foster and recommend that mutual understanding and respect which is the fruit above all of biblical and theological studies, and of brotherly dialogues.[40]

In the past, de-Judaizers of the Gospel like John Chrysostom began to divorce Christianity from Judaism. Modern scholars like Thoma who accept the asymmetry between the two are establishing the fact that "The Holocaust stands as a milestone for believing Christians of the inviolable oneness of Judaism and Christianity, based on the crucified Christ."[41] Restoring the Gospel to its matrix in the Hebrew Scriptures is the presupposition to this thesis. In God's revelation to the Chosen People are to be found the theological and historical roots of Christianity. The content of the revelation in the New Testament, however, must be construed not only with relevance to the Torah but in terms of post-biblical Judaism and the sad account of Christian anti-Semitism from the early days of the common era.

Here is the crux of the matter: the existential danger of a reversion to genocidal hatred of the Jews. Small wonder that the dangers which in the past "infested" the theological dimension should impel Thoma to systematize his research to give us an overview of "all the problems and malformations that have evolved from the Christian-Jewish encounter." Looking back on his experiences after World War II, he took stock of the Hitlerian ideology's attraction for some of his academic peers. After that, he came upon a very salutary insight:

> When the gas ovens of Auschwitz had ceased to smoke, when the Jews, contrary to the expectations of many people, became re-established in Israel, when it began to dawn on many Christians that they, too, bear responsibility for the mechanical destruction of the Jews under National Socialism, and when it became ever clearer how dangerous the situation in the Middle East could become for the peace of the world, only then — and unfortunately much too late — did Christians and Jews begin to reflect on it all and talk to each other.[42]

Only after locating the problem zones in theology does Thoma deal with the topic of Jesus Christ and his message in the context of early and rabbinic Judaism. He speaks of Jesus the Jewish rabbi with the proviso: "Whenever Jewish authors emphasize and elaborate on Jesus' Jewishness, they have at the back of their mind their own fate and the fate of their people."[43] One of his questions about the Christ, the Savior of the world whom Christians profess, leads him to a bridge-Christology. By scrutinizing the idea of imitation in the Hebrew Scriptures, he decides that this is the bridge between the earthly Jesus and the Risen Christ. Insofar as followers of Jesus here and now imitate Him in their daily lives will there be a lessening of "prejudice and arrogance toward the Jews, Jesus' brothers and ours."[44]

How weak the imitation of the suffering, dying and risen Christ has been can be tested in an observation by David Flusser. He says:

> I do not think that many Jews would object if the Messiah when he came again was the Jew Jesus. But

wouldn't many Christians be uneasy if they found that the messianic ideas of the Old Testament prophets were fulfilled, even though the Old Testament is also Scripture for them?[45]

Thoma is single-minded in his desire to make firm the foundations of human co-existence. He makes his own the words of Jules Isaac:

The glow of the Auschwitz crematorium is the beacon that lights, that guides all my thoughts. Oh, my Jewish brothers, and you as well my Christian brothers, do you not think that it mingles with another glow, that of the Cross?[46]

In that glow, Thoma foresees that in the Middle East there is a growing menace to the peace of mankind. In a short paragraph, he touches on the significance of the State of Israel not only for Israelis but for the entire Jewish people. Its genesis, a refuge from murderous anti-Semitism, ought to guarantee its acceptance. That this is not so the day-to-day confrontations attest. Thoma leaves it to a competent cadre of other Holocaust theologians to consider serious matters that call for our personal decision.

Two courageously vocal Christians, Alice and Roy Eckardt, have taken up a resolute position in their *Encounter with Israel*. They have no hesitation in establishing their assertion that:

Jews could not have become an integral people without the land. Even the "Canaanite" Israeli, by his very presence in the land of his ancestors, testifies to the historic link with Palestine.

. . . Jewish faith and Jewish peopleness developed as one; it is out of the question to say that one preceded the other. There is a saying in the Talmud: "Your Father is the Almighty; your mother is the congregation of Israel." Historically speaking, the most we can say is that the people of Israel were born out of the faith, and the faith was born out of the people of Israel.[47]

It is not to sacred but to secular history that we turn to uphold the right of Israel to exist as a sovereign, independent state. While it was only in 1948 that its statehood was granted, there never has been a time when Jews did not dwell in their Holy Land. Israel's relationship to that land must be evaluated in Jewish terms, that is, in recognition of the fact that Jews have never accepted the destruction of their right to be there. No matter where they might be in the Diaspora, pious Jews showed by their prayers for Palestine that they looked on themselves as surrogate custodians of their ancient heartland. The biblical renewal today has kindled in many Jews an encouraging sensitivity to their past, a feeling of oneness with all Jews who have ever lived. This is the clue to Jewish self-definition in a Post-Holocaust Age.

And the key to receiving Israel now lies in the word "Zion." We have known it as the City of David because David made it the capital of his kingdom. Much more significantly, by transferring the Ark of the Covenant there he constituted it as the center of the religious life of his people. That is why the prophets, in their turn, could ring the changes on its spiritual symbolism. Abba Eban directs our attention to the increasing importance of this symbolism when he writes:

> Zionism is nothing more — but also nothing less — than the Jewish people's sense of origin and destination in the land linked eternally with its name. It is also the instrument whereby the Jewish nation seeks an authentic fulfillment of itself.[48]

Modern Zionists have converted the biblical ideal into the political reality which we know. In spite of cruel hardships and unnerving vicissitudes, they persevered in their revolt against every sign of anti-Semitism which threatened to engulf them and this most especially in the Nazi period. In 1947, prior to the UN's "restoration" of Israeli independence, one of the spokesmen for its endorsement was none other than Andre Gromyko. In resounding words, he told his alert audience:

> During the last war, the Jewish people underwent exceptional sorrow and suffering. Without exaggeration, this sorrow and suffering are indescribable. It is difficult to express them in dry statistics on the Jewish victims of the fascist aggressors. The Jews in the territories where the Hitlerites held sway were subjected to almost complete physical annihilation.

... The United Nations cannot and must not regard this situation with indifference.

The fact that no Western European State has been able to ensure the defense of the elementary rights of the Jewish people and to safeguard it against the violence of the fascist executioners explains the aspirations of the Jews to establish their own state.[49]

The plight of Soviet Jewry makes us pause as we read. Where others were still reluctant to mention any kind of connection between the Holocaust and the Jewish dream of selfhood, Gromyko defended the rights of the Jews to their own political authority. What has happened in the intervening years to this Russian voice?

Alas! Not long after Gromyko's intervention, a very different idiom became the fashion in UN debates. Instead of Russian adherence to the Jewish ideal, the harshness of Arab altercations filled the chambers. Completely cut off from an older Arab tradition, the rallying cry became: "Zionism is racism." To all appearances, these latecomers to the international institution were ignorant of what Emir Feisal, representing the Arab world in the 1919 Peace Conference at Paris, dictated:

We Arabs, especially the educated among us, look with deepest sympathy on the Zionist movement . . . . We will wish the Jews a hearty welcome home . . . . We are working together for a reformed and revised Near East and our two movements complement one another. The movement is national and not imperialistic. There is room in Syria for us both. Indeed, I think that neither can be a success without the other.[50]

Would to God that the PLO might concentrate on this kind of language in reference to the argot of the Elders of Zion! And would to God that on November 7, 1980 the world had not been told of the new policy announced by the National Council of Churches: "The Palestine Liberation Organization at this time functions as the only organized voice of the Palestinian people and appears to be the only body able to negotiate a settlement on their behalf." The print was scarcely dry before the American Jewish Congress and the Anti-Defamation League charged that the draft lent credence to the role of the PLO.

Simultaneous Christian reaction came from Dr. Franklin

Littell. In his keynote address to the Sixth Annual Conference on *Teaching the Lessons of the Holocaust*, he energetically denounced "religious offices that apparently cannot distinguish between legitimate and illegitimate governments, terrorist bands and political formations of free men and women." In his role as president of the National Leadership Conference for Israel, he commented further on "the process of assassination and intimidation of moderate Arabs by which the PLO achieved such an exclusive position." Referring to what he called "The Church Bourbons," he objected: "Their thinking shows they have learned nothing from the witness of Christian martyrs in the German Church struggle, and nothing from the martyrdom of 6,000,000 Jews in the Holocaust."[51]

In the heat of an argument like this it is very difficult to determine where the lines are to be drawn. In calmer moments, it might be wise to look back to 1964 when the General Board of the National Council of Churches wrote the following into its resolutions: "The poison of anti-Semitism has causes of a political, national, psychological, social and economic nature." For NCC, this listing may clear the atmosphere. And in his turn, Dr. Littell will have to rethink the inferences to be drawn from his mention of the way in which the Nazi Party "functioned as the sole voice of the German people." The publicity given by the media to the NCC's posture relative to the PLO counteracts such a deduction as this.

If the denouncing of Zionism in the UN or the approbation of the PLO by Church bodies brings into the limelight the hazardous position of the State of Israel, perhaps it will arouse us from apathy to supportive action. Father Edward M. Flannery takes a dim view of such a wish in his discerning analysis of "Anti-Zionism and the Christian Psyche." He feels that Christendom's response to Israel still resembles Christendom's response to the Holocaust: stupid indifference, active opposition, overriding fear. The force undergirding such tendencies is the intense repudiation of any personal anti-Semitism![52]

On the grounds of historical validity, the Zionist, anti-Zionist battle should arouse our sympathy for our Jewish brethren. Any least hint that Christian antagonism toward them is somehow exerting an effective stimulus to the PLO operations in the Middle East must be a tocsin for us. We are obligated as human beings, after all the injustices inflicted on the Jews, to support the UN Resolution of 1948 and thus secure for them a good life in a land of their own. In addition, as Christians, we are bound to respect them because ". . . in view of the divine choice, they are most dear for the sake of their fathers. For the gifts and call of God are without recall." (Romans 11:28-29)

Especially for Jews like Elie Wiesel for whom the Divine Presence and the Covenant were shattered by the Holocaust must we have the openness he seeks. He replaces the Sinaitic covenant with what he designates as "the additional covenant." In solidarity, witness and sanctification of life, this new covenant will be the basis for contemporary Jewish self-affirmation. No matter how we regard his complete break with the past, we must admire his earnest commitment to the Jewish future. That is why we picture him as the undying witness to that spirit in man which knows: "Through centuries and generations to come, that to live as a man, as a Jew, means to say yes, to life . . ." Hence Israel must be the locus of the survivor, the site of revival where man can "take his fate into his hands."[53]

Complex as the reality of the State of Israel is for the Jew, it is equally complex for the Catholic. Of great importance in understanding the situation is the Vatican's non-approval of the State itself. The reason for this, usually unknown outside the Church, is that the common practice of the Vatican is to withhold official recognition from any country in a state of war or any country whose official boundaries are not sufficiently guaranteed by some international pact. Case histories can easily be found in the Vatican archives. So, the Holy See has not yet given any formal approval to the State of Israel. But there is another, and mayhap a more cogent reason for withholding its diplomatic, religious sanction. Because of the Holy See's solicitude for the Christian communities in Arab lands, the Papacy must take precautions against adverse reactions from opposing forces.

But if the Church qua institution must pay special attention to such restrictions, the same is not true of the individual Catholic. Today, some conservatives within the Church persist in acting as if the Diaspora is a punishment inflicted by God upon the Jewish people because they crucified Christ. For such, the State of Israel is a perverse act of defiance hurled at the Almighty by an unredeemed and unredeemable people. The teaching Church and the individual Catholic must cooperate in what looks like the perennial task of overcoming this racial hatred, this deadly ideology so very foreign to the good news of Jesus Christ.

Theologically, it is from within Judaism that Christians can come to know the State of Israel as a latterday testimony of

God's love for His chosen people. There we can appreciate the return of the Jews to Zion as God's renewed blessing on both the land and the people. From this standpoint, we can arrive at a deeper gratitude for our own faith as we recover the enriching roots of our religious heritage.

Judaism has never lost its vocation to be a light to the Gentiles. Martyrs of the Holocaust never betrayed their people's sense of responsibility toward us, the *goyim*. No matter how sinister the darkness which enveloped them, they managed to cling almost instinctively to their redemptive Calling. Just as their ancestors pledged themselves to God at Sinai, so they mutely but powerfully endorsed the Kiddush Ha-Shem, their way of sanctifying the Name. In so doing, they left as a legacy to their own nation the mindset of the Jews to live as Jews. And so they continue to communicate to all of humanity their indomitable will to be themselves. That is why contemporary Jews can thank God as they chant:

Am Ysrael chai! The people of Israel still live!

Here is the irrefragable bulwark against Hitler. The Fuhrer aimed primarily at the death of all the Jews on earth in order to purge the world of what was for him a "human substratum." Little did he imagine that the gehennas to which he consigned them would become enduring momuments to their memory. Neither did he conceive of the strength of survivors to rededicate themselves to the divine command of choosing life.

When Pope John Paul II met with some of these vital Holocaust survivors during his visit to Germany, he condemned the perverted theories of racism which had so violently under Nazism desecrated history. Speaking to a 24-member delegation of the Central Council of Jews in Germany, he told them:

> The innocent victims in Germany and elsewhere, the destroyed or scattered families, the cultural values and cultural treasures destroyed forever are tragic proof of where discrimination and disregard for human dignity can lead.
>
> . . . Concrete brotherly relations between Jews and Catholics in Germany receives a very special value against the dark background of persecution of Jews in this country.

Jewish-Christian history now as in the past goes through periods of hostility. Were we to gainsay the enmity expressed to the Jews in this latter half of the twentieth century we would have to be purposefully blind to what is happening on the national and international stage. Vivid accounts of murderous bombings, pictures of defaced tombstones, criminal attacks on individuals: hardly a day passes without some journalistic reference to one or the other. It is indeed sobering to test the record against the "General Declaration of Human Rights" which, on December 10, 1948, the UN pronounced to the world.

On the other hand, we must take heart from the dialogical advances which have been made between Jews and Christians. Were we to belittle such progress we would be impoverishing ourselves in the very depths of our being. In the liberal give and take of our meetings, some of us may disagree with Thoma's bridge-Christology; others may look on it as a decisive step forward in Christian theology. Again, some may discard the notion of the ongoing servanthood of Christ to the Jews; others may at the same time enthusiastically link it up with the imitation of Christ. Frequently, Christians surprise Jews by their approbation of Wiesel's new covenant theory; some Jews amaze Christians by classifying it as heretical.

What cannot be denied is that such constant interchange stimulates all of us to increased efforts at the eradication of every least trace of the teaching of contempt. We come to know more cogently that:

> Christians and Jews interpret and confess in different ways their faith in the One God who reveals Himself in history. The Torah, as the center of Jewish faith, is a divine plan and tool for the development of the world. Jesus takes that place in Christianity, as salvation for all men. In the face of such common ground as well as differences, the encounter between Christians and Jews must not be confined to a mere social meeting . . . . The more open and intensive such an encounter will be, the more candidly can we discuss that which separates the two groups.[54]

The revealed focus of unity in both covenants is love of neighbor. Working together in this unity, we are happily conscious of our interdependence as well as our independence. One result of this awareness is the reciprocity which enables us to strive for a genuinely Christian perspective of the Holocaust.

Notes

1. Eugene Borowitz, *How Can a Jew Speak of Faith Today?* (Philadelphia, The Westminster Press, 1969), p. 33.

2. *Op. cit.,* p. 34.

3. *Op. cit.,* p. 35.

4. Jacob Neusner, *Understanding Jewish Theology,* (New York: Ktav, 1973), p. 185 quoting Richard L. Rubinstein, *After Auschwitz,* pp. 153-154.

5. Max I. Dimont, *Jews, God and History: A Modern Interpretation of a Four-Thousand-Year Story,* (New York: Simon and Schuster, 1962), p. 388.

6. Arthur A. Cohen, *Thinking the Tremendum: Some Theological Implications of the Death-camps,* (New York: Leo Baeck Institute, 1974), pp. 17, 18.

7. *Op. cit.,* p. 21.

8. *Ibid.*

9. *Op. cit.,* p. 10.

10. Emil Fackenheim, *God's Presence in History,* (New York: N.Y. University Press, 1970), p. 84.

11. Jacob Neusner, *op. cit.,* p. 172.

12. Claire H. Bishop, *How Catholics Look at Jews,* (New York: Paulist Press, 1974), pp. 98,99.

13. John Pawlikowski, *Cathechetics and Prejudice,* (New York: Paulist Press, 1973), p. 120 quoting an article by Lee Belford in "The Churchman," Dec. 1970, p. 10.

14. Gregory Baum, *The Jews and the Gospel,* (New York: Newman Press, 1961), p. 5.

15. Raul Hilberg, *The Destruction of the European Jews,* (Chicago: Quadrangel Books, 1967), p. 555.

16. Jules Isaac, *The Teaching of Contempt,* tr. Helen Weaver (New York: Holt, Rinehart and Winston, 1964), p. 109.

17. *Op cit.*, p. 9.

18. *Jesus and Israel*, tr. Sally Gran (New York: Holt, Rinehart and Winston, 1971), p. 74.

19. Sacred Synod, *Documents of Vatican II*, ed. Walter M. Abbott, S. J., (New York: Guild Press, 1966), p. 660.

20. *Op. cit.*, p. 666.

21. Richard Lowry, *A Response to Clemens Thoma's Christian Theology of Judaism*, paper delivered at Jewish-Lutheran-Catholic Colloquium at Graymoor Ecumenical Institute, October 30, 1980.

22. Helga Croner, ed., *Stepping Stones to Further Jewish-Christian Relations*, (London: Stimulus Books, 1977), pp. vii, viii.

23. *Op. cit.*, p. 11.

24. *Ibid.*

25. *Op. cit.*, p. 15.

26. John Oesterreicher, *The Anatomy of Contempt*, (South Orange, Seton Hall University, n.d.), pp. 36, 37.

27. *Op. cit.*, p. 32, quoting Borowitz.

28. Alvin Rosenfeld, Irving Greenberg, ed. *Confronting the Holocaust: The Impact of Elie Wiesel*, (Bloomington: Indiana U. Press, 1978), p. 180.

29. *Op. cit.*, p. 181.

30. Sacred Synod, *op. cit.*, p. 661.

31. Eugene Borowitz, *op. cit.*, p. 23.

32. Clemens Thoma, *A Christian Theology of Judaism*, (New York: Paulist Press, 1980), quoting Rabbi Akiba, p. 132.

33. *Op. cit.*, pp. 133-134.

34. *Ibid.*

35. *Op. cit.*, pp. 128-129.

36. Helga Croner, *op. cit.*, p. 131.

37. John Koenig, *The Jewishness of Jesus,* paper delivered at Graymoor Ecumenical Institute, October 30, 1980, p. 1.

38. *Op. cit.,* p. 11.

39. *Ibid.*

40. Sacred Synod, *op. cit.,* p. 665.

41. Clemens Thoma, *op. cit.,* p. 159.

42. *Op. cit.,* p. 25.

43. *Op. cit.,* p. 107.

44. *Ibid.*

45. *Op. cit.,* p. 134.

46. *Op. cit.,* p. 152.

47. Eckardt, Alice and Roy, *Encounter with Israel,* (New York: Association Press, 1970), p. 247.

48. Chaim Herzog, *Who Stands Accused?* (New York: Random House, 1970), cf. p. 7.

49. *Op. cit.,* p. 8.

50. *Op. cit.,* p. 7.

51. Franklin Littell, press notice, Nov. 11, 1980.

52. Edward H. Flannery, *Anti-Zionism and the Christian Psyche,* cf. Eckhardt, op. cit., p. 222.

53. Rosenfeld and Greenberg, *op. cit.,* cf. p. 182.

54. Helga Croner, *op. cit.,* p. 147.

Chapter 5

AFTER THE HOLOCAUST: SOME CHRISTIAN CONSIDERATIONS

Alice and Roy Eckardt*
Department of Religious Studies,
Lehigh University, Bethlehem, Pennsylvania

First let us define our terms so that we are clear about our subject:

By "the Holocaust"[1] we mean the Nazi regime's intention and attempt to kill every Jew within its reach. That was the truth behind the Nazi terminology, however camouflaging it may have been intended to be at the time: *die Endlösung die Judenfrage* — the Final Solution of the Jewish Question. Other Nazi atrocities, however gruesome, massive, or unforgiveable, are not included under the word Holocaust. Only one people was selected for total eradication and that was the Jewish people. In the process they were dehumanized and treated as vermin or disposable matter in order to demonstrate the Nazi ideology. Every remnant of their faith and culture was to be demeaned and effaced. The purpose of this war against the entire Jewish people was presented as salvational in nature, and the reason was not what the Jews did or did not do but their "being." Even those Christians or other non-Jews who were killed for aiding Jews were punished for a decision which they had freely made. No choice or action was available to Jews by which they could save themselves. We

*ALICE and ROY ECKARDT are members of the Department of Religion Studies, Lehigh University. They have spent a recent year in Western Germany and Israel under a Rockefeller Grant, studying the consequences of the Holocaust for Christian and Jewish thinking and life.

must insist on this specificity, or we lose sight of the singularity of the Holocaust, and its significance, especially for Christianity.

Increasingly, as more attention is paid to this attack on the Jewish people, antisemites seek to diminish the numbers of victims or deny that the death camps ever existed. In the Communist countries of Eastern Europe, the very identity for which the victims perished is denied to them now; they have become Russian, Polish, or Lithuanian "victims of Fascism." A further recent development noticeable in our own country is a demand by other ethnic groups that their victims receive recognition in memorials to the Holocaust.

All of these tactics and developments act to obscure the absolutely unique plight of the Jewish people during the Nazi era, and also enable people to evade the soul-searching questions to which it should lead all of us. If the "Final Solution" were simply one more example of man's inhumanity to man (even if more extreme than most), and if Jews were only one of many peoples equally victimized by the German National Socialists, we then could treat it as an aberration of German history traceable to an unusual set of circumstances: a national trauma, an economic collapse, political instability under an unfamiliar form of government, the need for a scapegoat, and, of course, a demagogic genius who knew how to manipulate all of these factors to satisfy his lust for power and his vision of the world. How relatively simple, and how unthreatening such an explanation would be.

But we know it will not do, even though all those circumstances did exist in Germany prior to 1933. The explanation does not tell us why in the heart of Christendom the very people from whom originated the holy scriptures, apostles, and the confessed Lord of the church was not only singled out for annihilation but was, with rare exception, abandoned by the churches and Christian peoples. Not only were they abandoned, but frequently were reviled from pulpits and in theological works of the time, and pushed into the arms of the SS through collaboration of church officials in searching their records for evidence to establish "racial purity and impurity." A sociological-historical explanation does not satisfactorily tell us why these hapless people were also denied refuge in countries with avowed Christian and democratic traditions. Nor does it help us understand how a political party with the idolatrous, pagan, and inhuman impulses which the National Socialists exhibited could secure such sizable support from a country whose population was — at least on record — 95%

Christian; not to mention the laudatory support German clergy and bishops gave to the Nazi Government throughout most of its existence, including its military ventures. (The record of church – clerical and lay – behavior in Nazi-occupied countries is a more complex story, but is seldom little more than slightly better than the Third Reich, and at times, no better, perhaps even worse.)

There is no clearer way to demonstrate the Christian problem with the Holocaust than to cite a few specifics in the form of questions:

How are we to understand a German cardinal's letter sent to his clergy following the November 1938 *Kristallnacht*[2] telling them that this nation-wide attack on Jewish places of worship, businesses, homes, and persons was *not* a matter for church or clerical concern?

How are we to grasp the fact that in the years between 1939 and 1945 the only two references the Jesuit periodical *Civiltá Cattolicá* (published in the Vatican) made to Jews were in denunciatory ways in connection with the trial and crucifixion of Jesus? Moreover, those denunciations were not restricted to the past, but were brought up to date. For example, in December 1941 we read: ". . . the crime of the sons of the Synagogue has been repeated in every generation." And again in March 1942: "Those who were filled with 'malice,' and 'furious hatred' toward Jesus and who were responsible for his crucifixion are clearly identified in the Gospels and 'remain under the open accusation in front of the whole universe, even today'."[3]

How are we to accept that the best that Pastor Martin Niemöller was able to say regarding the "alien and uncongenial" Jews was a grudging acknowledgment that "God had seen fit to reveal Himself in the Jew, Jesus of Nazareth" and, therefore, this "painful and grievous stumbling block has to be accepted for the sake of the Gospel?"[4]

How are we to appropriate the truth that while the Warsaw Ghetto inhabitants were making their desperate last stand against machine guns, poison gas, and flame-throwers, the Christian part of the city observed Holy Week, and churchgoers paused on their way to or from Easter services to watch as Polish Jews hurled themselves from burning buildings?

How were we able, asks Father Richards of England, on "each December 28th (during World War II) to continue blithely commemorating the death of the Holy Innocents at Bethlehem, while showing such little concern, even after the news had reached us, that millions of other innocents were being done to death by a modern Herod at Belsen and Auschwitz?"[5]

And how are we to countenance *The Christian Century's* editorial comments after *Kristallnacht* that not only was it "highly inadvisable to let down our (American) immigration barriers" but "Christian ... citizens (of the United States) have no need to feel apologetic for the limitations (on immigration) . . . .?"[6]

The Holocaust and Christian responses to its various stages revealed the logic of the church's preponderant theology — a theology based on the conviction that a sterile and perverse Judaism had been replaced by the Christian Church as the carrier of God's Word and Authority, that the Jewish people were an evil "race" guilty of killing both God's prophets and Himself in his human incarnation, and thus bearing God's curse until they accepted the only means of salvation open to humankind: Jesus Christ.[7] Despite exceptions, this conclusion that the Holocaust is the culmination of the Church's teaching of contempt is the predominant perspective on the Holocaust to which we are forced by the mass of evidence. Unless we acknowledge that the church's own theology is the bearer and instigator of anti-semitism, and unless we see the Holocaust as "the final act" of all the "*practice sessions* of crusade, inquisition, and the like ...," (as) the practical implementation (by the German Nazis and their accomplices) of the dominant theological and moral conclusions of the church,"[8] we may not be shocked enough to engage in the theological and liturgical revolution that is required if we are to liberate ourselves and future victims from persisting genocidal impulses. For until Christian theologians are ready to create a theology free of any anti-semitic proclivities, the church will remain in the impossible situation it has always been in: on the one hand denouncing prejudice, hatred, and acts that flow from such feelings, while on the other hand providing the theological and liturgical foundation for that very antipathy that can break out in anti-semitic violence.

It should not have required the methodical murder of six million people, including one and one-half million children under fourteen years of age, to awaken individual Christians or theologians or the churches to the necessity of such revision. The consequences of the teaching of contempt were very evident throughout the centuries of regnant Christendom, and generally were justified theologically. But, if the Holocaust does not now sound the alarm bells for any of us who claim allegiance to the Creator God who loves all His/Her children equally, and who we believe suffers with those who suffer, then we had better abandon all talk about Christ and God, and join those who assert the right to make, remake, or destroy the world as they see fit. At least they are consistent!

Furthermore, as the Reverend Robert Everett points out, the failure to create a theology free of "traditional anti-semitic teachings would, in essence, provide a post-Holocaust theological justification for the murder of Jews and for their murderers as well."[9]

What then are some of the essentials of such a restructured and revitalized theology?

First, *the church needs to put an end to all teachings of superiority and claims to exclusive possession of the means of salvation.* This means purging ourselves of a "we" and "they" mentality that insidiously reduces the "they" to an alien and lesser status. The denial of common humanity to the Jewish people, so persistent throughout Christian history, is the hallmark of anti-semitism, Dr. James Parkes insists. (It is also, of course, the hallmark of racism.) The seeds of a future Holocaust are present whenever and wherever this denial of equal humanity persists.

The East German theologian Kurt Meier asserts that the Christian feeling of spiritual superiority was "an inclination toward the spiritual 'final solution of the Jewish people' long before Hitler began the physical annihilation."[10] We must therefore rid ourselves of the arrogant assumption that *we* understand God's will while *they*, Jews, do not. This requires very specifically rejecting *on principle* all missionary efforts directed to Jews (as Nes Ammim, the Christian moshav in Israel, has done). The position of the advocates of *Judenmission*—loving Jews and working to bring them home to God through Jesus, believing them "capable of reform" and of being "a source of blessing for the whole world" once they "have again been graciously received by God"[11]—is not the answer, no matter how superior it is to antipathy and hatred. The conversionist view is still, as our German colleague Dr. Rudolf Pfisterer puts it so succinctly, "a continuation of the Holocaust." In other words, the *best* of the Christian tradition is still directed to *ending* Jewish existence.

Moreover, from a theological perspective the missionary argument that "without the conversion of the Jews the Church would not find her fulfillment"[12] does not meet the fundamental issue that

> . . . conversionism constitutes an assault upon the foundation of the church. That foundation is the Israel of God. If the Jewish people are not the elder brothers within the family of God, it follows that the Gentiles, as reputedly adopted younger brothers, actually remain outside and without hope. The covenant into which Jesus the Jew ostensibly leads them becomes a delusion. Hence, the effort to convert Jews to Christianity is a veiled attack, perhaps unknowingly, upon the Christian faith itself. Conversionism is a theological impossibility — not for pragmatic reasons but for reasons of principle. Thus, it is not the *Endlösung* that brings about the Christian revolutionary's opposition to the missionizing point of view. However, the Final Solution has served to bring home the dreadful consequences of the erst-while Christian effort to convert Jews.[13]

Accordingly, we rejoice when we learn that a Dutch Mennonite pastor presented a statement to the Mennonite European Regional Meeting in 1977 calling for a clear affirmation of the Mennonite position as *co-heirs with Israel* to God's promises, full support for the "independent existence" of the Jewish people and their struggle to maintain that existence both in the State of Israel and elsewhere in the world, and contrition for Mennonite silence and inactivity during both the Holocaust and the struggle to establish the Jewish state.[14]

We endorse Krister Stendahl's conviction that we will not "come to the roots of anti-semitism unless we Christians learn . . . that our witness has specific limits within God's mysterious and all comprehensive plan," that there is to be a "God-willed co-existence between Judaism and Christianity in which the missionary urge to convert Israel is held in check."[15]

Closely allied to the foregoing argument that the church must abandon its displacement claims is a second essential corrective: *The church must cease once and for all its presentation of the Jewish people as the enemies of God and the children of Satan, as well as the murderers of God, for the issue is far more than a religious one.*

Precisely because both concepts of Jews as God's enemies and as the devil's offspring are to be found in the New Testament (in Paul and the Gospel of John), the church is obligated to dissociate itself decisively from such polemic.[16] Such inherently defamatory designations repeated over the centuries produced a demonic image of Jews which became embedded equally in folklore and literary classics.[17] This characterization of the Jewish people was grist for the mills of modern racial anti-semites and Nazi demagogues, and left church spokesmen with little ground on which to take a stand against accusations which could be rooted in scriptural passages as well as writings of the saints and reformers of the church. Dr. Peter von der Osten-Sacken writes that "the conclusion seems inescapable that the latent theological and religious anti-Judaism always present just below the surface can really be overcome only if the Jewish people are no longer defined in the light of the gospel as 'enemies'. . . ."[18]

As for the deicide accusation and consonant theology, we cannot relax under the illusion that the World Council of Churches' statement of 1961 and the Vatican II document *Nostra Aetate* of 1965[19] put an end to the problem. The weight of tradition is burdened by the New Testament texts which are regularly read during Holy Week and are incorporated (and sometimes expanded upon) in cinema or television productions.[20] The church's dilemma can be illustrated by reference to an article in a Berlin Protestant parish magazine of 1976, and comments on it by the Protestant scholar, Dr. von der Osten-Sacken. The author of the article writes, "Certainly it was the Jews who hanged God. This is an indisputable fact." In a valiant attempt to create solidarity in guilt, the author then warns the readers not to "seek the cross only in Palestine, among the Jews. It should be sought where it is set up anew every day . . . murderers of Christ, this is what we all are."

There are two difficulties in this brief passage, both of which are rooted in church history. The first is, as von der Osten-Sacken points out, that the bald statement, it is an "indisputable fact" that the Jews hanged God "cannot be taken back, modified, or restricted" once it is asserted. "In the form quoted it cannot be qualified, but is an absolutely anti-Judaistic dictum. The author speaks of 'the Jews,' he inserts 'God' for Jesus, and he describes the result of this pseudo-historical and pseudo-theological process as an 'indisputable fact,' although there is nothing factual about it and everything about it is disputable."

The second difficulty, as von der Osten-Sacken shows, is the absurdity of universalizing guilt for the crucifixion. To say we are all murderers of Christ is "both historically and theologically meaningless. For no one could murder the historical Christ a second time, nor can the risen Christ be murdered . . . . The form of solidarity which (some may thus seek) with 'the Jews,' who have allegedly 'hanged God,' consequently bears all the features of a pseudo-solidarity."

Professor von der Osten-Sacken concludes his own paper analyzing anti-Judaism in Christian theology and German New Testament studies, and its relationship to "political hostility to Jewry," with these words:

> . . . as long as the gospel presented and developed in the New Testament is constantly interpreted solely for the present time (apparently) and not simultan-eously criticized in the light of historical experience; if it is interpreted in the light of tacit assumptions which are not consciously modified, then students and parishes will continue to be conditioned by implicit Christian anti-Judaism for a possible political anti-semitism.
>
> In view of the experience of history, therefore, the Gospels' claim to exclusive truth must be open to the-ological criticism inasmuch as it lends the Gospel, proclaimed by human mouth and passed on by human hand, totalitarian features that are doom-laden and destructive . . . . Once the link between the Gospels' totalitarian claim and Christian hostility to the Jews is realized, a new light falls on the relationship between political anti-Judaism as a totalitarian ideology and Christian anti-Judaism. Both are then seen to be closely and unsuspectedly akin. That essential theological crit-icism of the Gospels' totalitarian claim must con-sequently involve a Christology which does not lead to a generalizing definition of the Jewish people as ene-mies of God and the Christian community.[21]

Third, *we must stop asserting that the cross constitutes the ultimate in human suffering.* By absolutizing the passion of Jesus in both its agony and its sense of Godforsakenness the church has been responsible for presenting and perpetuating a historical falsehood. Franklin Sherman reminds us that "the cross was the instrument upon which Jews were put to death . . . long (before) the time of Jesus" as well as for at least a century after.[22] Furthermore, thousands — no, millions — of individuals in countless times and places have suffered more cruel deaths. But it was in the dark abyss of the Holocaust that Jewish victims were subjected to unexcelled physical and mental anguish: Men were forced to choose which one member of their families might receive a cherished work permit which would enable that person to survive at least a little while longer. People were forced to engage in a race of death, knowing that to lose meant immediate death, and to win meant sentencing someone else to immediate death. Mothers faced the intolerable choice on occasion of abandoning a young child and thus having the chance of living (but thereby abandoning both Jewish and general standards of moral and loving behavior), or of accompanying the child to the gas chamber (giving up life to preserve love). Children watched in horror as other children were thrown alive onto a pile of burning wood knowing that they themselves were to meet the same fate.

The Godforsakenness of Jesus the Jew[23] has become non-absolute, if it ever was absolute, for there is now a Godforsakenness of Jewish children — and Jewish parents — that is the final horror.

> By making a self-serving and self-sustaining ideology out of the cross, the church could exalt the suffering of Christian martyrs as their faithfulness to the Lord, while representing identical Jewish martyrdom as God's punishment for their role in the crucifixion of the Christ and their continuing rejection of God's Messiah.

> The belief that God participates in humanity's suffering is a belief shared by many Jews. After the pain of Auschwitz only a suffering God can reach out and touch us from out of the whirlwind of the Shoa. But the symbol of God's participation in humankind's suffering must not perpetuate the suffering of Jews. There is no question but that we must avow that *the cross must never again be used against the Jewish people*, in any way. But is saying that enough? Sometimes words are also deeds; other times they are only bandages on a deep and festering wound. Can the cross be cleansed of the blood and tears of all the innocent people, especially Jews, who have been its victims? We do not have an answer. We only know and must testify that

for unknown numbers of Jews the cross is a terrifying sight and symbol,[24] and for very good reasons.

A fourth point to be made is that *the Holocaust not only exposed the extent of the church's anti-Jewish theology, but it also revealed the shallowness of its devotion to its own love ethic.* If a time of stress is a time that tests the viability of an ethic and its relevance for the behavior of its adherents,[25] then the credibility of the church's ethic of love — love of neighbor, love of the outcast, love of all God's children — was strained almost to the breaking point during the Nazi years. It was repudiated by the mass apostasy of church members in Germany and the occupied or satellite countries, and by the timidity of clergy and bishops who feared to test the faith of the faithful by asking them to stand fast against the spirit of evil abroad in the land, and, if necessary, to bear the cross of suffering rather than to sin.[26]

Did we need the "Final Solution" to teach us that "Christian anti-semitism is a direct contradiction of love as a guiding principle, and a malignancy which strangles the credibility of the Church's message"?[27] In 1933 someone in the Protestant church in Breslau, Germany knew this to be the case and tried to alert his fellow Christians to that truth. In the church weekly, in October, a brief paragarph was printed, entitled "Vision":

> Scene — A Church Service. The introit [Bat the opening of the service] comes to an end. The pastor stands at the altar. His opening words are, "Non-Aryans are requested to leave the church," No one makes a move. "Non-Aryans are requested to leave the church," he repeats. Again there is no movement. "Non-Aryans are required to leave the church at once." At this Christ comes down from the cross on the altar and quits the church . . . .[28]

Reading the churchmen's debates over the application of the Aryan Clause to the church, as well as some of the earlier racial anti-semitic literature, we are reminded forcibly that if Christians remain true to their confessed Lord, they will be ranged alongside the Jews whether they like it or not. We remind ourselves of Niemöller's reluctant acceptance of God's action in revealing Himself in a Jew of Nazareth. For the other side — racial anti-semitism — we refer to the 19th century German Eugen Dühring who, with logic and consistency, condemned

"Christianity of Palestinian origin" equally with everything Jewish. It was "itself Semitism," "offspring of the Jewish oriental racial soul," and Jesus himself is "drenched in draughts of Jewish tradition." Accordingly Dühring concluded (though with far less historical accuracy than logic), that since it was "impossible" to be "at one and the same time an intelligent convinced Christian and a serious anti-semite, the Christian Church as the No. 1 form of the 'Jew-Enemy' . . . sits together in the dock with Judaism."[29] We have to decide whether we will willingly sit in the dock with Jews — and Jesus of Nazareth — and accordingly know why we will take that risk, or whether we prefer to say "No, thank you," and therefore leave the church for some other association.

We believe that two of our students have evidenced some wisdom and insight that is relevant for our mutual concerns. One asserted that a "religion (and he was speaking of Christianity) cannot legitimately claim a divine relation with God while at the same time turning its back on human beings who are really extensions of God." The other expressed his belief that "the salvation of Christians can never happen as long as non-Christians are suffering."[30]

We will conclude with a few remarks on another note. For all who look into the dark abyss that the Shoa represents, the response of agony and despair is inevitable. For Jews there is the pain of remembering six million persons, killed to satisfy hatred and a perverse ideology; the torment of the mind and spirit over unfulfilled lives and the amputation of a major part of the body of Israel; and the hurt of abandonment.

For Christians the vicarious agony is compounded by guilt and shame which comes from being part of a community that contributed in one way or another, directly or indirectly, to mass murder — a crime for which no compensation can ever be made. The pain can become all but unbearable. What can we do? Ask God for forgiveness? Yes. But is that enough? Reconcile ourselves with Jews? Of course. But is that enough? The pain is searing. We need a gleam of light in the blackness of our despair. Yet we almost dare not look for it, for we fear that if we find it, we will use it to blot out even the memory of the darkness, and then cease our efforts of work for a truly humanized Christianity.

Our friend, Dr. Eva Fleischner, recently shared with us these mixed feelings of despair and fear of hope, and concluded that she must take the risk of celebrating hope when she finds evidence for it. We join her in reminding ourselves of another

Christian perspective of the Holocaust, no matter how miniscule: the perspective gained by learning about those who dared to care. The title of one book which tells about Germany's "silent heroes" epitomizes the situation in which these people had to be heroic in order to be true to their humanity and, in some cases at least, to their Christian ethic: *When Compassion Was A Crime*, written by Heinz David Leuner. In another book we hear from a Jewish survivor about a Reformed church congregation in Stuttgart, Germany which cooperated in sheltering however many Jews came into their midst. A book just published this year, *Lest Innocent Blood Be Shed*, tells the wondrous story of a French Protestant town, Le Chambon, which refused to abandon either the Jews fleeing from death or their belief that it was their responsibility to help all those in need. Again, *The Incredible Mission of Father Benoît* is the story of a Catholic priest who organized an underground movement in Southern France to provide Jews with false papers, hiding places, and guidance across borders into Spain, Switzerland, and Italy.[31]

If, for Abraham Heschel (and ourselves) the State of Israel enables us to "bear the agony of Auschwitz (and) to sense a ray of God's radiance in the jungles of history,"[32] so, too, the steadfastness and courage of those few Christians — individuals, families, pastors, and congregations — who defied the might and terror of the SS state to aid the outcasts help us to sense that love was not yet eradicated; that there is a spark we must nourish so that it may break forth as a blazing light.

Notes

1. The word "Holocaust" is not without symbolic problems since in biblical terms it meant a totally burnt sacrificial offering. "Shoa", means catastrophe but is a more general term. "Churban" is also used, but has the difficulty of being associated with the destruction of the Second Temple.

2. The night of November 9-10, 1938 "The Night of Broken Glass," was the occasion when more than 200 synagogues all over Germany were burned, Jewish shops and homes were ransacked and looted, Jews were beaten and killed, and at least 20,000 Jewish men were taken off to concentration camps. The letter was sent by Cardinal Faulhaber of Munich.

3. Charlotte Klein, "Vatican View of Jews, 1939-1962," *Christian Attitudes on Jews and Judaism* (London), #43 (August 1975), p. 12.

4. Martin Neimöller, as quoted in Richard Gutteridge, *Open Thy Mouth for the Dumb*, Oxford: Basil Blackwell, 1976, p. 103. The date was February 1938. A Niemöller sermon of 1935 included much of the *Adversos Judaeos* tradition of the church. It spoke of the Eternal Jew, forever on the move, without peace or home, his creativity turning everything to poison, reaping hatred and contempt from the world, burdened till the end of time with Jesus' Word of Judgment and "the unforgiven blood-guilt of their fathers" (p. 104).

5. H. J. Richards, "The Crucifixion and the Jews," London: Sisters of Sion, 1966, p. 12.

6. *The Christian Century*, November 30, 1938, as quoted in Hertzel Fishman, *American Protestantism and the Jewish State*, Detroit: Wayne State University Press, 1973, p. 58.

7. The detailed explication of this displacement theology and teaching of contempt has been done by a number of scholars, especially Jules Isaac, James Parkes, and Rosemary Ruether, and will not be reviewed here.

8. Robert Everett, "Christian Theology After the Holocaust," *Christian Attitudes. . .*, #50 (October 1976), p. 10.

9. *Ibid.*

10. Kurt Meier, *Christian Attitudes. . .*, #8 (October 1969), p. 17.

11. Philip Jacob Spener and Pastor Dannenbaum, as quoted in Gutteridge, *op. cit.*, pp. 326, 331.

12. Franz Delitzsch, in *op cit.*, p. 328.

13. A. Roy Eckhardt, "Christian Responses to the Endlösung," *Religion in Life*, 1 (Spring 1978), pp. 38-39.

14. Dr. Karel E. de Haan, *Christian Attitudes. . .*, #64 (February 1979), p. 10.

15. Krister Stendahl, in *Face to Face*, Fall/Winter 1977, p. 19.

16. Cf. Peter von der Osten-Sacken, "Anti-Judaism in Christian Theology," *Christian Attitudes. . .*, #55 (August 1977), p. 5.

17. It is no wonder that accusations of desecration of the Host, black magic, child murder, and poisoning of wells were attributed to a people believed to be working for the devil against God.

18. Von der Osten-Sacken, *op. cit.*, p. 5.

19. Neither document uses the word "deicide" but both urge that the events leading to the crucifixion not be presented in such a way as to impose responsibility upon the Jewish people of today. The WCC statement adds the phrase "responsibilities which must fall on all humanity, not on one race or community" (Third Assembly of the World Council of Churches, New Delhi, India, 1961). Both documents, along with many other church statements on Jewish-Christian relations are to be found in Helga Croner, ed., *Stepping Stones*, London: Stimulus Books, 1977.

20. A current film shown on television is Franco Zeffirelli's *Jesus of Nazareth.*

21. Von der Osten-Sacken, *op. cit.*, pp. 4, 5-6. Perhaps only a Christian of Germany could use such words, and make us listen to them.

22. Franklin Sherman, "Speaking of God After Auschwitz," *Worldview*, 17, 9 (September 1974), p. 3. Sherman mentions Josephus' reporting that Titus crucified so many Jews in 70 C.E. that "there was not enough room for the crosses, nor enough crosses for the condemned."

23. Cf. Jürgen Moltmann, *The Crucified God*, New York: Harper and Row, 1974.

24. Cf. Edward Flannery's account of being with a young Jewish woman who declared that the sight of the cross made her shudder, "like an evil presence" (*The Anguish of the Jews*, New York: Macmillan, 1965, p. xi).

25. Robert Willis, "Christian Theology After Auschwitz," *Journal of Ecumenical Studies*, 12, 4 (Fall 1975), pp. 494-5.

26. Donald Nicholls, "The Catholic Church and the Nazis," *Christian Attitudes. . .*, #64 (February 1979), p. 12.

27. Peter Gilbert, "Theological Impact of the Holocaust," *Christian Attitudes. . .*, #58 (February 1978), p. 12.

28. Breslau church weekly, *Evangelischer Ruf,* October 14, 1933, as quoted in Gutteridge, *op. cit.*, p. 100.

29. Eugen Dühring, as paraphrased by Gutteridge, *op. cit.*, p. 337.

30. Allen Delenick, 1977; James Boyer, 1979.

31. See, among others, H. D. Leuner, *When Compassion Was A Crime,* London: Oswald Wolff, 1966; Max Krakauer as reported in Gutteridge, *op. cit.,* Philip Hallie, *Lest Innocent Blood Be Shed,* New York: Harper & Row, 1979; Fernande Leboucher, *The Incredible Mission of Father Benoît,* Garden City, N.Y.: Doubleday & Co., 1969; Philip Friedman, *Their Brothers' Keepers,* New York: Holocaust Library, reissued 1978.

32. Abraham Heschel, *Israel: Echo of Eternity,* New York: Farrar, Straus and Giroux, 1969, p. 115.

Chapter 6

GENOCIDE AND RESISTANCE: CHRISTIAN PERSPECTIVES ON THE HOLOCAUST

Hubert Locke
Vice Provost for Academic Affairs,
University of Washington, Seattle

For over four centuries, Christendom and Western civilization have been defined in virtually synonymous terms.[1] For the greater part of this period, events and towering historical figures in the region which today comprises the two Germanys gave both shape and substance to this definition, making German culture a symbol of the highest achievements in the Western intellectual and spiritual tradition. Beginning with Luther and the Protestant Reformation, and extending through four hundred years of philosophy, music, science, literature, and technology, German history contributed to the development of Western society in a manner that is perhaps unparalleled by any other people, nation, or culture.

It must come as a major shock, therefore, for both Christendom and Western civilization to recognize that barely forty years ago, Germany also gave the modern world an unparalleled experience in human depravity and barbarism. That experience is rightly termed a watershed in modern history;[2] in its aftermath, it would be rational—a characteristic which is so highly prized in the Western intellectual tradition—to assume that neither Christendom nor Western civilization could be adequately described or discussed without taking that experience into account. Christendom has only of late begun to confront in any serious way the full dimensions of that experience and its grim implications for Christian teachings and values. Much of Western civilization continues to proceed as if that experience had never occurred.

The experience has come to be described in the literature as the Holocaust — the governmentally planned and efficiently executed murder of some six million European Jews. The precise historical referent is necessary since the term "holocaust" is apt to appear more frequently in modern usage in connection with the potential spectre of a nuclear conflagration than with an actual event of the recent past. What might potentially occur carries with it its own special horrors, but what has already happened is sufficiently horrendous, in and of itself, to warrant a term exclusively reserved for its description, unless there is a felt need to blunt the realities of the past by holding out the prospect of some cataclysmic insanity in the future.

I

Perhaps second only to the enormity of the Holocaust itself is the enigmatic response of Christendom and the Western world to it. Two post-war events may be seen as symbols of this response. As symbols, they do not represent the totality of reactions to the murder of six million Jews on the part of either Christian leaders or Western nations; symbolically, however, they characterize in dramatic form the failure to take the Holocaust and its implications seriously.

By the description of its own members, the International Military Tribunal at Nuremberg was designed to be the clearest and most definitive response possible on the part of the Western Allies toward the atrocities of the German Third Reich. The Tribunal engaged the combined efforts of three Western nations and the Soviet Union which sought to render a judgment on Germany set within the framework of international law. The Nuremberg trial, therefore, stands as a unique symbol of the significance which Western society attached to the events that transpired under German influence between 1933-45. That the tribunal, for all intents and purposes, wrote the law on the basis of which it subsequently tried twenty-two German defendants, that its chief aim was to make clear to the German people their collective guilt for the entire history of the Nazi period, or that commonly accepted principles of judicial procedure were either conveniently ignored or grossly violated, are criticisms of the Nuremberg proceedings which still echo in the literature some three decades later. Essentially missing from the critique of Nuremberg, however, is one simple fact. Of the twenty-two defendants, selected primarily as representatives of the major governmental and organizational structures through which the Third Reich carried out its twelve-year reign of death and destruction, none were chosen, tried, or convicted to represent the murder of six million Jews.[3]

The Nuremberg trial was based upon indictments which, in turn, were drawn up on four categorical offenses: war crimes, crimes against peace, crimes against humanity, and subsequently, the added crime of conspiracy to commit the first three offenses. From the outset, the American participants at Nuremberg aggressively pursued the conspiracy charge which, both in law and based on the evidence at the trial, was the weakest of the four criminal charges. By a series of convoluted procedural developments, three of the Western powers finally agreed to drop the charges alleging that the defendants conspired to commit war crimes and crimes against humanity and restricted the charge of conspiracy to crimes against peace.[4]

Between 20 November, 1945, when the Nuremberg trial began, and September, 1946, when the verdicts were announced, the evidence documenting the extent of a "common plan" to exterminate the Jewish populace of Europe and, more particularly, the deliberate and largely successful implementation of that plan, was overwhelming. If, in fact, the same fundamental questions raised during the Watergate inquiry thirty years later had been posed at Nuremberg regarding the genocide of the Jews – to wit: who knew? what did they know? when did they know it? – the evidence against a sizable number of Nuremberg defendants, witnesses, and others in custody who were not indicted in this trial would have been irrefutable. Yet the mass murder of the Jews was a minor and incidental part of the case which the American and British prosecutors placed before the Tribunal. They chose instead to offer elaborate, frequently contrived, and for the most part unconvincing arguments designed to prove that a conspiracy to commit aggressive war had existed as early as the founding of the Nazi Party in the 1920's. Why, one is led to ask, did the atrocities of the death camps find such a small place in the American and British cases for the prosecution?

Equally mystifying is the choice of the twenty-two defendants who were placed on trial. The diversity of their roles during the Third Reich and the disparity between those roles have been the subject of extensive, post-Nuremberg discussion and debate. What remains astonishing is the fact that although numbered among the defendants were such virtually meaningless figures

as von Papen, Schacht, and Fritzsche — meaningless when measured against the charges brought against them — other key
figures were never indicted or tried at Nuremberg. As Hitler's
Vice-Chancellor from 1933-34 and later German Ambassador to
Austria and Turkey, von Papen's role has been described as far
more one of personal intrigue and aggrandizement than any
key involvement in a conspiracy to commit war crimes, crimes
against the peace, or crimes against humanity. Fritzsche, in
turn, has been described as a "third-level propaganda official
and radio announcer, nothing more,"[5] while Schacht spent the
last two years of war in Dachau. None of these were respectable
figures; each was undoubtedly anti-Semitic to the core; all of
them had played a public part in the rise and the continuance
in power of National Socialism. But such was not the nature of
the charges brought against them and their acquittal was, therefore, not surprising.

There were, however, other German high officials in Allied
custody at the time of the Nuremberg trial who were case book
examples of crimes against humanity and even of the less sus-
tainable charge of conspiracy. Rudolf Hess, infamous comman-
dant of Auschwitz, was in Allied custody and actually appeared
at Nuremberg as a witness for the defense. S.S. Gruppenfuhrer
Otto Ohlendorf, commander of Einsatzgruppe D, who led one
of the notorious extermination teams on the Eastern front was
placed on the witness stand by the Americans and, it has been
noted, ". . . his matter-of-fact description of the mass killings
obviously chilled the Court."[6] Others were also in Allied custody:
Otto Dietrich, second in command to Goebbels; Walter Schel-
lenberg, head of Gestapo counterintelligence who appeared as
a witness against Kaltenbrunner and of whom it has been noted
that he was present for daily luncheon meetings at which plans
for the gas chambers were discussed; Ilse Koch, famed "Red
Witch of Buchenwald"; Irma Grese who was in charge of the
women's camps at Auschwitz, Ravensbrück, and Belsen; Fritz
Klein, chief S.S. doctor of Auschwitz — all these and others might
have been indicted and tried in what was to be *the* showcase
trial of German war criminals.

That these figures were subsequently tried and convicted in
the separate Allied and Russian military courts must be acknowledged but only heightens the incongruity.[7] The Nuremberg trial
was to represent the Allied effort to demonstrate "the dangers
of racism and totalitarianism" to the German nation and to the
world. As early as September 1944, U.S. Secretary of War Henry

Stimson wrote to President Roosevelt and Treasury Secretary Morgenthau:

> "It is primarily by the thorough apprehension, investigation and trial of all the Nazi leaders and instruments of the Nazi systems of terrorism such as the Gestapo, with punishment delivered as promptly, swiftly, and severely as possible, that we can demonstrate the abhorrence which the world has for such a system and bring home to the German people our determination to extirpate it and all its fruits forever."[8]

In light of subsequent developments and its final outcomes, the International Military Tribunal at Nuremberg leaves us with three unanswered questions—questions which should gnaw at the conscience of Western civilization for years to come:

1) Why did the Americans and British choose to ignore the mountainous evidence regarding the death camps as a major element in their cases for conspiracy and for crimes against humanity?
2) Why were defendants such as von Papen and Schacht indicted and tried while Hess and Ohlendorf were not?
3) Since the Tribunal had to write the law which it subsequently used as the basis for its proceedings, why did it not include the easily documentable fact of genocide as a "crime against humanity"?

II

The second post-war event is reflected in a series of events or non-responses of the Christian world to the Holocaust. It is symbolized by several leading journals in American Protestantism, one of which especially stands out for its historical significance with respect to this issue.*

On February 10, 1941, near the height of the unfolding drama

---

*Needless to say, American Protestantism does not represent the totality of Christendom any more than the International Military Tribunal at Nuremberg represented the full scope of the allied response to German war crimes. The response of American Protestant leaders, however, serves as a pivotal example of the problem under discussion; useful studies might be undertaken of responses of Christian leaders in other Western nations in the post-war period.

of terror and tragedy that was enveloping Europe, the first issue of a new bi-weekly journal, *Christianity and Crisis*, appeared on the American scene. As indicated by the lead editorial in the inaugural issue, the journal was envisioned as direct response to the unfolding events in Europe:

> "The tragic irony of the hour is that so many of the men in America whom this revolt against Christian civilization most concerns seem to be the least aware of its implications . . . The choice before us is clear. Those who choose to exist like parasites on the liberties that others fight to secure for them will end by betraying the Christian ethic and the civilization that has developed out of that ethic."[9]

In the same issue, the famed theologian, Reinhold Niebuhr, penned an article that, in retrospect, may be seen as a master statement of prophetic insight.

> "It is our purpose," wrote Niebuhr, "to devote this modest journal to an exposition of our Christian faith in its relation to world events . . . . Looking at the tragic contemporary scene . . . we believe the task of defending the rich inheritance of our civilization to be an imperative one, however much we might desire that our social system were more worthy of defense . . . . We think it dangerous to allow religious sensitivity to obscure the fact that Nazi tyranny intends to annihilate the Jewish race, to subject the nations of Europe to the domination of a "master" race, to extirpate the Christian religions, to annul the liberties and legal standards that are the priceless heritage of ages of Christian and humanistic culture, to make truth the prostitute of political power, to seek world dominion through its satraps and allies, and generally to destroy the very fabric of our western civilization."[10]

Niebuhr was, perhaps, more prophetic than even he himself realized. Exactly one year later, on February 10, 1942, Dr. Franz Rademacher, an ambitious young lawyer who was Chief of the Jewish Division of the German Foreign Office, sent a directive to all divisions of the Foreign Office announcing the reversal of Hitler's half-hearted plan to create a Jewish state on the island of Madagascar.

"The war with the Soviet Union," Rademacher wrote, "has in the meantime created the possibility of other territories for the Final Solution. In consequence, the Fuhrer has decided that the Jews should not be evacuated to Madagascar but to the East. Madagascar need no longer, therefore, be considered in connection with the Final Solution."[11]

By this time, Auschwitz was already operational, and by the summer the mass transportation and extermination of Jews had begun in earnest.

Niebuhr's article was not the only one to raise directly the question of the plight of Europe's Jewish populace. During the first four years of its publication, which coincided with the last four years of the war, other articles appeared on the same theme. In June, 1941, the Swiss writer, Denis De Rougemont wrote a penetrating essay entitled "On the Devil and Politics" in which he raised the question,

"Is Hitler the Antichrist? . . . . Hitler is more diabolical than is imagined by those who believe him to be the Devil in person, or the Antichrist . . . . In fact, the very thing that is diabolical about Hitler is the way in which he persuaded the Germans that all evil came from the Treaty of Versailles, or from the Jews, therefore from *others*. It is in such tactics that one recognizes Satan's handiwork among his delegates."[12]

Four months later a stirring article on anti-Semitism appeared, written by the renowned French Catholic philosopher, Jacques Maritain. In its opening paragraph, he declared,

"I have already spoken of anti-Semitism many times. I never would have thought that I would have to do so in connection with anti-Semitic laws promulgated by a French government—which are a denial of the traditions and spirit of my country."[13]

It is in the light of these clear perceptions of what was at work and at stake regarding the fate of European Jews, and which appeared so forcefully and unambiguously during the war years—and before the full extent of the extermination horrors became known—that the relative silence after the war on the part of American Protestantism is deafening. One can only speculate as to the possible reasons for the muted voices. It may be that American theologians became far more alarmed by the moral issues arising out of the atomic destruction which ended hostilities against Japan than by the human horrors which were discovered at Auschwitz, Treblinka, Sobibor, and Belzec. It may be that the spectre of the Senator from Wisconsin, Joseph McCarthy, who came to dominate the American political scene by 1950 and in whom many Protestant leaders thought they discerned a new Hitler, served to deflect their moral vision. It may be that the Christian predilection toward forgiveness and reconciliation overcame its inner compunction and its sense of moral outrage.

For whatever reason, we are left with the unmistakable impression that in the aftermath of the war, the moral vision of Christendom and its leaders became transfixed by and on other events on the national and international scene. Happily, there have been exceptions — the voice and writings of the American church historian Franklin Littell has been among the most persistent and outspoken in seeking to awaken the Christian conscience to the implications of the Holocaust for its own life and destiny. The esteemed educator in whose honour this volume has been prepared is also numbered among the few who have sought to examine the dimensions and complexities of Jewish-Christian relations from this perspective. The bulk of the record, however, is marked by a painful silence which only now, thirty-five years later, is beginning to be broken.

III

To raise critical questions about the Nuremberg Tribunal or the stance of post-war Christianity in relation to the issue of the Holocaust is not to indulge in the luxury of academic hindsight. The Tribunal had to wrestle, in the midst of the widespread chaos of the war's immediate aftermath, with circumstances for which there were no precedents either in law or in history, and within a hastily-constructed structural framework, the fragileness of which was apparent from the outset and which became the dominant theme in international relations almost as soon as the Tribunal ended. And if the attention of Christian leaders was diverted to other issues, at the least it can be said that they were issues of social justice and humanitarianism.

What perhaps may best be said thirty-five years later is that there remain vital questions of contemporary significance which arise out of the Holocaust, which speak both to Christianity and the Western world, which were not addressed by the Nuremberg Tribunal or by American Christianity in the post-war period, and which we ought to get about the task of addressing. To do so may well bring about a belated but welcomed era in Christianity's historic struggle with the claims of its own tradition, in Jewish-Christian relations, and in the recovery of the authentic humanistic roots of Western civilization and culture. Chief among these questions is the issue of professional ethics, individual integrity, and corporate responsibility.

IV

It has been repeatedly pointed out that the Holocaust was made possible by the corruption and collapse of any standards of ethics on the part of German professionals during the Nazi era. German civil servants, school teachers and university professors, engineers and doctors, lawyers and judges, clergy and scientists crumbled under the sway of the Nazi ideology — some fearfully, others reluctantly, many with enthusiasm. There were exceptions, to be sure, but they were relatively few in number and the longer the Third Reich lasted, the fewer the exceptions became.

The appalling ease with which German law and the courts were transformed into official instruments of terror, German scholarship became an intellectual rationalization for Nazi racism, German industries converted their research and manufacturing processes to the production of Zyklon B gas and the ovens for the crematoria, and the German civil service undergirded the whole, ghastly business with a grimly efficient and effective bureaucracy — all of this stands as one of the most painfully compelling warnings to the modern world. In an age which has come increasingly to depend on the knowledge of scientists, the skills of technicians, the expertise of professionals, and the competency of bureaucrats to manage the conduct of post-industrial societies, the German experience during the Third Reich demands a reexamination of the values and the interior constraints, the motivations and principles which guide these critical elements of our society as they go about their work.[14]

If our nation takes the Holocaust seriously, we should see groups of scientists and engineers, bar and medical associations, teachers, clergy, and police officer organizations — every guild and profession in our nation — addressing the fundamental issue of the adequacy of its internal standards of professional conduct, the formal preparation of its practitioners, and the professional values to which it subscribes, to withstand the totalitarian threat which always courses just beneath the surface of a democratic society. Businesses and corporations — particularly the multinationals — should reexamine their corporate policies and practices in the light of the same basic question: What was the role of institutions and individuals on the rise and power of the Third Reich, and what corporate and personal responsibility should exist in every society to guard against any possibility of its reoccurrence? Our generation can never atone for the evils of the past, but by a commitment to learning from that past, we can seek to insure a more decent and humane future.

Notes

1. The brief but penetrating "Preface" by Herbert Butterfield in W. Cowan, *Witness to a Generation* (1966) offers a cogent critique of this thesis.

2. Franklin Littell has used this term repeatedly to describe the historical uniqueness of the Holocaust; for a fuller treatment of this theme, see his *The Crucifixion of the Jews* (1975), esp. Chapter I.

3. The most recent historical treatment of the Nuremberg trial is B. F. Smith's *Reaching Judgment at Nuremberg* (1977). Smith observes, "the anguished cry of the Gestapo and S. S. camp victims . . . simply was not heard clearly at Nuremberg . . . witnesses to the great atrocities were used sparingly and those who did appear were seldom questioned in a way that brought their suffering and torment to life . . . . What the American team simply would not recognize was that, despite some reason for skepticism about atrocities in 1944, the central fact of 1945-46 was massive Nazi programs of human torture and extermination" (p. 88).

4. *Ibid.*, Chap. 5.

5.*Ibid.*, p. 292.

6. *Ibid.*, p. 89.

7. For biographical sketches of these figures and their subsequent fates, see R. Manvell and H. Fraenkel, *The Incomparable Crime* (1967).

8. Smith, *op. cit.*, p. 25.

9. Cowan, *op. cit.,* p. XVI.

10. *Ibid.,* p. 9.

11. N. Levin, *The Holocaust* (1968), p. 203.

12. Cowan, *op. cit.,* p. 8.

13. *Ibid.,* p. 12.

14. Only in recent years has substantive attention been directed toward an extensive examination of the backgrounds of many of the lesser bureaucrats who were part of the immense administrative machinery of the Third Reich and particularly of the death camps. For example, S. S. Gruppenfuhrer Ohlendorf, to whom reference was made earlier, was a research economist who held a doctorate in jurisprudence. Prior to his S. S. appointment, he had been director of the Institute for Applied Economic Science at Kiel. Hans Herman Kremer, whose diary of his brief assignment at Auschwitz is one of the classical accounts of sadism, was a Professor of Medicine at the University of Münster. Hans Frank, who spent the war years as Civilian Governor for the Occupied Polish Territories, was a brilliant German lawyer who at one point in his career directed the Nazi Academy of German Law (for fuller descriptions, see Manvell and Fraenkel, *op. cit.*; Littell, "Ethics After Auschwitz", *Worldview,* September, 1945; Smith, *op. cit.* et. al). As Franklin Littell has frequently observed, the Third Reich was not a scheme of illiterate savages in some remote jungle; the Third Reich and the murder of the Jews represented, in large measure, the "treason of the intellectuals."

Part III

THE FUTURE OF
JEWISH-CHRISTIAN RELATIONS

Chapter 7

FUTURE AGENDA FOR CATHOLIC-JEWISH RELATIONS*

Eugene Fisher
Executive Secretary for Catholic-Jewish Relations,
National Conference of Catholic Bishops,
Washington, D.C.

What is needed in Catholic teaching about Judaism today "is not merely the avoidance of blatantly anti-Jewish statements, but a complete and effective educational strategy for replacing" a past, negative portrait with one of greater historical and biblical accuracy, Dr. Eugene Fisher told participants in the International Jewish-Catholic Liaison Committee meeting in Madrid, Spain. The meeting, April 5-7, focused on how Christians and Jews teach about each other. Fisher is executive director of the U.S. bishops' Committee for Catholic-Jewish Relations. In his address he discussed some elements of an agenda for the future in Catholic-Jewish relations. Fisher said the agenda for the future needs to include more discussion of the relationship between the old and the new covenants; it needs to make clear the role of the Holocaust and Israel in contemporary Jewish consciousness. Moreover, the agenda for the future needs to examine the sort of introduction Catholic students are given to the Judaism of New Testament times. There is still urgent need to integrate the results of modern biblical scholarship with the treatment of New Testament themes in catechetical materials and in the liturgy itself,

*Reprinted by permission from *Origins*, Vol. 7: No. 47, May 11, 1978. This article was presented by Dr. Eugene Fisher as an address to the International Jewish-Catholic Liaison Commitee meeting in Madrid, Spain, April 5-7, 1978.

Fisher said. At one point he stated: "The next generation of Catholics could well be the first in almost two millenia to be raised with a positive understanding of how 'Jews define themselves in the light of their own religious experience.' " The text of Fisher's address follows.

This paper will attempt to assess the direction of current Catholic teaching, in the English language, concerning Jews and Judaism. By comparing present trends with those prevailing before the second Vatican Council's declaration, *Nostra Aetate* (n. 4), the hope is to isolate specific areas that might need to be addressed in future dialogues between Catholics and Jews, and within the Roman Catholic theological community.

Presumed here is at least a general knowledge of the problem, which is that over the centuries an anti-Jewish polemic became so pervasively intertwined with Christian understandings of Judaism that it came to constitute what Jules Isaac aptly termed a "teaching of contempt."[1] The theological content and historical impact of that former, highly negative approach have also been well documented.[2] More recently, however, beginning with the Second Vatican Council, great efforts have been launched to alter this negative portrayal and to replace it with an approach more in consonance with the authentic spirit of the message of Jesus toward his people.

While this paper will draw largely on the author's studies of the treatment of Jews and Judaism in current Roman Catholic educational materials published in the United States,[3] the 16 textbook series that I studied[4] included texts used in or adapted from religious education materials published in Canada and Australia. Based on articles reporting studies reported in English journals[5] it is also safe to assume that the British teaching materials are also comparable to, or at least within the same range as, that discerned for the American textbooks and teacher manuals in their treatment of Jews and Judaism.

In the early 1950's, the American Jewish Committee began to initiate a series of projects aimed at evaluating the treatment of intergroup relations in teaching materials produced by Catholic, Protestant and Jewish educators. To ensure against "reverse bias," educational specialists drawn from the respective faith communities were called upon to analyze the materials of their own groups following research designs suited to each. The Jewish self-study found almost no negative treatment of Christians, and in fact, very little mention of Christianity at all.[6]

The methodology for the Christian self-studies was pioneered by Dr. Bernhard Olson of Yale, whose statistical sampling of some 120,000 Protestant lesson units uncovered a disturbingly high percentage of anti-Jewish statements.[7] Judaism at the time of Jesus and thereafter was portrayed as degenerate and legalistic. Jesus and the disciples were shown as "somehow not Jews," while Judas and the enemies of Jesus among the Sadduccees and the temple priesthood were clearly identified as Jewish. The collective responsibility and divine retribution canards predominated in the portrayal of the Passion. The Holocaust and the State of Israel, the two central events of modern Jewish history, received virtually no attention and the history and nature of post-biblical Judaism were virtually ignored. Olson's findings were updated in a more recent study of Protestant texts in 1972. Distressingly, the author of this study was able to report almost no improvement over the earlier treatment.[8]

Such studies of the treatment of Judaism in educational materials are by their nature important indicators of the general consensus of feeling within a given religious community. Studies done of the patterns of American prejudice in turn show that "far from being trivial, religious outlooks and religious images of the modern Jew seem to lie at the root of American anti-Semitism."[9] My own textbook study sought to update earlier Catholic studies and so to provide an objective measure of change.

Catholic Teaching Before and After Nostra Aetate

Father Trafford Maher, S.J., of St. Louis University, supervised the Catholic self-studies. These focused not only on the treatment of Jews, but also on the treatment of other groups such as Protestants, blacks, etc.[10] They utilized modified versions of the criteria, analytic categories and statistical methodology originally developed by Olson.[11] The St. Louis studies uncovered a view of Judaism as negative and as stereotyped as that revealed in the Olson report for Protestant texts. Catholics and Protestants may have been divided on many theological issues in the late 1950's, but not in their common rejection of Jews and Judaism.

My 1976 study sought to ascertain whether and to what extent Catholic teaching had changed (hopefully for the better) as a result of the intervening period, which saw both the promulgation of *Nostra Aetate* in 1965 and the issuance of "Guidelines for Catholic-Jewish Relations" by the Secretariat for Catholic-Jewish Relations of the National Conference of Catholic Bishops in 1967. These guidelines aimed at specifying and implementing the general directives of the council concerning Jews.

My study was able to provide a strict measure of progress in the dialogue by utilizing exactly the same categories, criteria of judgment and statistical tools as those used in the St. Louis studies. In addition, by concentrating on catechetical materials and on the treatment of Jews and Judaism alone, I was able to pinpoint particular themes and periods with greater accuracy, while preserving the statistical base of comparison.[12]

The time between the St. Louis studies and my own was particularly frutiful for the dialogue and saw important official statements both in the United States and Europe.[13] These made explicit the positive implications of *Nostra Aetate* in a fuller way.[14] In addition, the earlier studies had made possible new insights into some of the more subtle dynamics of anti-Jewish prejudice to be found in the pre-conciliar texts.

After citing quotations from the Thering study, for example, (which, like mine, was limited to catechetical materials), one commentator noted that:

> "While all the above are scored positive (by Thering) for Jews, they clearly imply that the Judaism which is praised culminated in Christianity . . . . While the textbooks acknowledge the spiritual wealth of Judaism, they infer that these riches were totally absorbed by Christianity. Judaism's value as a religion appears to be exhausted in its contribution to the Christian heritage."[15]

Likewise, Olson had noted a dynamic by which the textbook author would generalize from individual Jews (such as Judas) or Jewish groups (such as the Pharisees) to all Jews at the time of Christ, and from all first-century Jews to Jews of any time and place.[16] The result was that statements which seemed at first to have minimal negative impact tended, when taken in context with the sequence of lesson units, to be much more harmful to the reader's image of Jews than would first appear.

I had then to develop a second set of criteria of judgment which could be applied independently to every reference to Jews and Judaism found in the study.[17] Predictably, I found that many statements which Thering would have scored as positive or neutral would have to be scored today as negative. Thus while following the Thering criteria, I discovered that Catholic religion materials are significantly more positive toward Judaism.

But I also noted that many subtle negative dynamics remain. We have moved beyond blatant stereotypy, but have not yet succeeded in fully uprooting the vestiges of ancient polemics.

For the study I analyzed each lesson of 16 major and representative religion series then in use in the United States, covering grades 1-12.[18] This enabled me to obtain an overall picture of the scope and development of attitudes toward Jews in the crucial years of a student's psychological development.

American Catholic textbooks are clearly more positive toward Judaism and historically more accurate than before the Second Vatican Council. Using the same criteria of judgment and applying the same statistical methods as Thering, I found a 50 percent higher ratio of positive to negative statements about Jews and Judaism than that reported by Thering in 1961.[19]

By analyzing these statements according to period and theme categories,[20] which Thering was unable to do in her more general study in 1961, I was able to isolate precisely the areas where improvement had been made and the areas where further work needs to be done to correct historical and/or theological inaccuracies.

The correlation of these findings with the statements of *Nostra Aetate* is most profound. Briefly, the Jewishness of Jesus and his disciples, along with the Judaic origins of many Christian practices are now frequently highlighted in the texts.[21] Again without citing examples (which can be found in full in my dissertation),[22] it is significant that no explicit references to the deicide or divine retribution charges, both of which were rebutted clearly in *Nostra Aetate*,[23] are now to be found in American textbooks. Statements referring to modern Judaism, or to Judaism in general, are likewise overwhelmingly positive in tone and often show a sensitivity nowhere attained in the texts studied by Thering in 1961.

The correlation between *Nostra Aetate* and the textbooks, however, holds equally for areas of negative portrayal of Jews and Judaism. Wherever the conciliar declaration was silent on an issue, or its language ambiguous, omissions and/or negative statements can be found in abundance in the texts.

Nostra Aetate, for example, did not seek to clarify the record on the Pharisees. My findings thus show that with only a couple of exceptions, the Pharisees today are as vilified and as maligned as they were in 1961. Likewise, the cautiously worded denial of collective responsibility for Jesus' death made by the council has been only moderately successful in combating this key element of the anti-Jewish polemic.[24] The idea that the Jewish people as a whole rejected Jesus during his lifetime is still the prevailing teaching in American Catholic materials. Indeed, negative statements connoting Jewish guilt in the events surrounding Jesus' trial and death still outnumber positive, historically accurate ones. As in 1961, the Roman role in Jesus' passion is largely overlooked. Little of the historical background and almost none of the insights of modern biblical scholarship are provided to the teachers in their manuals.

Even those textbook series which consciously seek to avoid implicating the Jews as a whole often fall short of the mark. Some, for example, replace the phrase "the Jews" with phrases such as "the enemies of Christ" in paraphrasing the passion narratives. But the reason for this is not explained to the teachers (the majority of whom, of course, were trained using preconciliar texts), so that the question can be raised and resolved for the students. The result, one must conclude, is that when the students participate in the Holy Week liturgy and hear the gospel narratives read (especially those of Matthew and John), they will inevitably identify "the Jews" as "the enemies of Christ." In short, there is an urgent and immediate need for integrating the results of modern biblical scholarship into the treatment of New Testament themes throughout our catechetical materials and in the liturgy itself.

What is needed is not merely the avoidance of blatantly anti-Jewish statements, but a complete and effective educational strategy for replacing the negative portrait with one of greater historical and biblical accuracy. Centuries of polemic have resulted in a general culture which has anti-Jewish stereotypes embedded in its very language patterns. American dictionaries, for example, regularly define "pharisaic" as "hypocritical" or "legalistic." The word "Jewry" is even defined in one dictionary as "ghetto"—thus identifying Jews as victims of oppression. Simply removing anti-Jewish pejoratives or making all references to Jews neutral in tone, then, will not adequately offset the effects of this general, anti-Jewish culture. A positive, corrective stance must be taken if ancient polemics are not to be perpetuated in our classrooms.

Also still prevailing in the treatment of the New Testament is the attitude that Judaism was a dead religion, suffocated by legalism and materialism by the time of Christ. This, too, was a theme not taken up directly by *Nostra Aetate* and so remains a prevailing pattern in our catechesis.

Likewise, there is an almost unbroken silence concerning Jews and Judaism in the entire period between the close of the apostolic writings and the middle of the 20th century. Judaism, even though presented sympathetically in most cases, is seen as essentially an Old Testament religion. There were found almost no references to the Talmud or to medieval Jewish thought or history. This fact reinforces in the student the notion that the Jewish people and their religion became theologically and historically irrelevant with the coming of Christianity. And again it is a theme not clearly taken up by Vatican II.[25] The supercessionist theory of the relationship between Judaism and Christianity (and between the Hebrew scriptures and the apostolic writings), then, is still the common teaching on the practical level. Despite the work of many leading Catholic scholars in the United States,[26] the basic theological understanding of Judaism remains virtually the same as before the council, though it may be articulated in subtler fashion today.

Agenda for the Future

"A task . . . as yet hardly begun" is how the American bishops described the need for constructing a renewed vision of the relationship between Judaism and Christianity in 1975. It is of great significance that most of the areas of negative portrayal of Judaism described above were specifically addressed in the 1974 guidelines issued by the Vatican Commission for Religious Relations with the Jews. While these guidelines have not yet had sufficient time to affect deeply the production of catechetical materials in the United States, the measurable impact of *Nostra Aetate* provides a basis for hope.

If the 1974 Vatican guidelines prove as effective as the directives of the council, one can confidently expect measured improvement in the catechetical treatment of the Pharisees, the crucifixion, the vitality of Judaism after the first century, and in the appreciation of a continuing role in its own terms of Judaism in God's plan for salvation. The next generation of Catholics could well be the first in almost two millenia to be raised with a positive understanding of how "Jews define themselves in the light of their own religious experience."

Before this can happen, however, certain key areas in the dialogue will need to be carried forward. In each, it should be noted, some form of official church pronouncements may well be needed if the insights of the dialogue are to be embodied in

practical changes in catechetical and homiletic treatment of
Jews and Judaism. A major lesson of the above analysis is that
only those areas which receive official and clear mandates by
the magisterium can be effectively renewed.

The following list is not intended to be exhaustive in scope or
in depth. It merely seeks to delimit three basic areas which,
from the perspective of the textbook studies, most need to be
addressed by this liaison committee of Catholic and Jewish representatives in furthering the dialogue so well, but only barely,
begun.

1. The Relationship Between the Covenants

This is the area of highest ambiguity in textbook treatments.
How, precisely, are we as Christians to understand the "permanent vocation" (1973 French bishops) or "permanent election"
(1967 American guidelines) of the Jewish people in God's plan of
salvation today? In what, precisely, lies the "perpetual value" of
the Hebrew scripture on its own terms that "has not been
cancelled by the later interpretation of the New Testament"
(1974 Vatican guidelines)? Are we as Christians in a position
today to delineate clearly the content and meaning of "those
promises" which "still await their perfect fulfillment of his
(Christ's) glorious return at the end of time" and those which
"were fulfilled with the first coming of Christ" (1974 Vatican
guidelines)?

It should be noted that this issue should be approached not
so much as a question of Christology as of eschatology. The
point of dialogue is not to accommodate one's own faith commitment to that of the other, but to work it out in such a way
that room is left within one's own vision for the validity of the
other's self-definition as a faith community. Is this possible for
Judaism and Christianity today?

It needs also to be stressed that, along with the internal reflections within each community, the proper forum for working on
such renewed theologies[27] is the dialogue itself. This implies, of
course, a completely new methodology for pursuing the process
of theology itself. The development of a dialogically founded
theological methodology may be the most crucial task before
this liaison committee. Common terminology and common criteria of procedure need to be developed, tested and used to
create a framework of common concepts that will have univocal
meaning for both groups.[28]

The fact that much of the development of our Christian theology of Judaism historically took place in isolation from contact with the living Jewish community, as the American bishops noted in their 1975 statement, both reveals the need and opens the way for this development. By using the internal Jewish concept of "sanctification of the name" (*kiddush ha-shem*),[29] the French bishops in 1973 were able to speak positively of an ongoing "vocation" or mission of the Jewish people in God's plan, at once unique to Judaism and complementary to, or at least compatible with, Christianity's internal view of its own sense of divine mission. Professor Tommaso Federici, in the first section of his paper delivered at the last meeting of the liaison committee in Venice, developed this insight even further in speaking of a Jewish mission for the proclamation of the One Name.

Such insights are not, of course, entirely new developments. Christian teaching since the time of the fathers has consistently held to a sense of Jewish witness. But this was essentially a negative view, by which the Jewish people were to be preserved in subjugation because their suffering could be utilized as a sort of inverted proof of Christianity.[30] What the recent developments are accomplishing, then, is a reassessment of an ancient theological tradition in the church, devoid of the negative polemics of its historical context, and offered honestly today as an utterance in the dialogue. Here, I believe, we can find a fruitful and solid basis for further exploration of the relationship between our two covenants in faith.

This dialogue, of course, is a two-way street, though not in the sense of a bargaining session. The Jewish community also has many misconceptions of the nature of Christianity, as well as a polemical tradition concerning Christians.[31]

In the Third National Workshop on Christian-Jewish Relations, held in Detroit in 1977, Rabbi Jacob Petuchowski suggested study of the Talmudic concept of the Noahide covenant as a way, from the Jewish side, for establishing an understanding of the role of Christianity in the divine plan in a way compatible with Judaism's internal self-understanding.[32] Such positive appreciations of the relationship between the covenants are only now beginning after a silence of almost two millenia on both sides.[33] But they offer great promise for the future.

2. *The Holocaust and the State of Israel*

The two central events of modern Jewish religious experience are the near-annihilation of European Jewry under the Nazi regime and the rebirth of the Jewish State of Israel. For Catholics to dialogue with Jews today, they must possess an understanding of these events and of the link between them within Jewish religious perception.[34] My textbook study showed that while these events are treated sympathetically whenever referred to, they are given scant treatment. And there is little or no direct confrontation with the theological issues they raise for Jews and Christians alike.

The relationship between land and people in Judaism has been explored on a scholarly level in Israel, in Europe and in the United States.[35] Yet, from the Catholic side one must note that, with the exception of those few individuals directly involved in the dialogue, there is little depth of understanding of Israel or the Holocaust generally within the American Catholic community.

The late Esther Feldblum opened her masterful study of the *American Catholic Press and the Jewish State* with the following quotation from Pope Pius X's response to Theodor Herzl's plea for support in 1904:

> "We are unable to favor this movement (Zionism). We cannot prevent the Jews from going to Jerusalem — (but) we could never sanction it. As the head of the church I cannot answer you otherwise. The Jews have not recognized our Lord, therefore, we cannot recognize you . . ." [36]

More recently the American bishops, while avoiding any particular religious or political interpretation, called for Christians to "strive to understand this link between land and people which Jews have expressed in their writings and worship throughout two millenia as a longing for the homeland, holy Zion." (NCCB, Nov. 20, 1975)

The difference between these two views provides an excellent measure of the progress made in Christian understanding of Judaism as a living reality. For this momentum to be maintained, however, the challenge offered by these two events, the Holocaust and the State of Israel, which are linked together as despair to hope, must be honestly faced by the church. From the point of view of the textbook studies, it can be clearly seen that our two communities stand today at a crucial turning point in our relations. We need more than ever before to work together, in a shared humility of vision, to build the kingdom of God.

3. New Testament Scholarship

Charlotte Klein, in her recent analysis of German Christian scholarship and its treatment of Jews and Judaism,[37] raises a crucial question: To what extent are we as Christians continuing to train our teachers and pastors in an understanding of first-century Judaism that is, at best, marred by triumphalism? The negative apologetical thrusts of such standard works as Schurer, Strack-Billerbeck and Kittel are well known.[38]

Yet these works, or works derived from them, still form the basic introduction to Judaism of the New Testament period that is available to American theology students and seminarians. Though Klein kindly notes that Anglo-American scholars tend to approach Judaism in a more objective manner, German scholarship is so highly regarded in the English-speaking world that her critique of those scholars must be considered valid for much of what is actually taught students in Catholic universities and seminaries in the United States. Her suggestion for a comparative study of the best of Christian scholarship thus represents an urgent need today.

Two of Klein's six points summarizing the general trends of biblical and theological scholarship are of particular importance here, and are equally pertinent to many Anglo-American authors:

1. Only some few real specialists in the departments of Jewish studies make a fresh examination of authentically Jewish sources. In most cases the material collected in certain works about the turn of the century is taken over as a matter of course and quoted, without bothering about the Jewish interpretation of the sources or considering how the Jews see themselves.

2. We often find that the same author when he expressly speaks of Judaism in an ecumenical context has a strikingly different approach from that which he adopts when he is dealing with the Christian religion and mentions Judaism more or less incidentally.[39]

The United States, possibly by reason of the size and vitality of the Jewish community, is blessed with a large number of excellent graduate programs, seminars and scholars dealing with these problems. However, works with the same lack of understanding of Jewish sources as those so trenchantly critiqued by

Klein are still standard fare in biblical and theologial courses in many American seminaries. The result is all too often the spread of misinformation regarding the nature of Judaism, especially concerning the biblical periods. The seminary curriculum itself thus needs to be revised to accommodate this distressing reality, and in a way much deeper than by simply adding units on Judaism.

Conclusion

Textbook studies such as my own cannot be taken in isolation from other trends influencing the life of the church. We have seen particularly how the readings of the liturgy and much that is current in contemporary biblical scholarship can modify and even defeat the best-intentioned efforts of religious education publishers.

The textbook studies reveal that great progress has been made in eradicating anti-Jewish polemics from our teaching. But this is only a beginning. Specific content areas, such as the relationship between the covenants, New Testament themes, the Holocaust and the State of Israel still need to be addressed. Further, specific programs need to be developed especially for the training of catechists and in the seminaries, for integrating into the curricula the best of the insights of modern Jewish and Christian scholarship. Much of the scholarly work to accomplish this already exists in the English language. Its results must be brought to bear in every key area of church teaching. Many American Catholic universities and seminaries already offer excellent courses in Judaism. These need to be augmented. More, existing courses and teaching materials used in seminaries need the same kind of critical analysis as that already given the grade- and high-school level materials. This would in itself help to raise the general level of sensitivity.

Notes

1. For Isaac's own definition of this concept, see especially: Jules Isaac. *Has Anti-Semitism Roots in Christianity?* (New York: National Conference of Christians and Jews, 1961); *The Teaching of Contempt* (N.Y.: Holt, Rinehart, Winston, 1964); and *Jesus and Israel* (English transl., N.Y.: Holt, Rinehart, Winston, 1971). For review and commentary on the significance of Isaac's work as applied to Catholic teaching see E.

H. Flannery, "Jesus, Israel and Christian Renewal,"*Journal of Ecumenical Studies*, IX:I (Winter, 1972), pp. 74-93.

2. E.g. especially James Parkes, *The Conflict of Church and Synagogue* (Sancino, 1934); *The Emergence of the Jewish Problem 1878-1939* (Oxford, 1946); *Anti-Semitism* (Chicago: Quadrangle, 1963); Edward H. Flannery, *The Anguish of the Jews* (N.Y.: Macmillan, 1965); Franklin Littel, *The Crucifixion of the Jews* (N.Y.: Harper and Row, 1975); F. E. Talmage, *Disputation and Dialogue* (KTAV-ADL, 1975); H. J. Schoeps, *The Jewish-Christian Argument* (N.Y.: Holt, Rinehart, Winston, 1963); Charlotte Klein, *Anti-Judaism in Christian Theology* (Philadelphia: Fortress, 1978). Of particular interest for the present study is Klein's chapter on "A Short Survey of Anglo-American Authors" (143-156) for present and future trends.

3. Eugene Fisher, "A Content Analysis of the Treatment of Jews and Judaism in Current Roman Catholic Textbooks and Manuals on the Primary and Secondary Levels," Ph.D. Dissertation, New York University, 1976. See also, Eugene Fisher, *Faith Without Prejudice: Rebuilding Christian Attitudes Toward Judaism* (N.Y.: Paulist, 1977, hereafter: "FWP"); "Furthering the Jewish-Christian Dialogue," *Professional Approaches for Christian Educators* (*PACE*, Vol. 7, 1976, "Teaching-A"); "Preparing for the Jewish-Christian Encounter," The Catechist (Nov., 1976); "Christian Teaching and Judaism," *SIDIC* (Vol. IX:3, 1976, 19-22); "Toward a Catholic High School Curriculum for Teaching about Jews and Judaism," *PACE* (Vol. 8, 1977, "Approaches-F").

4. See Table 1 (FWP. 126-7).

5. E.g. Srs. Mary Delly and Ann Moore, "The Old Testament in Christian Teaching," Christian Attitudes on Jews and Judaism Journal (London: No. 7, August, 1969, pp. 3-7); Sr. Ann Moore, "The Seeds of Prejudice: An Analysis of Religious Textbooks," The Sower (London: January, 1971): Louis Allen, "Jews in Popular Catholicism" The Month (London: November, 1975); Anthony Bullen, "Catholic Teaching of Judaism," Christian Attitudes (No. 39, December, 1974, p. 13); C. Klein, *op. cit.* (127-156).

6. Bernard D. Weinryb and Daniel Garnick, "Summary of Findings: The Dropsie College Study of Jewish Textbooks" (New York: The American Jewish Committee). Weinryb notes that in his study of 200 works only 14 percent of the lessons make any reference to non-Jewish groups; whereas some 50 percent-80 percent of Christian lesson units do so. While Christian texts must of necessity treat at length of Judaism to interpret its origins, the reverse is not true for Judaism. The result, however, is that Jewish students receive little or no information about Christianity and Christian beliefs beyond what may be picked up from

the general culture. Further studies are needed, however, before conclusions can be drawn as to Jewish conceptions of Christian beliefs and practices.

7. Bernhard E. Olson, *Faith and Prejudice* (Yale University Press: New Haven, 1963).

8. Gerald S. Strober, *Portrait of the Elder Brother: Jews and Judaism in Protestant Teaching Materials* (New York: National Council of Christians and Jews-American Jewish Committee, 1972).

9. Charles Glock and Rodney Stark, *Christian Beliefs and Anti-Semitism* (New York: Harper and Row, 1966, p. 205). On this subject see also Russell Allen, "Religion and Prejudice: The Patterns of Relationship" (unpublished Ph.D. thesis, Univ. of Denver, 1965); Gordon Allport, *The Nature of Prejudice* (New York: Doubleday Anchor, 1958, 413-425); B. Blum and J. H. Mann, "The Effect of Religious Membership on Religious Prejudice," *Journal of Social Psychology* (1960, Vol. 52, 97-101); M. B. Jones, "Religious Values and Authoritarian Tendency," *Journal of Social Psychology* (1958, Vol. 48, 83-89); C. and E. J. O'Reilly, "Religious Beliefs of Catholic College Students and Their Attitude Toward Minorities," *Journal of Abnormal Social Psychology* (1954 Vol. 49, 378-380); B. R. Sappenfield, "The Responses of Catholic, Protestant and Jewish students to the 'Menace' checklist,"*Journal of Social Psychology* (1944, Vol. 20, 259-299); A. W. Seigman, "The Relationship Between Religiosity, Ethnic Prejudice and Authoritarianism," Psychol. Rep. (1962, Vol. 11, 419-424). M. P. Strommen, *Profiles of Church Youth* (St. Louis: Concordia, 1963) validly points out that the data presented by Glock and Stark shows only a correlation between "orthodox belief" and anti-Semitic attitudes. But such correlations, in the absence of other evidence, cannot be taken to infer a *causal* relationship between the phenomena studied.

10. These studies took the form of three unpublished doctoral dissertations, for St. Louis University: Sr. Rita Mudd, F.S.C.P., "Intergroup Relations in Social Studies Curriculum" (1961); Sr. M. Linus Gleason, C.S.J., "Intergroup Relations as Revealed by Content Analysis of Literature Textbooks Used in Catholic Secondary Schools" (1958); Sr. Rose Thering, O.P., "Potential in Religious Textbooks for Developing a Realistic Self-Concept" (1961). It is significant that aside from a brief progress report issued by Maher for the Journal of the Religious Education Association (Vol. LV, No. 2, 133-138), the results of these studies were not published until over a decade later by John T. Pawlikowski, O.S.M., *Catechetics and Prejudice: How Catholic Teaching Materials View Jews, Protestants and Racial Minorities* (New York: Paulist, 1973); Pawlikowski notes that "here we have a reflection of the mindset of the pre-Vatican II church" (p.10).

11. Olson, *op. cit.*, 301-328; Thering, 82-99.

12. Fisher, "Content Analysis . . .," 37-64.

13. In addition to the American guidelines, one must cite: "Pastoral Orientations on the Attitude of Christians to Judaism," Episcopal Committee of the Roman Catholic Bishops of France, April, 1973; "Guidelines and Suggestions for Implementing the Conciliar Declaration *Nostra Aetate.*" Vatican Commission for Religious Relations with the Jews, Dec. 1, 1974; "Statement on Catholic-Jewish Relations," U.S. National Conference of Catholic Bishops, Nov. 20, 1975.

14. The 1967 American guidelines, for example, called for "an acknowledgment by Catholic scholars of the living and complex reality of Judaism after Christ and the permanent election of Israel alluded to by St. Paul (Rom. 9)." Likewise in 1973 the French bishops stressed the "permanent vocation" of the Jewish people in termsof a particular mission involving in Jewish terms, "the sanctification of the Name." Such notions today provide a solid basis upon which to construct a response to the poignant question of the bishop of Strasbourg. Arthur Elchinger: "Don't the Jews have a right to exist, not as future Christians, but as Jews?" (*L'Amitie, judeo-chretienne de France*, No., 2, 13-15, April-June, 1968).

15. Pawlikowski, *op. cit.*, 81.

16. Olson, *op. cit.*, 176. European studies have, of course, unearthed similar dynamics. See Houtart and Giblet, *Les Juifs dans la catechese* (Louvain: Centre de Reserches Socio-religieuses, 1969), and Klineberg, Tentori and others, *Religione e pregiudizio* (Rome: Pro Deo Free International University, Sperry Center, 1968). These are summarized in Claire Hutchet Bishop. *How Catholics Look at Jews* (New York: Paulist, 1974).

17. These criteria are listed in *FWP*, 141-151.

18. Included were 161 student texts and 113 teachers' manuals published between 1967 and 1975. See Table I for list.

19. *FWP*, 128.

20. See Tables 2 and 3. (Discussed in *FWP* 129-139).

21. *Nostra Aetate* stressed the point that Jesus, Mary and the apostles all "sprang from the Jewish people."

22. See note 3, above.

23. "The Jews should not be presented as rejected or accursed by God, as if this followed from the Holy Scriptures." (*Nostra Aetate*, no. 4). Denounced here is the notion that Jewish suffering, such as in the diaspora, was willed by God as a punishment.

24. "True, the Jewish authorities and those who followed their lead pressed for the death of Christ; still, what happened in his passion cannot be charged against all Jews . . . ." (*Nostra Aetate*, no. 4).

25. The seeds for a renewed theology of Judaism, however, were clearly present not only in *Nostra Aetate*, but also in *De Ecclesia*, the Dogmatic Constitution on the Church: ". . . this people remains most dear to God, for God does not repent of the gifts he makes nor of the calls he issues (cf. Rom. 11:28-29)" (Art. 16). The conciliar emphasis on the positive elements of Romans 9-11, as the American bishops noted in their 1975 statement, opens the way for an entirely new understanding of "the continuing relationship of the Jewish people with God."

26. Michael B. McGarry, C.S.P., surveys both formal church statements and the current range of theological opinion in this country in his *Christology After Auschwitz* (N.Y.: Paulist, 1977). Of note also is the doctoral dissertation of Monika Hellwig, "Proposal Toward a Theology of Israel as a Religious Community Contemporary with the Christian" (Catholic University of America, 1968). John Pawlikowski, O.S.M., analyzes this same material from a different perspective in his article, "Christ and the Jewish-Christian Dialogue," Chicago Studies (Vol. 16:3, Fall, 1977, 367-389).

27. I.e. A new theological understanding of Judaism by Christians and a new theological understanding of Christianity by Jews.

28. The medieval scholastic tradition may provide a precedent here. Scholars working in Arabic, Latin and Hebrew shared a common philosophical perspective, terminology, and set of theological questions. Today, such seemingly common terms as "sacred" and "secular," "grace" and even "faith" itself are understood in radically different ways by Jews and Christians. The result is "assymetry" of dialogue in which we often talk past each other rather than addressing each other's beliefs.

29. In the general sense as used in Jewish liturgy, rather than, strictly, martyrdom.

30. So Augustine: ". . . to the end of the seven days of time, the continued preservation of the Jews will be a proof to believing Christians of the subjection merited by those who, in the pride of their kingdom, put the Lord to death," "Reply to Faustus, the Magician" (12:9-13). Such

was also the consistent view toward the Jews of the medieval papacy. See Rev. Edward A. Synan, *The Popes and the Jews in the Middle Ages* (New York: Macmillan, 1965).

31. E.g., Joseph Kimchi, Isaac of Troki, Judah Halevi and others. See F.E. Talmage, editor. *Disputation and Dialogue: Readings in the Jewish-Christian Encounter* (New York: KTAV-ADL, 1975) for survey and selections. See also E. Fisher, "Typical Jewish Misunderstandings of Christianity," Judaism: A Quarterly Journal (Vol. 22:1, Spring, 1973, 21-32) for more recent adaptions of these arguments.

32. R. Jacob Petuchowski, "The Religious Basis for Pluralism," Origins (Vol. 6:47, May 2, 1977) 741-746. Medieval precedents are numerous. Prof. Sid Z. Leiman of the Kennedy Institute in Washington, D.C. cites the following, among others: Juda Ha-Levi, *Sefer ha-Kuzari* (tr. by H. Hirschfield, New York: 1946, p. 200); Moses Maimonides, *The Book of Judges* (tr. A. M. Hershman, New Haven: 1949, xxiii); M. Meiri, *Commentary on Baba Qamma* (to 113b); J. Vaavetz, *Maamar ha-Ahduth* (Ferrara: 1533, Chap. 3-9); E. Ashkenazi, *Commentary on the Passover Haggadah* (in *Migdal Eder*, N.Y.: n.d., 70); J. Emden, *Commentary on Aboth* (Amsterdam: 1751, ad 4:13). For an excellent summary of Jewish views of Christianity since the Enlightenment, including Mendelssohn, Geiger, Wise Rosenzweig, Buber, Sandmel and others, see W. Jacob, *Christianity Through Jewish Eyes: The Quest for Common Ground* (Cincinnati, Hebrew Union College Press, 1974).

33. See E. Fisher, "New Understandings of the Relationship Between the Covenants," *FWP*, 89-97.

34. For an excellent survey of recent thought on the Holocaust see John T. Pawlikowski, "The Challenge of the Holocaust for Catholic Theology," a paper presented to the Israel Study Group meeting, New York, March 5, 1978. On the theological relationship between the Holocaust and Israel, see especially "Cloud of Smoke, Pillar of Fire" by Irving Greenberg, "Rethinking the Church's Mission After Auschwitz" by Gregory Baum, and "The Holocaust and the State of Israel: Their Relation" by Emil Fackenheim, in *Auschwitz Beginning of a New Era? Reflections on the Holocaust*, edited by Eva Fleischner (New York: KTAV-ADL, 1977).

35. E.g., SIDIC, Vols. 7:2 (1974); 8:2 (1975); 9:1 (1976).

36. Esther Yolles Feldblum, *The American Catholic Press and the Jewish State* 1917-1959 (New York: KTAV, 1977) 1.

37. Sr. Charlotte Klein, *Anti-Judaism in Christian Theology* (Phila: Fortress, 1978) 3:7.

38. Klein may at times be faulted for overstatement but her basic thesis, that all too many Christian scholars speak "knowingly" of the nature of Judaism without validating their views from available Jewish sources is well taken.

39. *Ibid.,* 7.

Chapter 8

NEW REVELATIONS AND NEW PATTERNS IN THE RELATIONSHIP OF JUDAISM AND CHRISTIANITY*

Irving Greenberg
Director, National Jewish Resource Center
New York, New York

As this Sacred Synod searches into the mystery of the Church, it recalls the spiritual bond linking the people of the New Covenant with Abraham's stock.

For the Church of Christ acknowledges that, according to the mystery of God's saving design, the beginnings of her faith and her election are already found among the patriarchs, Moses and the prophets. (*Nostra Aetate*, Section 4, Par. 1,2)[1]

In His goodness and wisdom, God chose to reveal Himself and to make known to us the hidden purpose of His will . . . . This plan of revelation is realized by deeds and words having an inner unity. The deeds wrought by God in the history of salvation manifest and confirm the teaching and realities signified by the words, while the words proclaim the deeds and clarify the mystery contained in them. (Dogmatic Constitution on Divine Revelation, Chapter 1, Section 2)[2]

---

*Used by permission. This article appeared in the *Journal of Ecumenical Studies*, Vol. XVI, Spring, 1979. It was presented in preliminary form at the National Celebration of the Tenth Anniversary of the Declaration of the Relationship of the Church to the Jewish People of the National Conference of Catholic Bishops. A fellowship of the National Endowment for the Humanities in 1974-75 enabled the author to do much of the research and writing of this paper.

1. The Relationship of Judaism and Christianity: The Impact of History

Christianity grows in the bosom of Judaism. The statement, "Theirs (the Jews) is the sonship and the glory and the covenants and the law and the worship and the promises, theirs are the patriarchs and from them is the Christ according to the flesh" (Rom. 9:4-5), reminds us that initially Jesus could not be recognized as revelation except by Jews operating by Jewish categories of expectation and promise. The first followers shared the Jewish model of a covenant entered into through God's mighty acts in history. They accepted the principle that revelation is not finished and can be affected by later events in that salvation history. Because history is open, because humans have freedom even to disobey God, because God is neither fixed image nor possession, new events in history may illuminate the covenant or unfold new dimensions of covenant living. Christianity is the wager of faith of the original Jewish Christians that Christ's life was authentic revelation, validated by existing Jewish norms. Then Jesus' death made clear that he could not or would not fulfill the original expectations. This had to be seen as proof that he was a false Messiah or as new revelation of the character of Messianic salvation. Because the phenomenology of Jesus' revelatory power was so real, the faithful disciples did not yield even to the shock of the crucifixion. The disciples were in their most Jewish character in their perception that this tragedy did not end their revelation but rather shed new light on the nature of Messianic salvation.[3] Thus their acceptance of the resurrection as further event confirming the new covenant was deeply Jewish in its concept, even if its actual effect was to separate them from the Temple and from the ongoing Jewish worship and channels of atonement.[4]

The Christian Interpretation

However, the rootedness in Jewish salvation history and the shared norms of validation made Jesus' non-acceptance by other Jews especially problematic and troubling. The fact of common expectation made the ongoing, mainstream Jewish hope for other salvation threatening to the validity of Christianity. It had to be accounted for in the context of the shared fundamental that the Jewish people possessed authentic and original covenant, as well as hope. Given the disciples' conviction that they had experienced true revelation, they were unwilling to deny the phenomenology of salvation they had experienced. They could only understand the Jewish rejection as blindness, obduracy, hardness of heart – and these were all the more damning qualities for appearing in a group already blessed with illumination. In the words quoted in *Nostra Aetate*, "Jerusalem did not recognize the time of her visitation."[5]

The destruction of the Temple and the failed Bar Kochba rebellion of 132-135 confirmed this view. Although the mainstream of Jews did not accept their conclusion, the Hebrew Christians were "thinking Jewish" when they interpreted these events of destruction as being normative events with a religious message. These events confirmed the analysis – or even originated the analysis – that the old channel of salvation was stopped up and that a new channel was the valid one. It followed that a new people of God had been born. From there to the punishment and rejection theory of Jewish exile is not a big jump. Ironically enough, every step of this development had followed Jewish models and categories even if the net result was a repudiation of Judaism. The consequent insistence on the finality of Christ and the revelation in his life meant that Jews were condemned unless they saw the light. To someone like Paul who cared passionately about Jews, this reversal of destiny gave great anguish – enough to insist that they would ultimately see the light and be saved. The condemnation caused much less pain to Gentile Christians, and they could view it with equanimity or relish – or with a righteous sense of true faith triumphant.[6]

The Jewish Interpretation

By the same token, the Jewish community, faithful to Israel's covenant, could hardly be indifferent to Messianic claims or possible divine revelation. The community showed its openness to Messianic hope repeatedly before and after Jesus.[7] Jeremiah's words suggesting further illumination in history were always before its eyes. "Behold, the days will come, says the Lord, it shall no more be said: 'As God lives who brought up the children of Israel out of the land of Egypt' but: 'as God lives, who brought up the children of Israel from the land of the North, and from all the countries whither He had driven them . . . .'" (Jer. 16: 14-15; 23:7-8). Unhappily, each and every Messiah to whom the Jews opened up ultimately disappointed and could not bring final redemption. Rather than losing hope or yielding to despair, the bulk of Jews — or at least the saving remnant of Jews — continued to rely on God and the divine promises, and to hope again. Faithful to its covenant, trusting God's promises, Israel had to search its own heart and life when confronted with Jesus' Messianic claim and the later development — the announcement that Judaism, the original covenant, was over. In the experience of the destruction of the Temple and the crisis of faith which followed, Jews came to the same conclusion that Christians did in the crucifixion: their faith was not destroyed or shown to be false. They were being called to new forms of service and understanding while continuing on the way to the final salvation of the world.[8] Finding its religious life vital, the presence of God real, its trust in God's promises unbroken, the Jewish people could only conclude that Christian statements of supercession were false. It followed that Jews could only perceive Christianity as erroneous and Jesus as a false Messiah. The people could only conclude, sadly, that again a group of faithful Jews had responded in hope, only to discover (again) that the time had not yet come for fulfillment. As in the other cases, some Jews were too loyal to the new Messianic revelation to surrender it. Most Jews were faithful both to God as the Source who could and would yet generate redemption and to reality which yet proclaimed its resistance to that process.[9] They felt no need to cling to the new experience, since they were confident that God could and would bring true redemption in its time or when they were worthy.

True, this false Messiah was spectacularly successful in the world. Among some Jews, this fact alone evoked some special recognition or status for Christianity as a religion that had spread hope and knowledge of God and covenant throughout the world and thus brought final redemption closer.[10] Still, Christianity was intrinsically contradictory to Judaism's validity, precisely because of the shared assumptions. Therefore, faithfulness to covenant made contradicting Christianity religiously necessary and affirmative. The record of brutality and Jewish suffering brought on or contributed to by Christianity made it that much clearer that here was a false Messianism, one that might be dismissed by some as having lapsed into idolatry.[11]

The Modern Interpretation

For almost 1900 years, there was hardly any other faith option available to believing Jews or Christians. This typology is intrinsic in the central affirmations of both religions, due particularly to shared roots and assumptions. The movement away from these models started among Jews or Christians who had lost faith in the authority or credibility of shared roots and religious claims. They could use humanist and tolerance categories to change relationships. The liberal embarrassment at past hatred and prejudice combined with regret and shock of the climax of the Holocaust to set the stage for *Nostra Aetate*.[12]

The direction and content of *Nostra Aetate* were a vector of opposing forces. There was openness to fresh understanding of revelation in the Catholic Church, and there were those who believed this opened the door to a positive new understanding of Judaism. On the other hand the Church was still profoundly rooted in its classic heritage; its trust in the adequacy and fullness of its own religious life was still relatively unshaken, and it had strong institutional interests that resisted change. The perception of faithfulness to the magisterium combined with fear of undermining the faith of the masses to keep the declaration on the Jews fairly conservative The understandable result was *Nostra Aetate*, Section Four, an admixture of elements out of the re-thinking, tolerance, and traditional models. It sought to create new esteem and to open new options in Jewish-Christian relations, as in the deploring of Antisemitism and the ambiguous but pregnant citation that "He (God) does not repent of the gifts He makes nor of the calls He issues" (Rom. 11:28-29).[13] Still, as a document faithful to the finality of Christian revelation, *Nostra Aetate* was driven to come down on the side of the old traditional model of relationship. This accounted for such affirmations as "Jerusalem did not recognize the time of her visitation", that Christ made "Jew and Gentile . . . one in Himself"; that the authorities of the Jews and those who followed them had pressed for the death of Christ; and that most ambiguous sentence of all, "Although the Church is the new people of God, the Jews should not be presented as repudiated or cursed by God, as if such views followed from the Holy Scriptures."[14]

It was widely recognized in 1965 that all these ambiguities and ambivalences would have to be worked out in further development and that the final significance of *Nostra Aetate* would depend on the fruit it bore, e.g., on the direction the Catholic Church would take in explicating and developing its conflicted and conflicting views.

Since *Nostra Aetate*, the atmosphere of warm expectation and romance surrounding dialogue has cooled, as the radical hopes of the 1960's have been followed by the realism, disillusion, and sobriety of the 1970's. The Jewish perception of inadequate response by Christians to the crisis of the State of Israel's existence in 1967 and (somewhat less so) in 1973 has had a chilling effect. Jewish preoccupation with internal needs and Israeli survival and Catholic wrestling with internal trends unleased by Vatican II have been limiting factors. Still, dialogue has continued, and new areas have opened up; individual Christians have gone far in their new understanding of Judaism and its role in the divine economy of salvation. However, a comparison of the working document on Jewish-Christian relations ("Reflections and Suggestions for the Application of the Directives of *Nostra Aetate* 4," circulated on December 16, 1969) with the actual "Guidelines and Suggestions for Implementing the Conciliar Declaration, '*Nostra Aetate*'(n. 4)" issued on December 1, 1974,[15] shows there have been no theological great leaps forward at the institutional level.

The working document included important breakthroughs: recognition of the present and living reality of the Jews, who were given a Torah by God, within it a word that "endures forever," "an unquenchable source of life and prayer, in a tradition that has not ceased to enrich itself through the centuries." Similarly, it recognized that "fidelity to the covenant was linked to the land" and thus connected directly to the existence of the State of Israel. It affirmed that "the Old Testament should not be understood exclusively in reference to the New nor reduced to an allegorical significance."[16] By contrast, the promulgated guidelines omitted both the land and Israel and the Jewish Torah which endures forever.[17] The document hedges its acknowledgment that the history of Judaism did not end with the destruction of the Temple, with the insertion that the importance and meaning of Jewish tradition was "deeply affected by the coming of Christ."[18] Gone also is the simplicity of statement that "Jesus ... was a Jew," agreeing more than disagreeing with the Judaism of his time, and a critic from within.[19] Instead, there is "Jesus ... born of the Jewish people," bearing a new gospel message, perfecting the old which is "manifest in the New."[20]

Such theological hedging is not merely the result of political give-and-take in the church structures. It is intrinsic to the historically elaborated structure of the relationship of Judaism and Christianity. As long as the finality of Christian (and Jewish) experience of revelation is assured and dated to the opening round of their encounter and Christian formation, the coherence of Christian revelation, seen integrally, is in tension with the affirmations of Judaism's continuing integrity. Indeed, such affirmations remain subject to repeal by any resurgent Christian assertion of doctrinal adequacy or any proclamation that, in its transcendence, Christianity should not be dominated or reshaped by modern categories. (This neutral language is used to make clear that such thinking need not be fundamentalist.)

II. New Revelation and New Patterns

However, there has been a major development in the past decade: the crystallization of the awareness among many Jews and some others that this is a period of renewed revelation within Judaism. Aaron's staff has blossomed again, or, if you will, the olive tree has brought forth extraordinary and unexpected branches.[21]

In this generation two events have occurred of a magnitude that stamps them as major normative events in Jewish history. They are orientating events — pointing beyond themselves as models for living in the light of God's concern and working for the day when all humanity will live in its reality. They are the event of Holocaust — unparalleled tragedy and destruction — towering over the other great tragic watershed of 1900 years ago, the destruction of the Second Temple and the event of the rebirth of Israel — the experience of redemption as has not been experienced by Jews on this scale since the Exodus. Following the classic model, they illumine and fundamentally reinterpret the meaning and significance of the past 1900 years and the constellation of Judaism and Christianity.[22]

The Holocaust is a most radical contradiction of the fundamental statements of human value and divine concern in both religions.[23] The successful carrying out of the Holocaust and the response of Jews and Christians during this event are profoundly revelatory. For Christianity, the Holocaust reveals the demonic consequences and hateful potential present in its traditional picture of Judaism and the Jews, "the teaching of contempt" tradition. Notwithstanding the argument that Nazi Antisemitism is pagan, to the extent that the "teaching of contempt" furnished an occasion or presented stereotypes which brought the Nazis to focus on the Jews as scapegoats in the first place, or created a residue of Antisemitism in Europe which affected local populations' attitudes toward the Jews, or enabled some Christians to feel they were doing God's work in helping or in not stopping the killing of Jews — then Christianity is deeply implicated in the Holocaust.[24] This precedes the issue of church silence or actual complicity.[25]

Since the teaching of contempt goes straight back to the Gospel accounts, the Holocaust's fierce flames really reveal the privileged sanctuary of hate allowed to exist at the very heart of and in fundamental contradiction to the gospel of love which is the New Testament's true role and goal. The cancer is so deep that it is questionable whether anything less than full confession and direct confrontation with even the most sacred sources can overcome it. This is not said triumphalistically, but in reverence of Christianity. Repentence is a sign of life and greatness of soul. Those who deny are tempted thereby into repetition.[26]

There is further revelation — perhaps even more problematic. Much of the church's efforts and protests were for Jewish converts to Christianity and against forced divorces and other violations of Christian canons in the execution of the Holocaust — rather than against the principle. The picture of a silent Vatican is too simplistic. However, it turns out that so many of the protests were in defense of non-Aryan Christians. Despite knowledge of the dreadful atrocities going on, the lines and structures of human responsibility were narrowly drawn, apparently because of excessive emphasis on the significance of Christian belief as *the* category of solidarity and due to the placing of the Jews outside the pale. Thus, the German bishops and confessional or conscience Protestants who spoke a clear word against the Nazi Euthanasia policy did not speak such a word against the mass slaughter of Jews.[27] The late protests on Jewish *converts* in Poland and Hungary in 1943 and 1944 must be seen in the context of the terrible scenes of burning children alive and mass gassings known in exact detail by reports substantiated and forwarded to the Vatican by the Papal Nuncio.[28]

To put it cruelly and unfairly (because only in this way is the issue illuminated), one can translate the language of protest this way. If children believe in Jesus Christ as Savior and Word Incarnate, they should not be burned alive; their screams should not be heard back at the camp. If they do not believe in Jesus Christ as Savior and Word Incarnate, it is not *so* bad that Christians ought to risk speaking out. Nothing could be further from the message of Jesus Christ; nothing could make atheism more religiously and morally attractive an alternative. In short, the Holocaust reveals that the redemption and revelation of Christianity is inescapably contradicted by the constellation of its classic understanding of Judaism. It must choose between them. The conviction of the ongoing validity of Christianity demands that an alternative understanding exist. This conviction grows in part out of the testimony of true Christians who risked their lives and gave their all to save victims, and who resisted Nazism and went to their own Calvary out of concern for the crucified Jew. Unfortunately, they were a small minority.

In the same spirit, they do wrong who justify the silence of church or pope by prudential arguments, claiming that declarations would not have helped, or that, by Nazi fiat, Jews were outside the "flock" which a bishop might serve. If to be a Christian is to be willing to take up the cross to testify, there was hardly ever a more appropriate time to risk crucifixion than when children were being burned alive to economize on the one-half cent's worth of gas it cost to kill them. Besides, such arguments are an injustice to the actual record of the church. In Bulgaria, in France, and (at a late date) in Rumania, church intervention preceded those governments' ceasing collaboration and refusing to honor commitments already made to deport Jews. In two of the three countries which never agreed to deport their Jews (Finland, Denmark, and Italy), the dominant church denounced racialism or Antisemitism publicly even before the war. In Hungary in July, 1944, protests by the Vatican, among others, halted the deportations, but only after two-thirds of the Jews had been shipped out.[29] As Dr. Helen Fein says in her major study of Jewish survival in the Holocaust, "Church protest proved to be the single element present in every instance in which collaboration (with Nazi genocide) was arrested . . . ." On the other hand, successful segregation of the Jews is the most direct cause of Jewish victimization; segregation was most likely to occur in states in which the dominant church had failed to repudiate racial ideology.[30] The challenge is the extent to which theological categories and church interests dominate and suppress moral response—because of the attitudes toward Jews which grew out of the conviction of the unique, universal validity of Christianity.

Another issue illumined in the Holocaust is the classic "Israel of the Flesh" vs. "Israel of the Spirit" dichotomy. After all, is not "Israel of the Spirit" a more universal, more committed category? Yet, when absolute power arose and claimed to be God, then Israel's existence was antithetical to its own. "Israel of the Flesh" gives testimony by its mere existence and therefore was "objectively" an enemy of the totalitarian state. By the same token neither commitment to secularism, atheism, or any other religion — nor even joining Christianity — could remove the intrinsic status of being Jewish and being forced to stand and testify. This testimony, voluntarily given or not, turns out to be the secret significance of "Israel of the Flesh." A Jew's life is on the line, and therefore every kind of Jew gives testimony at all times.

"Israel of the Spirit" testifies against the same idolatry and evil. Indeed, there were sincere Christians who stood up for their principles, who were recognized as threats and were sent to concentration camps. However, "Israel of the Spirit" had only the choice of being silent; with this measure of collaboration, it could live safely and at ease. Not surprisingly, the vast majority chose to be safe. As Franklin Littell put it, when paganism is persecuting, Christians "can homogenize and become mere gentiles again; while the Jews, believing or secularized, remain representatives of another history, another providence."[31] And lest there be any question or hesitation of saying "Jesus was a Jew," let the Holocaust test speak. Were Jesus and his mother alive in Europe in the 1940's, they would have been sent to Auschwitz.

The Holocaust suggests that Christians (and Jews) have glamorized modern culture and underestimated evil. It suggests that, from now on, one of the keys to testimony in the face of the enormously powerful forces available to evil will be to have given hostages, to be on the line because one is inextricably in this fate. The creation of a forced option should be one of the goals of moral pedagogy after the Holocaust. This is the meaning of "chosenness" in Jewish faith.

The Christian analogy to this experience would be a surrender of the often self-deceiving universalist rhetoric of the church and a new conception of the church as the people of God — a distinct community of faith with some identification — that must testify to the world. There is a corollary to such a model: some strategy of designation and delineation that will identify this people. This is somewhat in tension with tendencies to formulate either a "religionless" Christianity or, at best, one less separated from the world. I believe there is merit in *both* poles of the tension. There may be a possible reconciliation of both needs through the choice of subtle forms of identification. Such a move will expose the church to persecution or worse from future rivals or tyrants, but this same step paves the way to an honest particularism that can recognize the existence of other peoples of God without surrendering its own absolute commitment or the command of its Lord. Thus, Christianity could live and testify in a truly pluralist world while preserving the ultimacy of its message.

The Holocaust profoundly reorients Jewish understanding as well. It reveals that Jews have not appreciated Christianity enough. This is a reflection of the general Jewish tendency to underestimate Christianity's redemptive contribution to the world, due to the bad experience Jews have had with it. Anger at Christian mistreatment has obscured the ambivalence and importance of Judaism in Christianity, which meant that Christians persecuted, but also kept alive and protected, Jews.[32] Even persecuting Christians gave Jews the option of converting, rather than styling the Jew as intrinsically demonic and beyond the right to exist. Rebuking the widespread, almost stereotyped, Jewish identification with secular, liberal modernity and against Christianity,[33] the Holocaust suggests that modern values created a milieu as dangerous as—more dangerous than—Christianity at its worst. Indeed, Jews have a vested interest in Christianity's existence. Russia, the society of secularism triumphant, has demonstrated again that secular absolutism is just as dangerous to Judaism as is an abusive Christianity, unchecked.[34]

The Holocaust warns of the danger of solidarity weaknesses in Jews and Judaism. These were exploited by the Nazis to divide and conquer Jews. It calls for a major strengthening of the human and ethical solidarity resources of Jewish tradition to stop another Holocaust from happening—and to insure that if others be the victims, Jews will not be indifferent or apathetic by dint of prejudice. This will take self-criticism and self-development and removal of every negative image of Gentiles or Christians or, for that matter, of women or other minorities.

For both religions, the Holocaust breaks the old secular-religious dichotomy. Who is the atheist? When the Einsatzgruppen in Simferopol, Crimea, could get up extra early on Christmas morning in 1942, to finish shooting the Jews before the others awakened—so as not to disturb the spirit of the holiday, some making it back in time for mass;[35] when Heinrich Himmler could demand belief in God of his SS men so they would not be like the atheistic Marxists;[36] when Jean Paul Sartre, fountainhead of atheism, could break with his Arab allies in 1967, refusing to allow another Holocaust, though the Pope remained silent; when the Satmar Rabbi's followers negotiated with terrorists: then the invisible church or synagogue has become a moral necessity. In these circumstances, secularity should be seen as the mask for those who give up the advantage of acknowledged faith (e.g., the church will try to save you in the Holocaust), because at such a time such advantages are blasphemous. Fear of God is defined biblically as inability to hurt — or unswerving reverence and care for — the image of God.[37]

Never again should official badge or professed religious belief allow murderers to escape condemnation and excommunication or allow victims to be excluded from the circle of humanity. Surrendering religious exclusivism or triumphalism is a crucial moral step.

Here the dialectic of the Holocaust makes its appearance again. It reveals that in pure secularity humans appoint themselves God and thereby become the devil. It warns that glorification of human autonomy can evoke the nemesis of human idolatry; that in the massing of science, technology, and efficiency exists the potential for mass killing, so that simple affirmation of human autonomy and human might is no longer morally tenable. This liberates Jews and Christians to be in tension with, as well as to celebrate, the secular city.

For both religions, the Holocaust reveals a fundamental shift in the ethics of power. The overwhelming force on the side of the murderers corrupted the murderers and frequently broke or added to the torment of the victims. The total absence of any check led to such phenomena as boredom, desire for variety in killing, playing with and tormenting the victims, and suppression of good will, since all the pressures and sanctions were toward being crueller to the victims. Moreover, the Nazi ability to exercise infinitely gradated power over them broke many people, leading them to sacrifice their most precious and beloved people and values, so that self-sacrifice and spiritual demonstration were obscured or suppressed. Witness this scene from the summer of 1944 at Auschwitz, portrayed by Tadeusz Borowski, a Polish inmate.

> They go, they vanish. Men, women and children. Some of them know. Here is a woman — she walks quickly, but tries to appear calm. A small child with a pink cherub's face runs after her and, unable to keep up, stretches out his little arms and cries: "Mama! Mama!"
>
> "Pick up your child, woman!"
>
> "It's not mine, sir, not mine!" she shouts hysterically and runs on, covering her face with her hands. She

wants to hide, she wants to reach those who will not ride the trucks, those who will go on foot, those who will stay alive. She is young, healthy, good-looking, she wants to live. But the child runs after her, wailing loudly: "Mama, Mama, don't leave me!"

"It's not mine, not mine, no!"

Andrei, a sailor from Sevastopol, grabs hold of her. His eyes are glassy from vodka and the heat. With one powerful blow he knocks her off her feet, then, as she falls, takes her by the hair and pulls her up again. His face twitches with rage.

"Ah, you bloody Jewess! So you're running from your own child; I'll show you, you whore!" His huge hand chokes her, he lifts her in the air and heaves her on to the truck like a heavy sack of grain.

"Here! And take this with you, bitch!" and he throws the child at her feet.

"*Gut gemacht*, good work. That's the way to deal with degenerate mothers," says the S.S. man standing at the foot of the truck.

"*Gut, gut, Russki.*"[38]

Out of this comes the realization that there has been a horrible misunderstanding of the symbol of the crucifixion. Surely, it is clear now that the point of the Gospel account is the cry: "My lord, my lord, why have you forsaken me?" Never again should anyone be exposed to such one-sided power on the side of evil, for in such extremes not only does evil triumph, but the suffering servant now breaks and betrays herself. Here is fundamental reorientation away from traditional Christian and medieval Jewish glorification of suffering passivity.

In the words of Rabbi Menachem Ziemba of Warsaw: "Sanctification of the Divine Name manifests itself in varied ways, at the end of the eleventh century or in the middle of the twentieth century. In the past during religious persecutions, we were required by the law 'to give up our lives even for the least essential practice.' In the present, Halachah (Jewish law) demands that we fight and resist to the very end with unequalled determination and valor for the sake of the sanctification of the Divine Name."[39]

Out of the Holocaust experience comes the demand for

redistribution of power. This accounts for the urgency with which Jews proclaimed the State of Israel after the Holocaust, and for the overwhelming worldwide shift of Jewry toward Zionism. Only the transfer of power to potential victims—power enough to defend themselves—can correct the new balance of power. This is the subterranean source of the enormous proliferation of liberation movements. This is a challenge to Judaism and Christianity to overcome those moral traditions which praise renunciation and suspicion of power and glorify defeat.

Here again the Holocaust gives us dialectical revelations: one should not romanticize the moral stature of the victims. The ability to use force is the ability to hurt; the tendency to give unlimited moral validity to erstwhile victims is false to the dialectic and encourages the worst tendencies in such movements. One must support a moral balance of power and dialectical and unceasing reconciliation and resolution of conflicts. Thus the right, the need for Israel to exist to protect past and potential victims of genocide, is corrected by concern for refugees. This concern intensifies morally as the threat to Israel's existence recedes, but we should never let concern for refugees become cover for genocide.

If the calling is to overcome crucifixion and prevent it from happening, then the religious concern must focus on resurrection. This is the religious equivalent of exploring the sacred dimensions of affluence and celebration. It is to work in real power situations and to eschew merely prophetic stances. Prophets can rely on spiritual power and make absolute demands for righteousness. Governments have obligations to protect people. This will involve calling upon the halachic resources of the Jewish tradition to judge specific situations and to reconcile conflicting claims and shifting facts. It means linking ultimate ends and proximate means in a continuing process. It cannot be done without some involvement, guilt, partial failures, etc. How can this be done without religion's blessing bloody arms or supporting an exploiting status quo? Dialectically it should be added that usually participation in the world leads to selling out to the status quo, unless one is refreshed by exposure to prophetic norms. Each religion will need the other's norms, strengths, and criticisms to save it from failing this challenge and to correct it along the way.

The focus on redemption/resurrection draws attention to the other revelatory event, the redemption which has taken place in this generation—the rebirth of the State of Israel. As difficult to absorb in its own way and, like the Holocaust, a scandal to many traditional Jewish and Christian categories, it is an inescapable part of Jewish historical experience in our time. And while it is a continuation and outgrowth of certain responses to the Holocaust, it is at the same time a dialectical contradiction to many of its implications.

> If the experience of Auschwitz argues that we are cut off from God and hope and the covenant may be destroyed, then the experience of Jerusalem affirms that God's promises are faithful and His people live on. Burning children speak of the absence of all value, human and divine; the rehabilitation of one-half million Holocaust survivors in Israel speak of the reclamation of tremendous human dignity and value. If Treblinka makes human hope an illusion, then the Western Wall asserts that dreams are more real than forces and facts. Israel's faith in the God of History demands that an unprecedented event of destruction be matched by an unprecedented act of redemption, and this has happened.[40]

This statement must not obscure the moral danger and profound ambiguity of a secular state carrying a religious message. One must be alert to the recalcitrance of the real to receive the ideal, the mixing of good and evil components in the real world, the danger of idolatry, the exhaustion of living in the tension of ideals and realities and the "Gott mit uns" tendency which could easily sell out God for idols. Not the least part of our hesitation is the actual cost in suffering, Arab and Jewish, which Israel's birth has entailed. Hence Israel's revelation is a very modern one — flawed, partial, real.[41] The moral danger is inescapable; the task is to become involved, to sustain the tension, to move beyond the easy stereotypes of law and gospel, to correct faults, and to minimize evil. It will take all the "Christian" testimony of the evil in human nature and all the "Jewish" testimony that the Messiah is not yet come to keep this secular revelation from degenerating into idolatry. It will take the fullest spiritual maturity of Jew and Christian to appreciate Israel in the real world it inhabits, and to protect it from the real dangers which its isolation poses to its very existence.

The Talmud tells that, after the destruction, God's might is shown in divine restraint from violating human freedom by intervening and preventing the evil, but divine awesomeness is shown in that the people of God still exist.[42] This revelation summons humankind to secularity, to create and rehabilitate the divine image in a human community. This is the ultimate testimony – perhaps the only credible one – which can speak of God in a world of burning children. And it summons humans to co-responsibility with God, that this fragile redemption be preserved and nourished.

It is a highly significant indication of the continuing operation of God's Spirit in the church that it instinctively moved in its renewal in a number of these directions even before it saw the significance of these revelatory events. Articulating and recognizing these signs will sharpen and deepen renewal and release powerful forces of the selfless love of God, open to all. *Nostra Aetate* was written with awareness of the Holocaust and of Israel, but as yet the revelatory significance was not grasped, even by the Jews. Hence, the document temporizes on the brink. The stakes now are considerably higher.

If Christianity finds the strength to admit the reappearance of revelation in our time, at one stroke this undercuts the entire structure of the "teaching of contempt" tradition. For the bringing forth of revelation truly affirms that God does not repent of giving gifts. At once, it restores God's gift of Christ to Christian Gentiles as an act of love, of broadening the covenant, rather than an act of cruelty which spiritually and physically destroys the original chosen people. It removes the shelter of legitimated hatred and allows Christianity to confront the evil in human hearts with the unqualified challenge of the command of love.

Nor does the recognition undercut the validity of the Gospel message. The further revelation clarifies Paul's affirmation that Jewish rejection of Christ paves the way for Gentile acceptance into the covenant. By a further act of grace the interpretation of supercession is found to be a way of stating the ultimate and valid experience of redemption's operating, a way that is no longer needed. It is a way which must be rejected, given its evil effects. The later revelation illuminates the earlier, giving the new interpretive key in God's unbroken promises. It is another case of what the Dogmatic Constitution calls "clearer understanding . . . enjoyed after they had been instructed by the (further) events."[43] (In that case, Christ's risen life; in this, further revelation.) For Christians, confirmation of the unfailing nature of the first covenant confirms the credibility and power of the second covenant.

Indeed the reappearance of revelation is an enormous gift in an age when secularism and scientism have all but undercut the sources and credibility of covenant faith, when Holocaust and history have all but overcome hope. The most powerful confirmation of religious hope is that crucifixion and resurrection have occurred in this generation – in the flesh of the covenanted people.[44] It is liberation from the tyranny of modern categories – a restoration of the old religious role of fighting idolatry. At the same time, the admission of the significance of secularity in this revelation gives great impetus to the Christian search for renewal in this world and for the appropriate understanding of divinity made incarnate in human context. It releases Christianity from timeless spirituality to find its word incarnate in the temporal lives of humans. If Judaism finds the strength and feeling to admit revelation in this time, then it too has the prospect of renewed hope and divine presence – much needed in an age in which secularity has shriveled many of the roots of faith.

Paradoxically enough, the security of its own confirmation; the restoration of the land, the covenantal sign, releases Judaism to ponder anew the significance of Christianity. It may well be that in its medieval state of powerlessness Israel, gnawed at by the contrast of hope and reality, could only push Christianity away – or, patronizingly, argue that the righteous of the Gentiles have a share in the world to come or that they have the Noachide covenant to live by. Given the axiom that Christian validity means Jewish invalidity, the people Israel could only trust the phenomenology of its vital religious life and the reliability of its God's promises and reject Christianity's claims. Confirmed now in its resumed redemption, shaken by the Holocaust's challenge not to put down others. Judaism can no longer give patronizing answers. It must explore the possibility that the covenant grafted onto it a way whereby God has called Gentiles to God. Of course, this invokes the principle, "by their fruits, you shall know them." When Jesus' Messianism led to hatred, exclusion, pogrom, it could only be judged false. If it now leads to responsibility, *mitgefühl*, sharing of risk and love, then its phenomenology becomes radically different. Suffice it to say – without irony – Christians have an extraordinary opportunity in this age: of showing the power of love and concern for Jews and the embattled beginnings of Jewish redemption, the State of Israel. Such a demonstration would give new seriousness among Jews to Christianity's own perception that it is a vehicle of divine presence and redemption in the world.

One of the gifts of such new possibilities is an end to easy Jewish identification of liberation with secularity and liberalism, and a much greater Jewish sense of pluralism, of Christianity as moral/religious balance wheel, of the need to preserve these values in a fast homogenizing world. Such rethinking would lead to a new sense of the preciousness of "parochial" education and of the need to husband resources of particular traditions, an area American Jewry has been slow and remiss in understanding — a mark of the continuing tyranny of easy modernity.

There is, of course, enormous Christian resistance to recognizing further revelation. After all, even Judaism and "observant" Jews have not yet given this revelation the centrality and response it deserves. Christian resistance is rooted in that fidelity to Christ which emphasizes the finality of Christ as revelation. In the words of the Dogmatic Constitution on Divine Revelation: "We now await no further new public revelation before the glorious manifestation of our Lord Jesus Christ."[45] The key word is "await." Sometimes revelation comes when it is not awaited. To rule out new revelation absolutely because the church possesses revelation already would be to be guilty of just the failure with which it (unjustly) charged Judaism and the Jews almost 2000 years ago. To rule out another revelation out of pride and importance in one's own revelation would be an egregious error. It would really be an attempt to preserve the church's triumphalism — since, clearly, the further revelation does not necessarily undercut the church's basic experience.

Rather, the church should appeal to the words of the Schema on Ecumenism. "Every renewal of the Church essentially consists in an increase of fidelity to her own calling . . . . Christ summons the Church as she goes her pilgrim way to that continual reformation of which she always has need insofar as she is an institution of men here on earth. Therefore, if the influence of events or of the times has led to deficiencies in conduct, in church discipline, or even in formulation of doctrine . . . (t)hese should be appropriately rectified at the proper moment . . . . There can be no ecumenism worthy of the name without a change of heart."[46] Thus the paradox: fear of new patterns bespeaks fear of the Christian capacity to sustain growth and catharsis. Confession of Christian guilt and affirmation of revelation is the statement of Christian hope unbroken.

It may seem incredible to speak of hope in a generation of holocaust and in a world where humans starve; where the survivors of the Holocaust, isolated, are constantly threatened with a repetition; where oil-purchased votes yield constant condemnations and assaults on the legitimacy of this fragile experience of redemption. Yet, this is the ultimate testimony of Judaism and Christianity: hope — to affirm life and its ultimate redemption.

The Christians who see the implications of the Holocaust and Israel are a prophetic leaven in the church who give hope that the church can be reborn, purged of its hatred, and rededicated to its mission of hope and its message of redemption to come from the world. True, the number of such Christians is still small — sometimes this suggests despair — but surely the number is no smaller than the band of twelve who started it 1900 years ago. To some Christians, such admissions risk the death of Christianity. Yet the reluctance to admit Israel's existence is the temptation to create a situation where another genocide can solve the Jewish problem — a genocide which can only destroy Christianity's final moral capital. True, for Christians to take up the new revelation is practically an invitation to be crucified. It is to confront the Gospel — and to admit that no one owns God's love. For 2000 years Christianity has taught that death to pride and triumphalism is rebirth to love and life. One hopes it has the resources to show this truth in its own life again.

For Jews, too, the unqualified confrontation with Christianity, without a priori dismissal, is a most painful prospect. For the Jews to accept the revelation of the Holocaust and Israel is to challenge existing denominational lines and to open up to fellow Jews and the world in a new, painful, risky, yet exhilarating, way.

This, then, is a moment of Messianic promise. In this generation which has seen the ultimate triumph of absurd death and meaninglessness can come a mighty rebirth in Judaism and Christianity, so that another volume of God's revelation may yet come out of this experience. "They that hope in God shall renew their strength," whatever their disappointments. If the risk is taken, later generations will tell how 4000 years after the Exodus and 2000 years after Calvary, Jews and Christians renounced the guarantees and triumphalism. They faced ultimate death, worked together, and overcame death with renewed life and extreme hatred with love, which is the divine presence in our midst. Truly, if this can be done, Judaism and Christianity are again models for the world, and this is a Messianic moment.

Notes

1. In Walter J. Abbott, ed., *The Documents of Vatican II* (New York: Guild Press, 1968), pp. 664-665.

2. Para. 1 in Abbott, *Documents*, p. 112.

3. This was the Jewish response to the destruction of the First Temple and later the Second Temple. See Salo W. Baron, *A Social and Religious History of the Jews* (Philadelphia: Jewish Publication Society, 1952), vol. 1, ch. 5; vol. 2, ch. 10, 11. See also I. Greenberg, "Judaism and History: Historical Events and Religious Change," in Jerry V. Duller, ed., *Ancient Roots and Modern Beginnings* (New York: Bloch Publishing, 1978).

4. Cf. in Jacob Neusner, *Early Rabbinic Judaism* (Leiden: E.J. Brill, 1975), "Emergent Rabbinic Judaism in a Time of Crisis: Four Responses to the Destruction of the Second Temple," pp. 34-49, especially pp. 41-43.

5. Abbott, *Documents*, p. 64.

6. Contrast Paul in Rom. 9-11 with the church's tradition. See on this Rosemary Ruether's *Faith and Fratricide* (New York: Seabury Press, 1974), pp 53ff., ch. 2.

7. See on this Gershom Scholem, *The Messianic Idea in Judaism* (New York: Schocken, 1971), and his *Sabbatai Sevi* (Princeton: Princeton University Press, 1973).

8. See on this my "Crossroads of Destiny: Responses to the Destruction of the Temple" (New York: n.p., 1975).

9. See Jacob Taubes, "The Issue between Judaism and Christianity," *Commentary*, Vol. 16 (December, 1953), pp. 525-533, especially pp. 531 ff.

10. See Jacob Katz, *Exclusiveness and Tolerance* (Oxford University Press, 1961), especially ch. 9, 10.

11. Katz, *Exclusiveness and Tolerance*, pp. 87, 89ff.

12. Irving Greenberg, "The New Encounter of Judaism and Christianity." *Barat Review*, vol. 3, no. 2 (June/September, 1968), pp. 113-125.

13. Abbott, *Documents*, pp. 666-668, 664.

14. *Ibid.*, pp. 664,666.

15. Fr. Cornelius Rijk (then director of the Holy See's office for Catholic-Jewish Relations), Fr. Edward Flannery (then executive secretary of the U.S. Bishops' Secretariat for Catholic-Jewish Relations), Abbot Leo Rudloff, O.S.B., of Jerusalem (consultant of the Vatican Secretariat for Promoting Christian Unity), Fr. Theodore deKruyt (a consultant on the unity secretariat), and Fr. S. LeDeault, "Reflections and Suggestions for the Application of the Directive of 'NOSTRA AETATE,' 4," text issued by Press Dept., U.S. Catholic Conference, December 16, 1969. Commission for Religious Relations with the Jews, "Guidelines and Suggestions for Implementing the Conciliar Declaration *Nostra Aetate* (n. 4)," (Rome, December 1, 1974).

16. Rijk, et al., *Reflections*, pp. 2-3.

17. Commission, *Guidelines*, pp. 1-2.

18. *Ibid.*, p. 5.

19. Rijk, *Reflections*, p. 4.

20. *Guidelines*, p. 5.

21. These words are said with great diffidence. These are the most solemn and serious affirmations that can be made. The official Jewish religious sectors and authorities were, by and large, just as unprepared for this as were most people.

22. My use of the word "revelation" in the rest of this section means that the event — like all revelations — leads to reorientation of the believers and is not merely an additional datum or nuance of understanding. See on this Paul M. van Buren's review of my essay cited below in *Journal of the American Academy of Religion*, Vol. 45, No. 4, p. 493.

23. See Irving Greenberg, "Cloud of Smoke, Pillar of Fire: Judaism, Christianity and Modernity after the Holocaust," in Eva Fleischner, ed., *Auschwitz: Beginning of a New Era?* (New York, KTAV, 1977) pp. 1-55.

24. *Ibid.* See also A. Roy Eckardt, *Elder and Younger Brothers* (New York: Scribners, 1967), Introduction and Part 1, and Franklin H. Littell, *The Crucifixion of the Jews* (New York, 1975).

25. Cf. such behavior as the Vatican's reaction to Vichy France's law of June 2, 1941, isolating the Jews and depriving them of their rights, that "in principle there is nothing in these measures which the Holy See would find to criticize," in Saul Friedlander, *Pius XII and the Third Reich: A Documentation* (New York: Knopf, 1966), p. 97; or Archbishop Grober's pastoral letter in Germany in March, 1941, indicating that

"the self-imposed curse, 'His blood be upon us and our children,' had come true terribly, until the present time, until today," quoted in Gunther Lewy, *The Catholic Church and Nazi Germany* (New York: McGraw Hill, 1964), p. 294; or the Vatican's help to thousands of German war criminals to escape after the war—including Franz Stangel, commander of Treblinka, mass murderer of over a million Jews! in Gitta Sereny, *Into That Darkness* (London: Andre Deutsch, 1974), pp. 289-323. On all this, see Helen Fein, *Accounting for Genocide: National Responses and Jewish Victimization during the Holocaust* (New York: Free Press, 1979), especially pp. 64-120. This outstanding study is now fundamental to any discussion of the relationship of Christian Antisemitism to the Holocaust. In a nutshell, Fein's work shows that the alienation from the other or the presence of categories of understanding that allow the victim to be isolated by the Nazis is the key to Nazi success in genocide. For a magisterial study of the background of this issue in Germany, see Uriel Tal, *Christians and Jews in Germany* (New York: Cornell University Press, 1975).

26. Cf. Greenberg, "Cloud of Smoke," pp. 20 ff.

27. Cf. Lewy, *Catholic Church*, ch. 9-11; John S. Conway, *The Nazi Persecution of the Churches* (New York: Basic Books, 1968), pp. 261-283. See also the as-yet-unpublished but very important Wolfgang Gerlach, "Zwischen Kreuz and Davidstern: Bekennede Kirche in ihrer Stellung zum Judentum in Dritten Reich." (Unpub. dissertation, University of Hamburg, 1970).

28. In her testimony at the Nuremburg trial, a Polish guard, S. Smaglewskava, revealed that in the summer of 1944, Jewish children were ordered to be burned alive to economize on the gas used for mass murder. "Their screams could be heard back at the camp," she reported in *Trial of the Major War Criminals before the International Military Tribunal* (Nuremburg, 1947, 1949), vol. 8, pp. 319-320.

29. Cf. Fein, *Accounting for Genocide*, p. 67; see also ch. 4.

30. Cf. *Ibid.*, ch. 3.

31. Franklin H. Littell, *The German Phoenix: Men and Movements in the Church in Germany* (Garden City, N.Y. 1960) p. 217. On the conflict of Nazism as a religion with Judaism and Jews, see Uriel Tal's very important essay, "Religious and Anti-Religious Roots of Anti-Semitism," Leo Baeck Memorial Lecture 14 (New York: Leo Baeck Institute, n.d.).

32. Yosef Yerushalmi, "Response to Rosemary Ruether," in Fleischner, *Auschwitz*, pp. 97 ff.

33. On Jewish modernity, see Milton Himmelfarb, *The Jews of Modernity* (Philadelphia: Jewish Publication Society, 1973), especially pp. 154-157, 158, 178; and Charles Liebman, *The Ambivalent American Jew* (Philadelphia: Jewish Publication Society, 1973).

34. See Himmelfarb, *Jews*, pp. 283-296, 343-360; and Greenberg, "Cloud of Smoke," pp. 14 ff.

35. *Trials of War Criminals before the Nuremburg Military Tribunals, under Control Council Law No. 10*, vol. 4 (The Finsatzgruppen Cases), U.S. v. Otto Ohlendorf, et al. (Washington, DC; U.S. Government Printing Office, 1952), pp. 500-503 and 215 ff.; cf. also p. 309.

36. Quoted in Roger Manvoll, *S.S. and Gestapo* (New York: Balentine, 1969), p. 109.

37. Cf. Greenberg, "Cloud of Smoke," pp. 45 ff; also "A Hymn to Secularists," dialogue of Irving Greenberg and Leonard Fein at the General Assembly, Chicago, November 15, 1974, cassette distributed by the Council of Jewish Federations and Welfare Funds, New York, 1975.

38. Tadeusz Borowski, *This way to the Gas, Ladies and Gentlemen* (New York, 1967), p. 87. Borowski's work is formally "fiction." It is actually memoir and its accuracy is verified by many personal witnesses.

39. Quoted by H.T. Zimels, "The Echo of the Nazi Holocaust in Rabbinic Literature" (n.p., 1975), pp. 63-64. Ziemba was killed by the Nazis on April 24, 1943. Initially, in August, 1942, he opposed armed resistance. See also the reflection on the loss of significance of martyrdom in Lawrence Langer, *The Holocaust and the Literary Imagination* (New Haven: Yale University Press, 1975), ch. 1.

40. Greenberg, "Cloud of Smoke," p. 32.

41. Cf. Irving Greenberg, *A Guide to Purim* (New York: National Jewish Conference Center, 1978), pp. 11-13. Cf. Jon Levenson, "The Scroll of Esther in Ecumenical Perspective," *Journal of Ecumenical Studies* 13 (Summer, 1976): 440-452.

42. Babylonian Talmud, Tractate Yoma 69b.

43. "Dogmatic Constitution on Divine Revelation" in Abbott, *Documents*, p. 124.

44. Some Christians have dared to develop the Holocaust/Israel tie in the model of crucifixion/redemption. I use this analogy with great trepidation. One must beware of its past associations and possible

misuse. Thus, for some Christians, the Holocaust is coopted to reinforce the crucifixion as credible Christian symbol (Moltmann). There is also the danger of dignifying the Nazi Final Solution as a necessary step on the way to salvation. Such a glorification can be avoided if the crucifixion is addressed through Holocaust categories, as total degradation and as a model of what should *not* be tolerated or allowed to happen rather than as redemptive suffering (see above). Cf. on this A. Roy Eckardt, "Christian Responses to the Endlosung," *Religion in Life* 47 (Spring, 1978): 33-45.

45. "Dogmatic Constitution on Divine Revelation," in Abbott, *Documents*, p. 113.

46. "Decree on Ecumenism," ibid., pp. 350-351.

Part IV

TENSIONS IN JEWISH-CHRISTIAN RELATIONS ARISING FROM MISSION AND LITURGY

Chapter 9

THE GOSPEL PASSION NARRATIVES AND JEWS

Paul J. Kirsch
Professor Emeritus of Religion, Wagner College,
Staten Island, New York

Clergy sometimes wonder if anyone is taking it to heart (or even listening) when they preach or read the scripture lessons at services of public worship; but thousands of Jews through the centuries could testify that after certain scripture lessons were read and commented on in Christian churches, their lives and property were in danger.

It was, of course, the Holy Week lessons and the other liturgy based on them, including homilies, that most required Jews to become invisible for a time. The annual reading of those New Testament lessons that portrayed the abuse and death of Jesus revived in many Christians the notions that the Jews had "rejected the Messiah" and had "crucified the Son of God" and thus deserved to be punished again.

Modern methods of studying the New Testament historically have put the story of the death of Jesus in a different and better light. Thus a great many Christian clergy active today have been inoculated against anti-Jewish interpretations of New Testament literature. But the New Testament as apprehended by the laity has not received sufficient attention. Is it possible that the "history of the passion" of Jesus still evokes for Christian congregations the old ideology that made "Christ-killers" of the Jews?

A major revision of the church lectionary has taken place recently. The Roman Catholic Church led the way, on the prompting of Vatican Council II (1962-65). The outcome was a three-year cycle of scripture lessons specifically appointed for each Sunday and major festival of the church year. The lessons for each

occasion are three in number, usually one from the Hebrew
Bible or Old Testament, one from the New Testament literature
other than the gospels, and one from the gospels. Other denominations were evidently ready for this concept. In such a three-
year cycle the whole wealth of the Jewish Bible and the New
Testament can be more fully and more fairly represented in the
church's lessons. The consequence has been that the Episcopal,
Lutheran, and Presbyterian churches and the United Methodist
Church, the United Church of Christ, and the other churches
cooperating in the Consultation on Church Union have largely
followed suit. Each church has made some modifications in the
Roman Catholic arrangement, in order to include portions of the
scriptures of special importance in its tradition. But for the
first time ever, American Christianity has a substantially common
lectionary.

There is some evidence that Christian relations with Jews had
a determinative effect on the development of the new lectionary.
The Vatican Council was sensitive to the relations of the church
with Jews, part of the "People of God." The Lutheran rescension
expressly claims to have been motivated in part by the desire to
avoid portions of the New Testament that could be mistakenly
apprehended as anti-Jewish.[1] Furthermore, the almost invaria-
ble inclusion of Old Testament portions in the lessons appointed
for each Sunday is a great gain. The splended wealth of the
Hebrew law, prophets, and writings is routinely tapped in Christian congregations. Christian preaching, which characteristically
lets itself be informed if not determined by the lectionary, thus
regularly celebrates religious insights that belong to Judaism.
The congruence and mutual support between the Old and New
Testament scriptures are regularly made visible.

Nevertheless a problem remains with those lessons that reflect
what has been called the "anti-Judaism of the New Testament."
The problem is especially evident in the lessons for Holy Week.
For the sake of simplicity (and because I am a Lutheran), let us
focus on the Lutheran lectionary.

The "long gospel" for Palm Sunday, the first day of Holy Week,
consists of the whole "history of the passion" according to each
of the synoptic gospels in successive years. The "short gospel"
is a substantial excerpt from the long gospel. Thus in 1979 one
heard the passion according to Mark; in 1980 one will hear the
passion according to Luke; and in 1981 the passion according to
Matthew. In the same churches, the lesson for Good Friday is
invariably the passion according to John.

In what follows I will discuss what may be the flash-points for anti-Jewish responses in each of these gospel lections. After that, I will discuss possible ways in which the lections can be put in such perspectives that the lay responses will be to individual and institutional *human sin*, rather than to Jews.

The Passion Narrative of Mark

Mark is not the worst offender among the gospel-writers, but he is an offender. He was presumably a member of the second generation of Christians, since it is likely that he published his gospel a little later than A.D. (C.E.) 70, and he does not claim and it is not claimed for him that he was an eye-witness to the events that he records. He can be identified as a member of what Norman Perrin called Hellenistic Jewish mission Christianity.[2] That is to say that Mark was brought up Greek-speaking and Jewish, or in a family that had been Jewish and coverted to Christianity, and was part of a movement that took special joy in the conversion of gentiles to the Christian way. Mark's fondness for gentiles appears in his identification as a gentile, i.e., as a Roman centurion, of the soldier who saw Jesus die and then said, "Truly this man was a son of God" (Mark 15:39).* Mark's pleasure in the fact that gentile Christians and Jewish Christians like himself were not obligated by the church to perpetuate the Jewish dietary laws appears when he reports that Jesus "declared all foods clean" (Mark 7:19).

In his passion history, Mark attributes to the "chief priests and the scribes" the intention "to arrest (Jesus) by stealth and kill him" (Mark 14:1). Clearly, the priests and scribes are Jewish religious leaders. Then Judas Iscariot, identified as "one of the twelve (disciples of Jesus), went to the chief priests in order to betray (Jesus) to them" (Mark 14:10). While Jesus is in the Garden of Gethsemane, after the last supper, Judas arrives with "a crowd with swords and clubs, from the chief priests and the scribes and the elders" (Mark 14:43). The indication of the chief priests, scribes, and elders identifies the authority behind the arresting group as the Sanhedrin or Council, a body of representative Jews who were associated with the high priest in administering Jewish self-rule under the Roman occupation of Judea. Jesus is taken "to the high priest," at whose place Mark says "all the

---

*All quotations from *The Holy Bible* are from the *Revised Standard Version*.

chief priests and the elders and the scribes were assembled"
(Mark 14:53). "Now the chief priests and the whole council sought
testimony against Jesus to put him to death" (Mark 14:55).

"The high priest asked him, 'Are you the Christ, the Son of the
Blessed?' And Jesus said, 'I am; and you will see the Son of man
sitting at the right hand of Power, and coming with the clouds of
heaven.' And the high priest tore his mantle, and said, 'Why do
we still need witnesses? You have heard his blasphemy. What is
your decision?' And they all condemned him as deserving death.
And some began to spit on him, and to cover his face, and to
strike him, saying to him, 'Prophesy!' And the guards received
him with blows" (Mark 14:61-65).

In the morning, "the chief priests, with the elders and the
scribes, and the whole council held a consultation; and they
bound Jesus and led him away and delivered him to Pilate. And
Pilate asked him, 'Are you the King of the Jews?' And he answered
him, 'You have said so.' And the chief priests accused him of
many things. And Pilate again asked him, 'Have you no answer
to make? See how many charges they bring against you.' But
Jesus made no further answer, so that Pilate wondered" (Mark
15:1-5).

Mark then makes reference to a custom of releasing one
prisoner at the Passover. Pilate asks "the crowd" whether he
should release the "King of the Jews." "For he perceived that it
was out of envy that the chief priests had delivered him up. But
the chief priests stirred up the crowd to have him release for
them Barabbas instead. And Pilate again said to them, 'Then
what shall I do with the man whom you call the King of the
Jews?' And they cried out again, 'Crucify him' " (Mark 15:10-13).
"So Pilate, wishing to satisfy the crowd, released for them
Barabbas; and having scourged Jesus, he delivered him to be
crucified" (Mark 15:15).

The Roman soldiers further mock and abuse Jesus, and then
they crucify him. Passersby mock Jesus. "So also the chief priests
mocked him to one another with the scribes, saying, 'He saved
others; he cannot save himself. Let the Christ, the King of Israel,
come down now from the cross, that we may see and believe' "
(Mark 15:31-32).

Then "Joseph of Arimathea, a respected member of the council, who was also himself looking for the kingdom of God, took
courage and went to Pilate, and asked for the body of Jesus"
(Mark 15:43). Pilate, hearing that Jesus was already dead, grants
the body to Joseph. He wraps the body in a shroud, buries it in a

tomb hewn out of rock and rolls a stone against the door of the tomb (Mark 15:44-46).

It has frequently been noted by commentators that the gospel-writers are very circumspect in their depiction of Pontius Pilate, the Roman procurator of Judea. The evangelists are all part of a missionary thrust that is furthering the expansion of the Christian movement among Jews of the diaspora and, with more success, among gentiles ("God-fearers") who have previously been attracted by Jewish monotheism and ethics and regularly attend synagogue worship. These writers' circumspectness is guided by the wish to avoid, in the broad missionary field of the Roman empire, the appearance of proclaiming a redeemer and a faith that have already come under the condemnation of the Roman imperial government. The consequence is that Pilate is pictured as reluctant to execute Jesus and as almost forced to do so to keep the peace. In Mark's view, Pilate knows that Jesus was accused before him out of "envy" on the part of the chief priests, and he tries to release Jesus. It is the Jewish authorities and the crowd they control who press Pilate to order Jesus' death.

Let us note that Pilate need not be looked at in such an excusing way. It certainly was in the interest of the Roman empire to be on guard against any Jewish messianic movement as a threat to Roman rule in Judea. Furthermore, Pilate is known to secular history as a severe and cruel protector of Roman interests, who was later, A.D. (C.E.) 36, removed from office by Rome because he was needlessly provocative of unrest. Therefore, any Roman governor of Judea, and Pilate more than most, ought to be credited with abundant motivation of his own to nip in the bud any Jewish movement that was calling its leader "Messiah."

The effect of Mark's concern practically to exonerate Pilate is to put almost all the responsibility for Jesus' death on Jewish figures. The "whole council," including representative members of the priests, scribes, and elders, finds Jesus worthy of death. Among these elements, the high priest and the chief priests are most implicated by Mark. The high priest conducts the hearing given to Jesus and leads the way in finding Jesus guilty of blasphemy and worthy of death. The chief priests deal with Judas; they lead in producing testimony against Jesus; they accuse Jesus before Pilate; they stir up the crowd to ask for the release of Barabbas and the crucifixion of Jesus. Although these priests are not identified as Jewish by Mark, it was clearly obvious to

Mark's contemporary readers that they were Jews. It may be only slightly less obvious to Mark's modern hearers that they were Jews. On the other hand, that the "whole council" was not unanimous or even entirely present at the condemnation of Jesus is implied in the episode that shows Joseph of Arimathea, a member of the Council, giving Jesus a respectful burial.

Is it necessarily anti-Jewish to show the chief priests, including the high priest, as the prime movers of the events that led to Jesus' death? It is, unless two clarifications are made. First, as already shown, the historical role of Pontius Pilate in the death of Jesus and Pilate's probable motives must be made manifest. Secondly, it has to be made clear that the chief priests are not to be construed, in whatever they did, as representatives of Judaism as such. They are properly seen (a) as not at all constitutive of Judaism as we know it and as it has been for the last 1900 years, and (b) as motivated in the case of Jesus by political considerations.

It was only a few years after the death of Jesus that warfare initiated by Jewish Zealots broke out against the Roman occupation of Palestine. The consequence of the war, A.D. (C.E.) 66-70, was the destruction of the temple and of Jerusalem itself. The temple has never been rebuilt. The type of Judaism that thought of sacrifices at the temple as its chief rites perished with the temple, and so did the priesthood that presided over those rites. Never since A.D. (C.E.) 70 has there been a Jewish priesthood. Therefore, the concerns that caused Jewish priests to be opposed to Jesus disappeared from Judaism 1900 years ago.

More importantly, the high priest and the chief priests had political reasons to oppose Jesus even if they had no quarrel with him religiously. The high priest was, in the Roman system of governing Judea, the chief political officer of the Jews and the one responsible for administration of Jewish self-rule. The high priest thus answered to the Romans for law and order in Judea. In the nature of his position he would dread any messianic movement, which could only mean to him insurrection against the Romans. The Romans, most certainly as represented by Pilate, could be counted on to suppress insurrection with a vengeance against all Jews. Precisely what happened to Jerusalem and the temple and priesthood in A.D. (C.E.) 70 — total destruction — must have been what the priests feared when they saw Jesus being hailed as the Messiah. Thus their action to eliminate Jesus (and a dangerous movement) was dictated to them by considerations of survival, not only their own, but Jerusalem's.

The Passion According to Luke

The passion narrative as it appears in Luke's gospel, chapters 22 and 23, is largely based on Mark's gospel. In a number of instances in which it differs from Mark's, it is all the more concerned to locate the responsibility for Jesus' death among Jews and to picture Pilate as acting reluctantly and under great pressure from Jews.

At the beginning of Luke's account, "the chief priests and the scribes were seeking how to put (Jesus) to death; for they feared the people" (Luke 22:2). That is, "the people" could have been expected to resist any public arrest of Jesus. Thus Judas agreed with "the chief priests and captains" as to how he might betray Jesus to them "in the absence of the multitude" (Luke 22:3-6). Thus far Luke seems more concerned than Mark to establish the innocence of the Jewish people of Jerusalem.

While Jesus is at prayer on the Mount of Olives, "there came a crowd," led by Judas (Luke 22:47). The crowd is then identified as "the chief priests and captains of the temple and elders" (Luke 22:52), including "the slave of the high priest" (Luke 22:50). It seems improbable that the chief priests and elders would have been part of the arresting party. "The captains" are members of the temple police. But evidently Luke is bent on identifying the real culprits who sent the police. Jesus is seized and led into the high priest's house (Luke 22:54). "The men who were holding Jesus mocked him and beat him" (Luke 22:63). These men were, of course, the employees of the high priest.

"When day came, the assembly of the elders of the people gathered together, both chief priests and scribes; and they led him away to their council, and they said, 'If you are the Christ, tell us'" (Luke 22:66-67). Jesus' answer asserts that "from now on the Son of man shall be seated at the right hand of the Power of God" (Luke 22:69). The council takes this as Jesus' avowal of his messiahship and that as enough to charge him with before Pilate. "Then the whole company arose, and brought him before Pilate" (Luke 23:1). There they accuse Jesus, saying, "'We found this man perverting our nation and forbidding us to give tribute to Caesar, and saying that he himself is Christ a king'" (Luke 23:2). These are charges that Pilate ought to take seriously, as implying insurrection against Roman rule. But Pilate is completely unconvinced and unimpressed and says that he finds no crime in Jesus (Luke 23:4). Luke thus implies that the Council's charges against Jesus are false and that Jesus' messiahship has been deliberately misrepresented to Pilate by the Council.

At this point Luke has another source than Mark and he relates that, because Jesus was a Galilean, Pilate sends him to Herod Antipas, the ruler of Galilee and Perea, who is in Jerusalem for the Passover. The "chief priests and the scribes" go along and accuse Jesus before Herod (Luke 23:10). "Herod and his soldiers treated (Jesus) with contempt and mocked him" and sent him back to Pilate (Luke 23:11). Herod was Jewish and his soldiers were probably Jewish.

"Pilate then called together the chief priests and the rulers and the people, and said to them, 'You brought me this man as one who was perverting the people; and after examining him before you, behold, I did not find this man guilty of any of your charges against him; neither did Herod, for he sent him back to us. Behold, nothing deserving of death has been done by him; I will therefore chastise him and release him'" (Luke 23:13-16). Those addressed clamor for the release of Barabbas instead and for the death of Jesus. Twice more, four times in all, Pilate asserts his conviction of the innocence of Jesus and his intention to release him, but to no avail. The chief priests and the rulers and the people keep insisting that Jesus be crucified, "and their voices prevailed. So Pilate gave sentence that their demand should be granted" (Luke 23:23-24). Pilate releases Barabbas; "but Jesus he delivered up to their will" (Luke 23:25). This extraordinary way of putting it suggests that Jesus was turned over to the Jews for execution; but of course only Romans carried out executions by crucifixion in Judea, and Roman soldiers crucified Jesus. "And the people stood by, watching; but the rulers scoffed at him, saying, 'He saved others; let him save himself, if he is the Christ of God, his Chosen One!'" (Luke 23:35). "The rulers" here are the members of the Sanhedrin or Council, who had accused Jesus to Pilate.

As we saw was the case in Mark's narrative, so also here in Luke's the responsibility for Jesus' death is placed upon the Jewish authorities, pre-eminently the chief priests. Pilate's relative innocence is even more insisted on than in Mark, for Pilate finds no crime in Jesus and tries four times to release Jesus; he is simply overpowered by Jewish insistence on Jesus' crucifixion. The role of the Jewish "multitude" is depicted ambiguously. On the one hand, they call to Pilate for Jesus' death without the explicit encouragement of the priests. But they do not mock Jesus while he hangs on the cross, and when they have seen Jesus die they return home "beating their breasts" (Luke 23:48).

We may be encountering in some of this material sources that Luke used which were friendlier than he to the Jewish multitude and fairer in showing the people's despair at Jesus' death. In contrast to Luke's view of "the Jews," the Roman centurion who had been watching the crucifixion is said to have "praised God, and said, 'Certainly this man was innocent' " (Luke 23:47).

The writer of the gospel according to Luke is also the author of the New Testament book of the Acts of the Apostles. The statements in Acts about the death of Jesus show how thoroughly Luke has taught himself that all the guilt for Jesus' death belongs to Jews. For example, when the apostle Peter is called upon to justify, before the high priest and the Council, his healing of a cripple and his preaching of Jesus and the resurrection, Peter is portrayed as saying, "Rulers of the people and elders . . . be it known to you all, and to the people of Israel, that by the name of Jesus Christ of Nazareth, *whom you crucified*, whom God raised from the dead, by him this man is standing before you well" (Acts 4:8-10, italics mine). Any Roman complicity in Jesus' death has fallen out of the picture entirely. And what Luke has taught himself he is still capable of teaching to others.

The Passion According to Matthew

Matthew's narrative of Jesus' passion is read in chapters 26 and 27. Matthew is considered to be, like Mark, a man of the Hellenistic Jewish Christian community. He has decided that the true fulfillment of Judaism lies in acceptance of Jesus as the Messiah; and he is not only competitive, in the style and content of his writing, with the developing rabbinic Jewish tradition, but he is resentful of that Judaism which continues its development without regard to Christian claims made on behalf of Jesus. His competitiveness is evident in the scorn he casts upon the Pharisees, the founders of post-temple Judaism (Matthew 23:1-36). His conviction that the Christian community constitutes the true Israel is evident in his version of Peter's confession of his faith about Jesus.

Mark, too, had described Jesus as asking his disciples who they thought he was. When Peter says, "You are the Christ (Messiah)," Jesus responds by charging the disciples to tell no one (Mark 8:29-30). The implication is that to believe that Jesus is the Messiah in the traditional sense is to expect Jesus to raise an army and to drive out the Romans. The Jewish public's hopes for something like this are not to be connected with Jesus.

Furthermore, Jesus proceeds to revise the disciples' own expectations as to what he will do as "Messiah." He will suffer many things and be put to death (Mark 8:31). Thus Jesus seems in Mark to be assimilating what "Messiah" means in his case to the current conception of the expected "Son of Man," who is typical of the saints and martyrs of the Most High (cf. Daniel 7). Perhaps, in Mark's view, Jesus is also pulling the meaning of "Messiah" as it relates to himself in the direction of the suffering Servant of the Lord, portrayed in Isaiah, chapter 53.

The treatment of the same story in Matthew's gospel does not so much deny what Mark suggests as to add a new line of thought. Jesus' reply to Peter's assertion that Jesus is the Messiah is to say, "Blessed are you, Simon Bar-Jona! For flesh and blood has not revealed this to you, but my Father who is in heaven. And I tell you, you are Peter, and on this rock I will build my church, and the powers of death shall not prevail against it" (Matthew 16:17-18).

The striking thing here is the first appearance in the gospels of the word translated as "church." What Matthew has done here is to pre-empt for application to Jesus' followers a Greek word (*ekklesia*) that had previously been used by Jews to refer to themselves. When the Hebrew Bible had been translated into Greek, *ekklesia* was used to translate the Hebrew (*qahal*) for "assembly of Israel." Thus *ekklesia* (literally, "called out") had connotations of "chosen people" or "people of God." Matthew's usage has the effect then of saying that the Christians are the new chosen people, or the new Israel. The implication is that the Jews who have not accepted Jesus as the Messiah are no longer chosen people. We may, therefore, expect that Matthew's treatment of the passion narrative will be imbued with this kind of conviction.

To a very considerable degree, Matthew's account of Jesus' passion follows Mark's version. Again it is the "chief priests" along with "the elders" who are most active in planning and seeing to Jesus' arrest; it is the chief priests who deal with Judas; the "chief priests and the whole council sought false testimony against Jesus that they might put him to death" (Matthew 26:59). It is the high priest who asks Jesus directly whether he is the Christ. Although Jesus' reply is ambiguous ("You have said so," Matthew 26:64), the high priest declares that Jesus has uttered blasphemy, and the Council concurs and finds Jesus deserving of death. The chief priests and the elders have Jesus bound and delivered to Pilate, and they accuse him before

Pilate. What Jesus is accused of is not stated, but evidently it was insurrection, because Pilate's first question to Jesus is reported as, "Are you the King of the Jews?" (Matthew 27:11).

Matthew alone has a story to the effect that Pilate's wife sent word to Pilate during Jesus' trial: "Have nothing to do with that righteous man, for I have suffered much over him today in a dream" (Matthew 27:19). The value of the story to Matthew, who believes in such dreams, is not only that Jesus is righteous and therefore innocent of the charges against him, but that even a Roman could see that. When Pilate, therefore, offered to release Barabbas or Jesus, "the chief priests and the elders persuaded the people to ask for Barabbas and destroy Jesus" (Matthew 27:20).

Matthew alone has the story that Pilate washed his hands "before the crowd, saying, 'I am innocent of this man's blood, see to it yourselves' " (Matthew 27:24). Commentators take this as a most improbable event. Pilate was accountable to Rome for his administration. He would have had to think that if he was publicly on record as convinced of Jesus' innocence, he had to release him, and that if he sentenced Jesus to death he had to be able to defend the execution as required by Jesus' guilt. But this legend appeals to Matthew because of the way it asserts Jesus' innocence in Roman eyes and portrays Pilate as no worse than a weak man, who was overpowered by the chief priests and the (Jewish) people.

This brings us to the single most regrettable sentence in the whole New Testament. When Pilate has washed his hands, "all the people answered, 'His blood be on us and on our children' " (Matthew 27:25).

What Matthew probably intended by this story, written in the 90's of our era, was to convey his belief that Jerusalem had been destroyed and most of its inhabitants killed by the Romans in A.D. (C.E.) 70 because of Jerusalem's rejection of Jesus. Thus he was saying that it was precisely the people who said these words and their immediate children (and perhaps grand-children) who, forty years later, paid with their blood for their complicity in the death of Jesus. If that was Matthew's opinion, it was severe enough.

But one has to shudder when one thinks about what the annual repetition of these lines for 1900 years as Christian *scripture* has brought upon Jews. "All the people" said these words. Therefore, one is led to believe that all the Jews in Jerusalem said them with one voice. The words also envision "the Jews" as very sure of themselves, willing to take not only upon themselves but upon their descendants for all time to come the full responsibility for the death of Jesus. No others, not the friends and defenders of Jesus among the people, not even the Romans, have any responsibility for Jesus' death. Naively heard, it is as if these words proclaim, "Yes, we Jews are the Christ-killers, and we are perfectly willing to answer for it forever." It is depressing to think of this message coming year after year, with the authority of scripture, to Christians with any inclination at all to be anti-semitic.

When Matthew has reported that Pilate sentenced Jesus to be crucified, and that the Roman soldiers mocked Jesus and ridiculed the idea that he could be king of the Jews and then crucified him, he too tells that the "chief priests, with the scribes and elders, mocked him, saying, 'He saved others, he cannot save himself' " and more to the same effect (Matthew 27:41-42). As in the other synoptic gospels, the Roman authority is seen as very reluctant to sentence Jesus. The Jewish authorities, chief priests and elders, and the Jewish people are vehement and self-righteous in their determination to do away with Jesus.

The Passion According to John

The passion narrative from John's gospel is the one destined to be heard most often, being appointed for reading every year on Good Friday.

John's gospel, almost certainly the last to be written, shows some signs of dependence on the earlier gospels or on some of their sources. On the other hand, either the writer had other sources than those of the synoptic gospels, or he very freely and imaginatively re-interpreted the synoptic material.

It is a peculiarity of John that he generally refers to the opposition to Jesus simply as "the Jews." What this may say is that, in the time and place of John's writing, Jews and Christians were rival and mutually opposed communities, each claiming to be the true people of God. John apparently read this mutual opposition between Jews and Christians back into Jesus' time. Thus "the Jews" comes to be, in his gospel, a code for "Jews who opposed Jesus." This usage can lead the hearer of this gospel to forget that Jesus and his disciples themselves were Jews. With few exceptions in John, "the Jews" are the villains. Noting this does not prepare us to expect from John a careful and judicious account of Jesus' death.

The reading of the passion narrative from John begins with chapter 18. "Judas, procuring a band of soldiers and some officers from the chief priests and the Pharisees" went to the garden where Jesus was in order to have him arrested (John 18:3). The mention of soldiers is interesting. "Soldiers" can only mean Roman soldiers; and if they were part of the arresting party, then the Roman governor of Judea is indicated as himself interested in Jesus' arrest and trial. This is historically probable in the highest degree, as we have seen in our previous discussion of Pilate's role. But since John himself sees the death of Jesus as the work of "the Jews," the story of the soldiers must have been in John's source and left "uncorrected" by John's own prevailing opinion.

John's text is the only one among the gospels that implicates the Pharisees in the plot against Jesus. The Pharisees are pictured in the other gospels as having controversies with Jesus about the oral Torah, but they are never named as among those who wanted to do away with Jesus. In the synoptic gospels it is primarily the chief priests and, back of them, the Sanhedrin or Council who take the initiatives against Jesus. The council is explained in the synoptics as the chief priests, scribes, and elders, under the presidency of the high priest. The "scribes" are *sopherim*, men of the book, that is, experts in the interpretation of the sacred books of the law, the "laws of Moses." There were scribes of the Pharisee party, to be sure; but there is no reason to suppose that all *sopherim* were Pharisees. Since the Pharisees and the Sadducees, or priestly party, had acute differences regarding the interpretation of the Mosaic law, it is necessary to assume that there were also *sopherim* or legal experts of the Sadducean party. John's specific mention of the Pharisees as joining the chief priests in sending police to arrest Jesus may be another consequence of reading back into Jesus' time the opposition that John himself and Christians in his time and place are experiencing from Jews. When John writes, the temple and the chief priests have disappeared. The lively Jewish community that he is in opposition with is, therefore, made up of Pharisees. For the Pharisees were the Jewish party that knew how to survive the loss of the temple and the sacrificial system. It was Pharisees who realized that Jews had an atonement, in deeds of lovingkindness, equal to the defunct sacrificial system. Thus John's way of writing has the effect of fixing responsibility for Jesus' death not only on the chief priests, who were extinct as a class when he wrote, but also on the variety of Jews his readers are familiar with in their own time.

Jesus after being arrested is taken to Annas, who is described as father-in-law of the high priest. A former high priest himself, Annas is evidently still effectively in power as head of the high-priestly family. He questions Jesus about his disciples and his teaching, but Jesus says only, "Ask those who have heard me." Jesus is then taken to the current high priest, Caiaphas, and from Caiaphas' house to the praetorium (John 18:12-28). The implication of this account is that the high priests Annas and Caiaphas take it upon themselves to accuse Jesus to Pilate.

"So Pilate went out to them and said, 'What accusation do you bring against this man?' They answered him, 'If this man were not an evil-doer, we would not have handed him over.' Pilate said to them, 'Take him yourselves and judge him by your own law.' The Jews said to him, 'It is not lawful for us to put any man to death' " (John 18:29-31). In John's view, the high priests are now accompanied by "the Jews," and it is "the Jews" who want Pilate to execute Jesus.

Pilate then asks Jesus, " 'Are you the King of the Jews?' Jesus answered, 'Do you say this of your own accord, or did others say it to you about me?' Pilate answered, 'Am I a Jew? Your own nation and the chief priests have handed you over to me; what have you done?' Jesus answered, 'My kingship is not of this world; if my kingship were of this world, my servants would fight, that I might not be handed over to the Jews; but my kingship is not from this world.' Pilate said to him, 'So you are a king?' Jesus answered, 'You say that I am a king. For this was I born, and for this have I come into the world, to bear witness to the truth. Everyone who is of the truth hears my voice.' Pilate said to him, 'What is truth?' After he had said this, he went out to the Jews again, and told them, 'I find no crime in him. But you have a custom that I should release one man for you at the Passover; will you have me release for you the King of the Jews?' They cried out again, 'Not this man, but Barabbas' " (John 18:33-40).

John is making a number of points in this way of telling the story. One is that Jesus does indeed admit that he is a king — that is, the Messiah — but he is not the kind of king that Pilate needs to worry about as a threat to Roman rule. The idea of kingship here is thoroughly spiritualized; it is not political or of this world; it has to do with bearing witness to the truth. Thus Pilate has no reason of his own to execute Jesus and is willing to release him. Secondly, the real enemies of Jesus are "the Jews."

Jesus' "own nation and the chief priests" have handed him over
to Pilate. But they knew as well as Pilate did that Jesus' type of
kingship was no threat to Roman rule, and hence they have lied
to Pilate in accusing Jesus to him. Thirdly, there is the most
curious claim that if Jesus' kingship were of this world, his
servants would fight in order that Jesus might not be handed
over to "the Jews." This seems to imply that if Jesus did want to
set up a this-worldly messianic kingdom, of the very kind many
Jews were looking for, he would have to fight *the Jews*! This
makes no sense whatever historically. It only indicates the depth
of John's animosity toward "the Jews."

After Jesus has been scourged on Pilate's orders and the soldiers have mocked Jesus and put a crown of thorns on his head,
Pilate again tries to release Jesus. He says that he finds "no
crime in him." But, "when the chief priests and the officers saw
him, they cried out, 'Crucify him, crucify him!' Pilate said to
them, 'Take him yourselves and crucify him, for I find no crime
in him.' Then the Jews answered him, 'We have a law and by
that law he ought to die, because he has made himself the son
of God' " (John 19:6-7). In the synoptic gospels, Jesus never called
himself the Son of God. At most, he permitted himself to be
called son of God in the honorary sense in which the Messiah
was called the son of God, as in Psalm 2. However, in John's
gospel, quite unhistorically, Jesus is frequently spoken of and
spoken to as the Son of God in a non-honorary and substantial
sense. In the light of the synoptic gospels, it is historically most
improbable that the chief priests would have leveled against
Jesus before Pilate the charge that he had made himself the Son
of God. It could not have meant anything actionable to Pilate.
But for John himself it is evidently one factor in the hostility
between Jews and Christians in his time that Jews resent Christian claims that Jesus is the Son of God.

Pilate is depicted by John as "more afraid" when he hears
that Jesus made himself the Son of God. He asks Jesus, "Where
are you from?" Jesus does not reply. When Pilate says to Jesus,
"Do you not know that I have power to release you, and power
to crucify you?", Jesus replies, "You would have no power over
me unless it had been given you from above; therefore he who
delivered me to you has the greater sin" (John 19:8-11). Here
John puts it on the lips of Jesus himself that those who accused
him to Pilate have the greater sin.

"Upon this Pilate sought to release him, but the Jews cried
out, 'If you release this man, you are not Caesar's friend; every-

one who makes himself a king sets himself against Caesar!'"
(John 19:12). Here John's "Jews" are more friendly to Caesar
than Pilate is and know Pilate's bloody business better than he
does. Again, Pilate "said to the Jews, 'Here is your King!' They
cried out, 'Away with him, away with him, crucify him!' Pilate
said to them, 'Shall I crucify your King?' The chief priests
answered, 'We have no king but Caesar.' Then he handed him
over to *them* to be crucified" (John 19:14-16, italics mine). Here
again we have, as we had in Luke's account, an apparent handing
of Jesus over to the chief priests to be crucified. Historically,
there was no such thing, of course; only the Romans conducted
crucifixions in Judea. But the imprecision is continued by John
in the next verses, where we read, "So *they* took Jesus, and he
went out bearing his own cross . . . to Golgotha. There *they*
crucified him" (John 19:17-18).

Joseph of Arimathea is again reported as claiming the body of
Jesus and burying it. But Joseph is introduced by John as "a
disciple of Jesus, but secretly, for fear of the Jews" (John 19:38).

All the gospels have explicitly made Jewish priests, scribes,
elders, and people responsible for the suffering and death of
Jesus. John seems to exceed the rest by his frequent designation
of these parties collectively as simply "the Jews." Is it any wonder then that Glock and Stark found so many members of American Christian churches believing that "the Jews were the group
most responsible for crucifying Christ," and that "the Jews can
never be forgiven for what they did to Jesus until they accept
him as the True Savior," and that "the reason the Jews have so
much trouble is because God is punishing them for rejecting
Jesus."[3] The reading of these gospel narratives of the passion
must be the chief source and reinforcement of anti-Jewish feelings and actions among Christian church members. What is to
be done about this?

Some Proposals

There is no use talking about abandoning these passion
narratives, or even about publishing them in expurgated or
revised form. No church would consider for an instant any
editorial modification of any New Testament texts. The reason is
that the texts are sacred scripture. Nor will the passion lections
be abandoned. For the sacrificial death of Jesus is absolutely
central in all Christian theology of atonement, forgiveness, and
reconciliation with God. Jesus' death is seen as indispensable,

because it is effective in taking away the sins of the world.

It is important to note here that for Christian theology, Jesus' death is effective without regard to what particular persons or institutions had any part in bringing about Jesus' death. In fact, if attention is drawn to the historical involvements of particular persons in Jesus' death, its saving function may be frustrated. Whatever persons and institutions entered the causative process, they are taken by Christian theology as symbolic or representative of universal human sinfulness. It was human sinfulness, which is present in all mankind, that killed Jesus.

Here is the way the apostle Paul sees it: "For God has done what the law, weakened by the flesh, could not do: sending his own Son in the likeness of sinful flesh and for sin (or, as a sin offering), he *condemned* sin in the *flesh*" (Romans 8:3, italics mine). "The flesh" is universal human nature. God comdemned sin in universal human nature when he exposed what violence sinful human nature was capable of doing to the good man Jesus. Thus God made all of us Christians aware of sin and disgusted with it in ourselves because of what sin did to Jesus. Once we have experienced that revulsion against our sins, then "the law of the Spirit of life in Christ Jesus has set (us) free from the law of sin and death" (Romans 8:2). The power of sin over us has been broken, and we want to be on Christ's side, obedient to "the law of the Spirit of life in Christ Jesus."

It is thus a necessary consequence of Christian theology with reference to the death of Jesus that any blaming of other particular persons or institutions for Jesus' death is emphatically excluded. Unless the death of Jesus is blamed on *human sin*, including our own sins as Christians, and has turned us against *our own sin*, it has lost its salvific effect for us. Thus blaming the death of Jesus on Jews is not merely a regrettable side-effect of the gospels, and unfortunate for the Jews—it is a disaster for Christians in that it prevents the death of Jesus from doing its work for us; it prevents us from being saved by that death.

Nevertheless, the passion narratives still have the power to distract us into thinking of "Jewish" guilt. If they cannot be rewritten or abandoned, what can be done with them to make their theological meaning unmistakable?

(1) There are hundreds of thousands of instances every Sunday in which the church's lections, having been reprinted, are placed in the hands of worshippers in order that they may follow the readings with their eyes. Furthermore, in some churches (Lutheran churches, for example) the printed lections

are fitted out with brief prefaces. Footnotes would accomplish the same purposes. Such prefaces or footnotes are necessarily brief, but it is intriguing to think about what they might achieve in preventing anti-Jewish reactions to some of the lections. For example, when the lection represents Pilate in the too excusing way that we have observed, the preface might say something like this: "Pilate as defender of Roman imperial interests in Judea was mortally afraid of Jewish messianic movements and had his own political reasons, however much they are obscured here, to want Jesus and his movement brought to a quick end."

When the lection points to the chief priests calling for Jesus' death and urging the (Jewish) people to do the same, the preface might say something like this: "Christian readers need to remember here that the priests and people are not to be thought of as Jews, or as though they are representative of Judaism; they are to be seen as representative of the misunderstanding of Jesus, defensiveness, and general sinfulness that characterize mankind, including ourselves. If the events described here do not turn us against our own sins, they are unable to save us."

Although the illustrative material from the New Testament that has been discussed in this essay has been drawn almost exclusively from the passion narratives, it is not to be thought that anti-Jewish material in the New Testament is limited to the passion narratives. For example, passing reference was made to Matthew's diatribe against the scribes and Pharisees: "Woe to you, scribes and Pharisees, hypocrites . . ." (Matthew 23:1-36). The sort of prefaces being called for here would be directed to preventing anti-Jewish impressions and fostering appreciations of Judaism on a weekly basis throughout the church year.

The prefaces that are already in use and that this writer has read have not attempted to do anything about the detracting and even hostile images of Jews in some portions of the New Testament. The concern to avoid suggesting and reinforcing anti-Jewish attitudes is not yet as strong in the churches as it must become. But this is a programmatic essay. The concern here is with what can be done.

If prefaces of the kind suggested here were regularly printed, they would reach some special groups in addition to the laity in general: that is, the clergy, volunteer Sunday School teachers, and the smaller number of Christian day school teachers. The clergy, who preach regularly on the lections, would find in the prefaces ideas on which they could expand in homilies. At the very worst, they would be unlikely to take exception to the prefaces or to challenge them in their sermons. Lay teachers in church religious education programs are also in good position to take up what they would find in the prefaces and to expand upon and reinforce their positive perspectives in their teaching.

(2) Something more than the brief prefaces called for above needs to be prepared for the Christian clergy, that is, long prefaces for every lection in the church year in which Jews are described, discussed, or referred to. I have already claimed that modernly educated clergy have been inoculated against anti-Jewish expressions in the New Testament. If this is true, their preaching ought already to be healed of anti-Jewish biases. But it is not clear that preaching has the needs of the laity in this area sufficiently in mind. The long prefaces, designed to be of assistance in sermon-preparation, should explicitly recommend two concerns: (1) that lay misunderstandings of Jewish roles in the story of Jesus be corrected, and (2) that the Jewishness out of which Jesus came be presented in the favorable light that it deserves.

Such long prefaces to the lections would also assist Christian clergy in instructing lay Sunday School and day school teachers as to how best to deal with the portions of the New Testament that have put Jews in a bad light, and as to how to have the fullest appreciation of the Jewish elements in the Christian heritage. The lay teachers may be happy to study a book of such prefaces on their own.

The long prefaces being proposed here would be similar to the parts of this essay that were devoted to interpretation of the passion narratives of the gospels. Their over-all purpose would be to relativize the all-too-human elements in the New Testament that denigrate Jews. The New Testament is to Christians what Torah is to Jews, that is, word of God. The New Testament therefore tends to be heard by lay Christians who have not had much education in biblical studies as absolute, as if it were the very *words* of God. But the New Testament was composed by human writers, who were very much conditioned by the hostilities among which they wrote. The necessary task is to expose the human elements in the New Testament scripture for what they are.

For most of the common era, Christian teaching has been the primary source of anti-semitism. In the last two centuries, Jews have been subjected to secular anti-semitism as well. It is hard to believe that secular anti-semitism would have occurred, or at any rate would have been as vicious, if it had not been prepared for and reinforced by religious anti-semitism. The power and unlimited inhumanity of anti-semitism have been abundantly and horrifyingly demonstrated by the Holocaust. Therefore, Christianity is called upon to do what only it can do, and what it must do for its own integrity as well as for the well-being of Jews, and that is to purge itself of anti-Jewish misunderstandings and the attitudes and actions based on them. For the church to correct the anti-Jewish elements of its utterances at worship and to learn to speak well of Jews when it is at worship are clearly necessary and major components of this self-reform.

Notes

1. *Contemporary Worship 6, The Church Year Calendar and Lectionary*, Philadelphia: The Board of Publication, Lutheran Church in America, 1973, p. 17.

2. Norman Perrin, *The New Testament: An Introduction*, New York: Harcourt Brace Jovanovich, 1974, p. 150.

3. Charles Y. Glock and Rodney Stark, *Christian Beliefs and Anti-Semitism*, New York: Harper and Row, 1966, pp. 59, 62 and 64.

Chapter 10

JESUS: BOND OR BARRIER
TO JEWISH-CHRISTIAN RELATIONS*

Cynthia L. Bronson
Priest Associate, Christ and St. Stephen's
Episcopal Church, New York, New York

I have been asked to share my thoughts regarding the topic
Jesus: Bond or Barrier to Jewish-Christian Relations?

Soon after beginning the preparation for this discussion, I
realized that any response to this inquiry involves much more
than I had originally supposed because the question can be
addressed – and answered – from more than one perspective.
To begin with, we need to clarify who it is we're talking about
when we say "Jesus." Is it to the historical man of Nazareth or to
the exalted Christ that we are referring? Is such a separation
superficial or is it necessary? Beyond this, should we separate
the Jesus of the Gospels and his teaching from subsequent
Christian history with its pogroms and persecutions in the name
of Jesus – or must we?

Let me begin by saying that as a believing Christian I find the
differentiation made between the "historical Jesus" and the
"exalted Christ" to be somewhat undesirable, or at least unnecessary. When I say the name of Jesus – for example, during
prayer – I do not automatically plug into one or the other, but
am referring both to that life as we can discover it in Scripture
and the Christ of faith which has been preached throughout
two Christian millennia. I believe that for the confessing Christian any such distinction is ultimately meaningless.

*This article was originally presented before the Committee on Jewish
Relations of the Episcopal Diocese of New York on November 24, 1980.

Yet, for all that I have just said, it is precisely such a separation that is needed to discuss the topic at hand. For example, if we decided to approach the subject through a study of his life and teachings, we could go on for thirty-three years — Jesus' lifetime! — discussing such topics as:

Jesus: How Faithful Was He to the Law?

or:

Jesus: Where Can He Be Placed Within Judaism?

or:

Jesus: How Does His Teaching Compare/Contrast with Contemporary Pharasaical Thought?

or:

Jesus: Did He Really Consider Himself the Messiah?
And What Did the Title Mean to Him?

If we were to spend our time devoted only to the teachings of Jesus, or his relation to the Torah, etc., my own bias (and one I believe to be well-substantiated) is that we would necessarily come to the conclusion that Jesus is much more of a bond than he is a barrier between Christians and Jews. As Pinchas Lapide has expressed it, Jesus was Jewish in spirit in at least six respects:

1.) in his hope
2.) in his eschatology
3.) in his Jewish ethos
4.) in his blind trust in God
5.) in his very Jewish messianic impatience
6.) in his Jewish suffering[1]

Beyond this, Lapide feels a bond because of:

1.) Jesus' setting in life; the whole physical background
2.) the languages of prayer and worship — Hebrew and Aramaic
3.) the understanding of the Bible and its interpretation along rabbinical rules
4.) Jesus' oriental imagination — i.e., his parables were directly meant for the Jew familiar with the Bible

5.) the mutual concern for the land, or what Lapide refers to as "this anxious love for Israel with its thirst for redemption."[2]

Even where Jesus appears to be at odds with his milieu — in disputing with the Pharisees, for example — it could also be argued that he was only being faithful to a tradition in which the greatest luminaries were provokers of lively opposition among the people, from Moses on.

If you like we could also find verses such as Matthew 5:17 — "Do not think that I have come to abolish the Law or the Prophets; I have not come to abolish them but to fulfill them" — in order to emphasize that Jesus saw himself within the mainstream of Judaism. Christians might approach the subject in this way for a variety of reasons, not the least of which might be so that we can say to our Jewish friends, "See - he really *is* one of yours -and you can welcome him back as a brother!"

Yet, as important as this kind of discussion is, it is not adequate to dialogue on our question only from the perspective of the life of Jesus. Is Jesus a bond or a barrier? I believe that this can only begin to be answered for us when we examine the Christ of faith. For I believe, in the words of Jacob Jocz that, "Jewish reclamation of the historical Jesus is of no real significance to the Church or to the Synagogue. The discussion between Jews and Christians transcends historical interest, and is essentially a discussion of faith."[3] That is precisely what Lapide is referring to when he states that "what really separates us are 48 hours from the first Good Friday onward . . . just two days, but they are, of course, the decisive days on which more or less the whole of Christology rests."[4]

What is of the most concern to me for the purpose of this presentation is that I address myself to the recent efforts of certain Christian theologians in the interest of Jewish-Christian relations.

All of us are aware that there is a current trend within the Church to rediscover our Jewish roots; or, as this process has been called by Robert Gordis of the Jewish Theological Seminary and others, "the re-Judaizing of Christianity." I certainly consider myself to be a disciple of this theological re-thinking and believe with all my heart that great, great good will come from such a searching. Yet, I'm worried and my concern is directed specifically toward what certain Christian theologians are doing with the exalted Christ (again, making a distinction I do not care for) in their sincere (and I have no doubt about this sincerity) attempts to re-evaluate the Christian tradition in light of the Holocaust and for the improvement of Jewish-Christian relations. In the interest of time, let me cite *one* example, and one particular theologian. I do this in the hope that I do not misrepresent him in my desire to compress his thought succinctly.

In a paper entitled, "The Resurrection and the Holocaust," one of A. Roy Eckhart's major concerns is the importance of being faithful to Jewish categories of thinking and life. This leader in the field of Jewish-Christian relations states that "a genuine rediscovery of Jewishness *has to mean* the taking of historical fact with utter seriousness."[5] He says that because of the qualified extent to which Christian faith can accept new revelatory moments, Christianity has reduced history to a collection of interstices between an original past truth, the Resurrection, and a decisive coming, the Parousia, which, in the Christian's eyes, are the only truths that count. The logical outcome of this kind of schema is that even an event of such catastrophic proportions as the Holocaust has no real ultimate significance. Eckhardt believes — and for the most part I agree with him — that it is the teaching of a *consummated resurrection* which lies at the heart of Christian hostility to Jews and Judaism. However, for him, the cure to this cancer is not to be obtained by doctoring the resurrection; rather, he feels that we must excise it totally from the particular place it now holds within the Christian faith.

Eckhardt writes:

> "That Jewish man from Galilee sleeps now. He sleeps with the other Jewish dead, with all the disconsolate and scattered ones of the murder camps and with the unnumbered dead of the human and non-human family. But Jesus of Nazareth *shall* be raised. So, too, shall the small Hungarian children who were burned alive at Auschwitz . . . ."[6] Eckhardt says that the only way the hell of the Holocaust can be defeated is through the hope of a future resurrection, not one that is past. Eckhardt believes that this is the only possible conclusion, if we Christians, "who are calling for a reaffirmation of Jewishness mean what we say."[7]

I believe that what Eckhardt is saying about "consummated event" is extremely important and I also agree with Rosemary

Reuther that a discussion of "fulfilled vs. unfulfilled messianism" is at the heart of Jewish-Christian conflict and/or understanding. Nevertheless, even though I consider myself to be "meaning what I say" in my re-affirmation of Jewishness, I would consider this point in a different way — by the process of reinterpretation *without* removal. While I agree with Eckhardt that the resurrection of Jesus is not a "consummated event" as traditionally understood, I can affirm the thought of Paul van Buren much more when he says that the resurrection of Jesus Christ is not God's *last* word — but it is *a* word. And what I hear that word saying to me is this:

> "The resurrection of Jesus Christ means that the image of God cannot be destroyed; it gives the certainty that the path of the Torah is the right path; that the Word of God which requires us to do justice, to love kindness, and to walk humbly with our God can be trusted and discloses a future for us, and is a source of hope."[8]

In my view, there are a number of points within the Christian faith at which Christians are at the same time closest — and farthest — away from Jesus. The resurrection, when viewed from the perspective I have just shared, is one such point. Another is the Cross. It is precisely at the point of the Crucifixion, where Christians are brought by faith closest to the mystery of suffering — and hence, to Auschwitz and the Jewish people — that Jews undoubtedly feel the farthest from Christianity.

In the words of Jacob Jocz:

> "Thus, Church and Synagogue face each other; between them stands Jesus Christ. The Synagogue's "no" and the Church's "yes" are *not* no and yes to each other - but no and yes to Jesus of Nazareth, the son of God."[9]

I do not mean to imply by my above remarks that I consider Jesus' sonship to be dependent on whether or not he was raised, or that I think Eckhardt is somehow denying that sonship, for I do not. But I do not understand why in Eckhardt's mind the resurrection of Jesus seems to preclude a future event which will redeem all. Beyond that, I believe a personal reaffirmation of my Jewish heritage does not have to mean that I now must think only in Jewish categories. I also believe that Judaism and

Christianity must not be afraid of living creatively in eternal challenge to each other.

Is Jesus a bond or barrier? I have tried to give a few examples which show how he can be both of these, although I prefer "creative point of tension" to the word "barrier." I do not consider this to be an "either/or" situation. And yet, there is something larger, a "yes" to which we both can assent, the "yes" to which Roy Eckhardt was referring. We share the same hope, as we serve the same God. As a Christian, I believe that my hope *is* the Jewish hope: into which Christians have access through Jesus Christ; the hope "that reaches out beyond ourselves, for the renewal and completion of God's creation."[10]

Notes

1. Pinchas Lapide, in a paper "Is Jesus a Bond or Barrier? A Jewish-Christian Dialogue" with Hans Kung, *Journal of Ecumenical Studies*, p. 468.

2. *Ibid.* p. 467.

3. Jacob Jocz, *The Jewish People and Jesus Christ*, SPCK, London, 1954, p. 9.

4. Pinchas Lapide, "Is Jesus a Bond or Barrier?" p. 472.

5. A. Roy Eckardt, "The Resurrection and the Holocaust" (unpublished paper, p. 6).

6. *Ibid.* p. 13.

7. *Ibid.* p. 12.

8. Coos Schoneveld, in a paper, "Preface and Postscript," American Jewish Committee, Jerusalem.

9. Jacob Jocz, *The Jewish People and Jesus Christ*, p. 321.

10. Paul van Buren, *Concerning the Way*, Seabury Press, New York, 1980, p. 196.

Part V

ATTITUDES TO BE
DEVELOPED IN EDUCATION

Chapter 11

INTRODUCING JUDAISM:
THE FIRST COURSE AND ITS PROBLEMS

Jacob Neusner
Professor of Religious Studies,
Brown University,
Providence, Rhode Island

Lee A. Belford has devoted his career to improving relations between Jews and Christians through education. It is appropriate, therefore, to pay tribute to him by a discussion of an aspect of "religious education" not commonly deemed relevant to the work of educationists. I mean the academic study of religions in colleges and universities. In this paper I outline diverse approaches to an introductory course on Judaism to be given in an academic setting. My intent is to broaden the frame of discourse on the nurture of close and intimate religious and intellectual ties between Jews and Christians. For what we do in colleges and universities, in its way, may help people through learning and interpretation to understand and respect one another. In that way the distinctive task of the university — the acquisition of learning for the purpose of insight and understanding — may be carried out for the benefit of this other, and important, enterprise, the one of interfaith relations.

I

THE ELEMENTARY COURSE

An introductory course in a university, strictly speaking, is any course which has no prerequisite. Since, in the humanities (excluding language studies), it is unusual to require a prerequisite, most courses in fact introduce not only the subject but also the discipline. This is so without regard to the location of the course within the program of studies, that is, whether it is deemed for beginners or for advanced students, bears a low or a high number. And, it must be said, even courses for which a student must qualify by taking a prior subject in fact impose few demands; instructor's permission commonly replaces that prior course. So, in all, for the humanities, most of what we do is to introduce some part of the subject we teach. Our work is perpetually elementary.

There are courses, nonetheless, which address themselves to the fundamental issues of a subject or field. These serve to draw students to work in that field, on the one side, or to tell students pretty much all they will ever know about that field, on the other side. That is, they conventionally serve as the first experience of a student in the given subject, and, it is understood, they may also serve as the last. Or students may decide to take further subjects in that field. In the former aspect these courses fall under the category of performing "service," in that students from many different departments may elect them and, in the latter, they take their places as part of the "major."

It is the ambiguity of such courses and their clientele which makes teaching them especially interesting. We have to speak with many voices, portray our subject with multiple vision, address the most private issues and those accessible to our discipline and its modes of discourse, all at once.

There is a taxonomy of such courses to be specified. One type of introductory course presents the rudiments of a discipline, for example, explains the several methods used in the academic study of religions. A second type, which is quite distinct, presents the fundamental facts of a given religion, or of a given phenomenon affecting diverse religions, e.g., Judaism, or the nature of religious society. In this type, the methods used in the course may not be made explicit but, since data never speak for themselves but are given a voice by one method or another, methods once more require explication. A third type introduces the subject, "religion," or delineates the subject by some distinctive trait, for instance, "Catholicism-Protestantism-Judaism" or "the religions of the West" or "the religions of the Orient." This is a variation on the second type. What these three types of courses have in common is that they attempt to survey a vast range of material. The normal mode is to block and choose, that is, block out a wide range of data and choose, for careful study, some quite specific and concrete problem. This choice is to be suggestive for a wider range of issues.

A quite distinct kind of introductory course will present a much smaller topic or problem than "Judaism" or "Methods in the study of religions" or "the religions of the west" or "religion and society." It may take up instead a very narrow theme, such as "American Judaism" or "Zen Buddhism" or "medieval Christianity." Now as soon as I give these topics, the reader will have wondered how one may characterize them as "narrow" yet, compared to the earlier ones, they clearly represent another, and more limited, sort of course entirely. Yet, I maintain, these too in fact constitute introductory courses so long as students are not required to elect antecedent ones on that very subject, e.g., "religions in America" before "American Judaism," or "medieval history" before "medieval Christianity," or "Judaism in Europe" before "American Judaism." If a course does not directly relate to the materials of its successor, that is, of the course which it serves as prerequisite, then the successor-course is not an advanced course in any material sense. Since students begin the subject, the course introduces that subject. True, a "methods-course" will define how we approach a given subject. But it will not provide the student with knowledge of that subject, and, therefore, as I said, the course which does provide the elementary facts and undertake their preliminary interpretation must be deemed introductory.

I argue this proposition with some care so that the repertoire of suitable subjects for introductory courses on Judaism may be broadened. There is no reason that we should assume we know just what must be done for an introduction, that is, describe the "beliefs and practices of Judaism," or assume there is a normative course of some one kind, e.g., a history of the Jews or a history of Judaism. There is no limit to the range of topics and problems upon which we may draw for our introductory course, except our own imagination and academic conscience. These are criteria for the exercise of our taste and judgment on what is to be introduced and how we propose to introduce our subject. First, we have limited time. So we must choose something important, with lasting intellectual consequences. Second, the students have little preparation for the subject. The gentile and Christian ones have none, and their impressions are vague and vapid. The Jewish ones emerge from an educational system which, at best, imparts a smattering of

Hebrew. But they have rich access to their own memories and experiences, and these require sorting out and examination. Since we do not propose to teach Judaism under a scheme of intellectual *apartheid,* with one course for Jews, another for others, we have to find a set of questions and issues relevant to, and within the grasp of, students of diverse character. Third, and still more important, in introducing our subject we have to take full account of its context, that is, academic work. It follows that what we teach should be continuous with other studies in the university and department (discipline) in which we teach, and not with the system of Jewish or Christian schools, of whatever character, out of which some of our students emerge. The social definition of our setting, therefore, is the university and its intellectual continuum. A student coming into a course on Judaism should not have reason to wonder whether, in this setting, he confronts essentially distinctive modes of thought, an agendum of learning fundamentally different from that which governs other courses in the humanities. These seem to me some of the important criteria in the decisions to be made on how to teach introductory courses on Judaism in departments of religious studies.

By now it should be quite obvious that no one course may claim to exhaust the possibilities of introduction. Any course is a very small and concrete, but wholly practical, judgment upon elevated issues of the intellect. It is applied reason and practical and practiced learning. Each instructor, therefore, will make judgments and decisions. Of greater consequence, as we learn from what works and what does not work, and as our own tastes and ideas change, the character of our courses, even when they bear the same title, will change, too. It is unthinkable to me that a course, even using pretty much the same textbooks and following the same sequence of themes and problems, will essentially replicate itself from one year to the next. Our courses are the expression of ourselves. If we repeat them unchanged from year to year, it means we either have made no mistakes, or have not learned from, or even recognized, the mistakes we have made.

These general observations will take on greater meaning when brought to bear upon several specific examples of introductory courses I have given. I offer my own work as an example not to be followed but to be explained and criticized. All we have to offer is experience, the concrete example of a theory followed at one time and dropped in favor of some other. Teaching is an art, at which no one can claim to excel all the time, or needs to admit to constant failure either. To learn how to practice an art, all we are able to do is to see how others have practiced it, to learn from their errors, and perhaps to copy their successes and hope they work for us, too. If I claim for myself any merit at all, it is merely the courage to admit in public to what I have done in my classroom, and to offer for the experiment and criticism of others the sorts of things which, over twenty years of teaching, I have come to think worthwhile.

II

THE PURPOSE OF A COURSE-SYLLABUS

What I present for analysis are the syllabi of a number of courses given over the past few years. The purpose of a course-syllabus should be specified. It is not merely a "bibliography." Unlike the practice in European and Israeli universities, we do not merely hand out lists of books and expect students to find their own way. Perhaps we should. But our educational tasks are distinctive and would not be well served in such a way. A syllabus in our hands specifies some things and signals others by indirection. It specifies where a student should be at a particular time, what books a student should possess, what pages in those books should be read for a given session. Students learn best when they know where they are in the unfolding of a subject, and they are (for good or ill) happiest when they know what is expected of them and believe they can meet those expectations. A syllabus is therefore essential, in our approach to teaching, to provide the students with a clear sense of the order and structure of a course (assuming the course is a well-planned and orderly exposition of its subject).

But a syllabus serves a second purpose, and this is why it should be analyzed and carefully unpacked. It states a theory of the subject and makes decisive judgments about how the subject should unfold, what comes first and what comes second. In all, it makes an emphatic statement of a theory of the logic of its subject. A course lacking a theory of the subject simply presents information, but no ideas, and surely no insight. A course which teaches a subject in one way, and not in some other, because of a larger theory of the character and inner logic of the subject, will provide a measure of insight. For the ideal is for a student to see not merely the traits of the subject, but how the subject works. Taking apart the theme of the course and seeing its inner parts — these are, in my judgment, the worthwhile modes of learning. Finally, a course which teaches a subject in such a way as to exemplify a larger problem or to point toward the greater potentialities and implications of this particular chapter of learning is the highest goal. That is when a university becomes worthy of its name: a place of discourse on many things, but from the perspective of encompassing reason. Occasionally I find myself able to teach a course on Judaism from which students learn something about the nature of religion. I may succeed in so shaping a subject as to illustrate a larger problem of interpretation, a larger scheme of knowledge. On those rare moments I should be prepared to claim success for my work. In the syllabi that follow, these goals are going to be detected principally in the introductory statements about the purpose of a course, in the headings of the several units of a course, and in the character of the reading which I assign.

One thing will become obvious at the outset. I have edited or written the majority of the books which I use in my elementary courses. The reason is that most of these books are anthologies, with the opinions of many different scholars amply represented. I brought them into being for diverse kinds of courses which I teach. A very few of them are wholly under my authorship and speak out of my own scholarly work. I regard it as a responsibility of scholars to address students with a clear and accessible account of the main, and usable, results of disciplined learning. This I have done. A few of them are out-and-out textbooks, in which I provide what I conceive to be a coherent account of the subject mainly in my own words, not as an anthology, and also not as an account of my own scholarly work. These generally serve to provide a framework for my larger pedagogical work. To assess the courses outlined here, it may be necessary to consult the specific readings assigned in the several anthologies. Otherwise the shape and structure of the readings will hardly be clear.

In recent years I have made fairly extensive use of movies. Very belatedly, I have noticed that students learn effectively through what they see and hear, because they are raised on television. Instead of bemoaning that self-evident fact, I have decided to try to make use of it. The main educational task is to use the various movies to exemplify important problems, to allow the students to derive both information and understanding from what they see. This requires not only the showing of movies but, obviously, discussion of what one is to look for, before the movie, and analysis of what one has seen, afterward. It is principally for the modern phase of the history of Judaism that movies are useful as primary sources. I tend to look for different ones from one year to the next, mainly because I find it dull to see ones I have already seen. But there are types of movies which remain the same, and for certain units, these types will prove useful every year.

One type of movie must help the students see the shift in the role and aspirations of women in Judaism, which I regard as a critical subject for contemporary study. For this purpose *Hester Street* is exceedingly effective, and *I Love You, Rosa* may serve as well. There are numerous effective movies on the destruction of European Jewry, and one valuable exercise is to analyze the different viewpoints of the movie-makers upon the common subject under discussion. *The Eighty-First Blow*, for example, proves to yield nearly as much insight about the operative civil religion of the State of Israel as it does about the events of 1933 to 1945. The reader will notice that I invariably cancel class on the day of a movie. The reason is that I want the students to take the movie seriously and to regard it as integral to the work of the course. I also advertise the movie so that people in the University and community feel free to come. The costs are negligible. (We enjoy the support of the Bureau of Jewish Education of the Jewish Federation of Rhode Island in this connection, as well as in bringing lecturers, whose presentations are integrated into several courses in Judaic studies.)

III

A CHRONOLOGICAL INTRODUCTION TO THE HISTORY OF JUDAISM

The first course for consideration is the most conventional. It is an "Introduction to Judaism" which introduces the subject along essentially historical and chronological lines. It outlines the several periods in the history of Judaism and describes the principal traits of the "Judaism" expressed in those periods. Since what emerges is a rather one-dimensional account of this and that, not a cogent picture of a religion, Judaism, I made the critical conceptual issue of the course the problem of defining Judaism out of the diverse data assembled along the way.

The problem of this course is to define "Judaism," in particular to solve the dilemma of finding appropriate definition for a diverse and ancient religious tradition. The course consists of lectures and sections. Reading assignments, which average 100 pages a week, are to be completed by the section meetings at which they are to be discussed.

Introduction to the course. The problem of defining a definition. Recommended: Neusner, *Understanding Rabbinic Judaism*, pp. 405-411.

I. The Biblical Foundation of Judaism
Neusner, *Way of Torah*, pp. 1-8.
Kaufman, "The Biblical Age," in Schwarz, *Great Ages and Ideas of the Jewish People*, p. 3-92.
Spiegel, "Amos vs. Amaziah," in *Life of Torah*, pp. 31-40.
Genesis 1-2.
The Book of *Amos*.
The Book of *Deuteronomy*.

II. Varieties of Judaism before A.D. 70, Sectarian and Normative
Ralph Marcus, "The Hellenistic Age," in Schwarz, *Great Ages*, pp. 95-142.
Geza Vermes, *The Dead Sea Scrolls in English*, pp. 11-68, 69-94, 149-68.
Apocrypha: Ecclesiasticus: Jesus Son of Sirach, Chapters 24, 35, 36, 38, 44-50.
New Testament: *Matthew, Romans* 9-11, *Galatians*.

III. Pharisaism Before 70
Neusner, *From Politics to Piety: the Emergence of Pharisaic Judaism*, pp. 1-45, 81-154.

IV. Rabbinic Judaism: Origins and Character
Neusner, *Way of Torah*, pp. 9-28.
_____, *There We Sat Down: Talmudic Judaism in the Making*, pp. 19-140.
_____, *Understanding Rabbinic Judaism*, pp. 11-23.
Recommended: Gerson Cohen, "The Talmudic Age," in *Great Ages*, pp. 143-214.

V. The Religious Life of (Rabbinic) Judaism

Neusner, *Life of Torah*, pp. 17-24, 81-150.
Guttmann, "The Religious Ideas of Talmudic Judaism," in *Understanding Rabbinic Judaism*, p. 37-52.

VI. **Philosophy, Mysticism, and Rabbinic Judaism**

Abraham Halkin, "The Judeo-Islamic Age," in *Great Ages*, pp. 215-65.
I. Twersky, "Maimonides," in *Understanding Rabbinic Judaism*, pp. 185-212.
Neusner, *Way of Torah*, pp. 50-57.
Gershom G. Scholem, "General Characteristics of Jewish Mysticism," in *Understanding Rabbinic Judaism*, pp. 243-76.
Recommended: M. Kaplan, "Medieval Jewish Theology," in *Understanding Rabbinic Judaism*, pp. 133-46.
Abraham J. Heschel, "The Mystical Element of Judaism" in *Understanding Rabbinic Judaism*, pp. 277-300.

VII. **Jews and Judaism in Modern Times**

Salo Baron, "The Modern Age," in *Great Ages*, pp. 315-419.
Neusner, *Way of Torah*, pp. 61-94.
Louis Ginzberg, "Israel Salanter," in *Understanding Rabbinic Judaism*, pp. 353-82.

VIII. **American Judaism**

Neusner, *American Judaism: Adventure in Modernity*, pp. vii-viii, 1-86, 143-54.
Emanuel Rackman, "Orthodoxy"; Abraham J. Feldman and Jakob J. Petuchowski, "Reform Judaism"; and Theodore Friedman, "Conservative Judaism," in *Life of Torah*, pp. 155-83.

IX. **Contemporary Judaism and Zionism**

Baron, "The Modern Age," in *Great Ages*, pp. 420-54.
Jack Nusan Porter and Peter Dreier, eds., *Jewish Radicalism*, pp. 1-50.
Neusner, *Life of Torah*, pp. 205-34.

X. **Conclusion**

Neusner, *Way of Torah*, pp. 95-99.
_____, *Life of Torah*, pp. 5-16.
Reading period assignment: Neusner, *Invitation to the Talmud* (Harper & Row).

IV

AN ANALYTICAL INTRODUCTION
TO THE SYSTEMS OF JUDAISM

While the course outlined above proved interesting, it seemed to me a fresh approach would promise more useful insight. Specifically, I wanted to see whether, instead of simply outlining a sequence of "Judaisms" and asking whether it was possible to define "Judaism" out of the diverse data produced over the centuries, I might entirely eliminate the issue of historical chronology. What is important *about* "Essenism" or "Hasidism" or "Talmudic Judaism," after all, is not when these kinds of Judaism flourished but, rather, *how* they worked. What is it that we learn from them which might prove helpful in the analysis of contemporary expressions of Judaism and of other religions? For that purpose, analysis of a *system* within Judaism, with due respect for its particular historical and social setting, seemed to me a preferable experiment. The opening paragraph spells out the problem.

The reader will notice that the page-assignments are considerably smaller than in the earlier course. As I learn more about teaching, I have come to prefer that the students read a smaller number of pages with great care, rather than a larger number in a rushed and often sloppy way. In the former sort of assignment lies the possibility of learning.

This course explores the proposition that, at various points in history, the Jews have set forth distinct and distinctive "systems" — ways of living and world-views — which defined and explained the worlds in which they lived. Each of these systems, moreover, had to deal with certain constants, characteristic of the Jews as a group for the whole of their history. The course addresses three problems: (1) description of some of the systems of Judaism (specifically: Biblical, Essene, Rabbinic, Zionist, Reform, and American), (2) the interpretation of these systems by reference to the world meant to be explained by them, and (3) the comparison of the several systems subject to description and interpretation.

I. **Introduction to the Course**
II. **Two Biblical Systems**
Read: The Book of Deuteronomy, The Book of Leviticus.

III. The Essenes' System
Read: Geza Vermes, *The Dead Sea Scrolls in English*, pp. 11-52, 69-148.

IV. Out of the Holocaust: Formation of the Rabbinic System
Read: Neusner, *Between Time and Eternity*, pp. 1-46.
Neusner, ed., *Understanding Jewish Theology*, pp. 11-62.

V. The Maturing of the Rabbinic System: Talmudic Judaism
Read: Neusner, *There We Sat Down*, pp. ix-xx, 19-140.

VI. Traits of (Rabbinic) Judaism
Read: Neusner, *Between Time and Eternity*, pp. 47-114.
Neusner, ed., *Understanding Jewish Theology*, pp. 89-148.

VII. The Crisis of Modernity: Tradition and Change
Movie: "I LOVE YOU, ROSA"
This is instead of a class session.
Read: Neusner, *Between Time and Eternity*, pp. 115-30.
Neusner, ed., *Understanding Jewish Theology*, pp. 229-70.
Neusner, *American Judaism: Adventure in Modernity*, pp. 1-13.

VIII. Theological Systems and Modernization: Reform Judaism
Read: Neusner, ed., *Understanding Jewish Theology*, pp. 149-64, 196-214, 259-70.
Neusner, *Between Time and Eternity*, pp. 130-45.
Neusner, *American Judaism, Adventure in Modernity*, pp. 117-42.

IX. Assimilationism as a System of Judaism
Movie: "THE JAZZ SINGER"
This is instead of a class session.
Read: Philip Roth, *Portnoy's Complaint*.
Neusner, *American Judaism: Adventure in Modernity*, pp. 61-86.

X. Zionism as a System of Judaism
Class lecture: David Goodblatt, University of Haifa
Read: *Between Time and Eternity*, pp. 145-54.
Understanding Jewish Theology, pp. 73-88.
American Judaism: Adventure in Modernity, pp. 87-116.

XI. "The Holocaust" and Judaism
Movies: "NIGHT AND FOG," "GENOCIDE"
Read: *Understanding Jewish Theology*, pp. 163-94.
Between Time and Eternity, pp. 154-66.
Elie Wiesel, *Gates of the Forest*.

XII. **American Judaism**
Read: *Between Time and Eternity,* pp. 166-76.
American Judaism: Adventure in Modernity, pp. ix-xx, 15-34,
35-60, 143-54.

FINAL

You will be asked to describe two or three "systems" in the
history of Judaism, to compare them to one another, and to
evaluate each in terms of the on-going tasks of any system
put forward out of Judaism. The final must be typed. It may
go from 10 to 15 pages, but no longer than that. The work of
systematic analysis, not description, is at the center of the
assignment.

V

A PARTICULAR TOPIC (I)
AMERICAN JUDAISM

It should not be thought that the only kind of introductory
course is one which tells the whole story, from beginning to
end, of the history and structure of Judaism. Another kind of
elementary or "first course" is one which takes a specific topic
and raises questions in the analysis of that topic. The results of
this analysis will, in due course, serve for the study of quite
fresh themes. A fair exemplification of this kind of course is one
on American Judaism, a very attractive subject for our students,
because nearly all of them have studied American history, and
most of them have some impressions of, or even experience
with, Judaism as it is formulated in this country and in Canada.
The readings in the anthologies, *Understanding American Judaism,* are quite diverse and introduce a wide variety of movements
and viewpoints.

The purpose of this course is to analyze and interpret the
nature of religion in modern and contemporary times, using
Judaism in America as the specimen. What does it mean to
"be religious"? What are the ambiguities of religiosity? What
does it mean not to "be religious"? What are the complexities
of secularity? How does inherited religious culture change

and, at the same time, affect the nature of change? These questions intersect with another set. What is American about American Judaism? What is Judaic, carrying forward abiding phenomena of classical or Rabbinic Judaism? And there is yet a third set of questions: What is the meaning of "Jewishness," the ethnic, professedly non-religious congeries of social and cultural traits emergent in contemporary American Jewish life?

I. Asking the Question
Neusner, *American Judaism: Adventure in Modernity,* pp. vii-viii, 1-3, 143-53.
Neusner, *Understanding American Judaism,* I, pp. xvii-xxv, 3-65; II,303-26.
Chapman, *Jewish-American Literature,* pp. 279-99.

II. Uprooting and Replanting
Neusner, *American Judaism: Adventure in Modernity,* pp. 4-9.
Glazer, *American Judaism,* pp. 12-78.
Handlin, *The Uprooted,* pp. 7-57, 85-104.
Chapman, *Jewish-American Literature,* pp. 238-53.

III. First Fruits: Children and Grandchildren
Nathan Glazer, *American Judaism,* pp. 79-129.
Oscar Handlin, *The Uprooted,* pp. 105-269.
Chapman, *Jewish-American Literature,* pp. 193-207, 37-45, 307-309, 569-86.

IV. American Judaism as Religion
1. *The Rabbi*
Neusner, *American Judaism: Adventure in Modernity,* pp. 35-60.
Neusner, *Understanding American Judaism,* I, pp. 103-14, 141-215.

V. American Judaism as Religion
2. Reform and Conservative Judaism
Neusner, *Understanding American Judaism,* II, pp. 3-104, 195-218, 247-302.

VI. American Judaism as Religion
3. Orthodoxy
Neusner, *Understanding American Judaism,* I, pp. 269-84; II, pp. 105-94.

VII. The "American Jewish Way of Life"
Neusner, *American Judaism: Adventure in Modernity,* pp.

9-13, 15-34, 61-85.
Neusner, *Understanding American Judaism*, I, pp. 69-101.
Marshall Sklare, *America's Jews*, pp. 103-54.

VIII. **Modes of "Jewishness"**
   1. Culture
Philip Roth, *Goodbye Columbus.*
Chapman, *Jewish-American Literature*, pp. 694-727, 654-64, 346-50, 387-406.

IX. **Modes of "Jewishness"**
   2. Zionism, Israelism
Neusner, *American Judaism: Adventure in Modernity*, pp. 87-116.
Porter and Dreier, *Jewish Radicalism*, pp. 51-118.
Sklare, *America's Jews*, pp. 210-23.
Chapman, *Jewish-American Literature*, pp. 546-59.

X. **Modes of "Jewishness"**
   3. Radical Jewishness, New Jews, Women
Nathan Glazer, *American Judaism*, pp. 151-86.
Porter and Dreier, *Jewish Radicalism*, pp. 1-50, 149-78, 243-72.
Suggestions for reading period assignment:
The Immigrant Experience:
Moses Rischin, *The Promised City. New York's Jews, 1870-1914.*
Mark Zborowski and Elizabeth Herzog, *Life Is with People.*
The History of American Jews:
Henry L. Feingold, *Zion in America.*
Oscar Handlin, *Adventure in Freedom.*
Zionism and American Jews:
Melvin I. Urofsky, *American Zionism from Herzl to the Holocaust.*
American Jewish Literature:
Allen Guttmann, *The Jewish Writer in America: Assimilation and the Crisis of Identity.*
A Novel of American Judaism:
Ludwig Lewisohn, *The Island Within.*
A theological novel:
Arthur A. Cohen, *In the Days of Simon Stern.*
Some American Judaic Theologians and Theologies:
Richard L. Rubenstein, *After Auschwitz.*
Mordecai M. Kaplan, *The Future of the American Jew.*
Herman Wouk, *This Is My God.*
Alan W. Miller, *The God of Daniel S.: In Search of the American Jew.*
Milton Steinberg, *A Partisan Guide to the Jewish Problem.*

"Radical Jewishness," etc.:
J. Neusner, ed., *Contemporary Judaic Fellowship: In Theory and in Practice.*

VI

A PARTICULAR TOPIC (II)
ZIONISM

Yet another introductory course takes up not a conventional phenomenon of Judaism, such as American Judaism, but rather a single movement. For this purpose I select one of two movements which have reached their full promise both in theory (theology, ideology) and in social expression and institutional potentiality, Reform Judaism and Zionism. Zionism is much easier to teach, because of the cogency of its theoretical issues and because of the clearcut beginning, middle, and end which, in the nature of things, the movement exhibits. In the past I have tended to end the course in 1948. In the present version, I have chosen to devote a good deal of attention to Zionism in America and, more especially, to the Zionist analysis of American Jewry and of American Judaism.

This course explores the diverse theoretical systems which, before 1948, reached the conclusion that the Jews should create a Jewish state, and which further explored the character of that state after it would be brought into being, the politics required to accomplish that goal, the definition of the meaning of "being Jewish" created in the light of that goal, and the diverse other powerful intellectual forces subsumed under the movement of Zionism. The stress is on the interplay between political and social theory, on the one side, and the political and social realities of the Jewish people, on the other.

I. **The Formation of Zionist Theory**
Introduction to the Course
Hertzberg, *The Zionist Idea,* pp. 14-100.
Zionism in the Nineteenth Century
Howard Sachar, *A History of Israel,* pp. 3-36.
Hertzberg, pp. 116-40, 178-98.

Herzl
Amos Elon, *Herzl*, pp. 97-186, 221-47.
Sachar, pp. 36-63.
Hertzberg, pp. 204-30.
II. **Zionist Theory as Politics and Eschatology**
Zionist Theory to 1948:
Ahad HaAm. Klatzkin
Sachar, pp. 65-138.
Hertzberg, pp. 247-77, 314-28.
Under the Mandate: Zionism and Socialism
Sachar, pp. 138-62, 163-94, 249-78.
Hertzberg, pp. 329-97.
Movie: I LOVE YOU, ROSA.
Zionism and the Intellectuals
Hertzberg, pp. 467-544.
III. **Zionism as Actuality: Israel and America**
Zionism and the State of Israel
Sachar, pp. 580-614, 667-740.
Hertzberg, pp. 545-620.
Movie: THE JAZZ SINGER.
Israeli Zionism Today
Rael Jean Isaac, *Israel Divided*, pp. 1-73, 138-63.
Sachar, pp. 740-838.
Evening lecture on Israeli life today, David Goodblatt, Haifa
University.
Movie: NIGHT AND FOG. THE HOLOCAUST ("World at War").
American Zionism and Palestinism ("Pro-Israelism")
Yonathan Shapiro, *Leadership of the American Zionist Organization*, pp. 3-76, 207-61.
The Zionist Critique of American Jewry
Ben Halpern, *The American Jew*, pp. 11-69-97-160.
The Zionist Claim Upon American Jewry
Hillel Halkin, *Letters to an American-Jewish Friend*, pp. 1-76, 153-246.

VII

**A PERSONAL COURSE
JUDAISM IN LATE ANTIQUITY**

Finally, I provide the syllabus of a course in which I introduce not a subject or a problem but something quite particular: my own work in its context. I think students should have access to the scholarly interests of professors, even though, in the nature of things, the larger work of teaching will require attention to larger and more representative aspects of a subject. Still, once in three or four years I give a course in which, in the main, the students read my work in the context of its larger historical and methodological setting: Judaism in late antiquity. The present version of the course required far too much reading and seemed to me to yield greater capacity to speak learnedly of problems of method than to form intelligent accounts of the character of the Judaism of ancient times and of the substance of its sources. I doubt that I would again offer the course in this particular formulation. But it may provide some idea of one approach to the problem of teaching one's own scholarly *oeuvres*, which I think does have a valid place within the undergraduate curriculum.

The problem of this course is the description of Judaism out of the diverse sources – literary and archaeological – of the period 70 through 640.

Introduction to the course
I. **The World of Late Antiquity**
The Tripartite World of Ancient Times: Iranian, Roman, and the Third World of Semitic and Other Peoples.
Peter Brown, *The World of Late Antiquity: from Marcus Aurelius to Muhammad*, pp. 7-188.
M. Avi-Yonah, *The Jews of Palestine: A Political History from the Bar Kokhba War to the Arab Conquest.*
II. **The Formation of Rabbinic Judaism**
The Definition of Rabbinic Judaism
Neusner, *Between Time and Eternity*, pp. 1-114.
Neusner, *Understanding Rabbinic Judaism*, pp. 1336.
The Formative Period of Rabbinic Judaism: Yavneh
Neusner, *First-Century Judaism in Crisis: Yohanan ben Zakkai and the Renaissance of Torah*, pp. 1-200.
Neusner, *Eliezer ben Hyrcanus*, vols. I-II.
Neusner, *Development of a Legend: Studies on the Traditions concerning Yohanan ben Zakkai.*
Neusner, *A Life of Yohanan ben Zakkai.*
III. **Mishnah**
Neusner, *Invitation to the Talmud: A Teaching Book*, pp. 1-87.

Neusner, *A History of the Mishnaic Law of Purities*, II, pp. 221-56.

Neusner, *The Rabbinic Traditions about the Pharisees*, Vol. III.

Neusner, *Modern Study of the Mishnah*.

IV. **Talmud**

Neusner, *Invitation to the Talmud*, pp. 87-247.

Neusner, *Formation of the Babylonian Talmud*.

V. **Talmudic Judaism**

The Use of Talmudic Evidence for the Study of Judaism

Neusner, *Talmudic Judaism in Sasanian Babylonia*, pp. 3-12.

Neusner, *A History of the Jews in Babylonia*, III, pp. ix-xxi, 272-338; IV, pp. 183-278.

Neusner, *A History of the Jews in Babylonia*, I (2nd ed.), pp. 122-78; II, pp. 92-125; III, pp. 41-271; IV, pp. 73-182.

Cases, History, and History of Religions: the Rabbi

Neusner, *Talmudic Judaism in Sasanian Babylonia*, pp. 25-138.

Neusner, *A History of the Jews in Babylonia*, V, pp. 1-342.

VI. **Synagague Art**

The Art of the Synagogue and the Religion of the Rabbis

Ernest Namenyi, *The Essence of Jewish Art*, pp. 1-80.

Erwin Goodenough, *Jewish Symbols in the Greco-Roman Period*, XII, pp. 1-157.

Pierre du Bourguet, *Early Christian Painting*.

Neusner, *Early Rabbinic Judaism*, pp. 139-87.

Smith, Review, *Journal of Biblical Literature*, 86 (1967), pp. 53-68.

Bernard Goldman, *The Sacred Portal: A Primary Symbol in Ancient Judaic Art*.

Dura Europos and Its Synagogue

Goodenough, *Jewish Symbols in the Greco-Roman Period*, XII, pp. 158-98.

Carl Kraeling, *The Synagogue*, pp. 321-63.

Neusner, *Early Rabbinic Judaism*, pp. 188-208.

J. Gutmann, *The Dura-Europos Synagogue*.

A. D. Nock, "The Synagogue Murals of Dura Europos," in *Harry A. Wolfson Jubilee Volume*, II.

E. Bickerman, Review, in *Harvard Theological Review*, 58 (1965), pp. 127-51.

A. D. Nock, *Essays in Religion and the Ancient World*, ed. Zeph Stewart, I, pp. 459-68; II, pp. 877-918.

VII. **Archaeological Evidence of Judaism**

The Magical Bowls

Neusner, *A History of the Jews in Babylonia*, V, pp. 217-44.
Neusner, *Talmudic Judaism in Sasanian Babylonia*, pp. 13-24.
M. Margaliot, ed., *Sefer Harazim.*
M. Smith, "Hekhalot Rabbati," in A. Altmann, ed., *Biblical and Other Studies.*
Neusner, *History of the Jews in Babylonia*, V, pp. 343-75.
VIII. **Christian Writers on Judaism**
Aphrahat
Neusner, *Aphrahat and Judaism*, pp. 1-18, 19-67, 84-112, 123-95, 242-44.
Neusner, *Aphrahat and Judaism*, pp. 68-83, 113-22, 196-241.
Robert Murray, *Symbols of Church and of Kingdom.*
A. Lukyn Williams, *Adversus Judaeos: A Bird's Eye View of Christian Apologiae until the Renaissance.*
George F. Moore, Christian Writers on Judaism, *Harvard Theological Review* 14 (1921), pp. 197-254.
IX. **Talmudic and Contemporary Judaism**
The Uses of Talmudic Judaism by Modern Jews
Neusner, *Between Time and Eternity*, pp. 115-76.
Neusner, *Contemporary Judaic Fellowship in Theory and in Practice*, pp. 1-50, 67-74, 121-48, 239-70.
Neusner, *Contemporary Judaic Fellowship*, pp. 51-66, 75-120, 149-238.

VIII

CONCLUSION

These syllabi are offered not principally to serve as models but primarily to stimulate others to give thought to the potentialities of the "introductory course." One kind of course which I do not offer is an introduction to Jewish religious belief and practice, to "the theology of Judaism," and to similar, essentially theological kinds of courses. The reason is that I think such courses obscure the critical problematic of studying Judaism as a contemporary religion. They impose upon the study of Judaism categories of greater value for the study of Christianity. The definition of what it is that we study when we study religion seems to me to require attention to religion not as theology and ritual but as an expression of a world-view and a way of living, as a mode of organizing society and creating and expressing culture.

In these aspects the data for the Judaic experience are remarkably rich.

Moreover, within that definition supplied to us by anthropology, not theology, we are able to take seriously the "Jewishness" of people whose expression of Judaism diverges from the patterns conventionally understood as "religious" — no required believing, little church-going, for instance. These people experiment, in ways I think particularly interesting, with the potentialities of the Judaic tradition in the circumstances of modern and contemporary society. What is important about Judaism, so far as the Jews of modernity shape and express something legitimately deemed to fall within the tradition of Judaism, is not their irreligiosity (and I am not prepared to concede they are not "religious" in important and suggestive ways). It is their capacity to revise and reshape inherited culture and tradition into something fully expressive of their humanity.

In short, Judaism must tell us how to introduce Judaism — Judaism, and not Christianity in its more conventional phases, or the model of any other important religion of our own day. Judaism will for its part make a contribution to the shaping of the definition of religion and of the agendum for the study of religion. But it can do so only when the interesting issues yielded by Judaism are permitted to stand at the head of the scholarly program. Telling our students "what the Jews believe" and how "the Jews practice their religion" describes only a part of the data and, in my own judgment, not necessarily the most interesting part. Indeed, I should claim that the reason the study of Judaism finds so comfortable a niche in the humanities is the very complexity of the human data to be learned and interpreted.

The relevance, finally, of introductory courses such as these to the larger theme, "attitudes to be developed in education," may be stated in only a few words. Gentile and Christian students acquire in courses such as these both information and familiarity. To them Judaism is not alien anymore. It is a religious tradition, with distinctive traits and beliefs, which they feel confident they understand, in some appropriate way, and are able to interpret. It is the strangeness of Judaism to the Christian which in some part makes Judaism appear to be threatening, disreputable, and fearful. Then all of the unfortunate words about "the Jews" or "the Pharisees" in the New Testament take on immediate and terrible meaning. With understanding and a sense of appreciation, by contrast, comes the capacity for respect and even esteem.

College courses about Judaism do not engage in apologetics. But they do, and should, provide the occasion for illumination which leads to understanding. If we understand a religion, we can comprehend the religious convictions and observances of its adherents. It is this quest for understanding of Judaism which I think is well served by the sorts of introductory courses I have outlined here, and by those many other kinds of introductory courses which others may develop. As tens of thousands of college students encounter courses such as these, it seems to me likely that a fresh and sound appreciation for Judaism will make its way and vastly improve the intellectual encounter of Christian and Jew. Surely this is a kind of enterprise well in accord with the life's work of Lee A. Belford. For if, in the words of Salo W. Baron, anti-Semitism comes in part from "dislike of the unlike," then through learning, the different may be made, if not less different, at least more familiar and more readily understood.

Chapter 12

AN INCONCLUSIVE UNSCIENTIFIC POSTSCRIPT

Paul R. Carlson
Executor Director, Northeastern Pennsylvania
Congregations in Christian Mission,
Scranton, Pennsylvania

A small group of rather sophisticated Southern Presbyterian women had gathered for their monthly study of the Gospel of Mark. As with Circle groups across their denomination,[1] they had previously considered the background of this Gospel, and now they were about to engage in a study of Mark's use of the title, "Son of David."

Hot stuff. Huh?

The lesson writer herself had defined "Son of David" as an expression of "a nationalistic and military feature" of the messianic expectation of the Jews of Jesus' age.[2] It was especially popular, she noted, among ". . . the Zealots, the revolutionaries of the day, because of their expectations of a nationalistic, warrior-type king." As "a descendant of David," she said, Jesus is portrayed in Mark as ". . . the true King of Israel, a royal Messiah."[4]

> Jesus reinterprets the popular expectation from a Messiah being a national deliverer to a Messiah who brings sight to all who will see and understanding to all those who will hear . . . Jesus, the Son of David, reaches out in love and compassion to bring healing to all people and to all nations.[5]

All hints of triuimphalism aside, Circle members zeroed in on a single question that dangled provocatively at the end of this lesson in the study guide. The question was this: "Is the state of

Israel today related or not to the historic past tied to the title 'Son of David'? How?"[6]

Even if one grants that the editors inadvertently missed the lower case "s" in reference to a sovereign state, one still finds the question itself rather awkward. In its most neutral form, is it possible that the writer intended to ask: Regardless of the relationship of the modern Jewish State to the historic past (i.e., the Biblical period), is the State of Israel today tied to the title "Son of David"? If so, how? Or, perhaps, two questions actually were intended: (1) Is the modern Jewish State in any way related to that of the Biblical period? (2) Is the State of Israel today tied to the title "Son of David"? If so, how?

Whatever the case, this small group of Southern Presbyterian women appeared to be less interested in messianic designations and far more concerned about gas tanks, American tax dollars, and what Anwar Sadat himself repeatedly called "Jimmy's Treaty."

There was little doubt from the ensuing discussion that the question for these women was how world Jewry could be so presumptuous as to even think that there could be any relationship between the State of Israel today and the Israel of the Biblical period. For example, Lulane, a college graduate and former Peace Corps volunteer, expressed bewilderment, if not hostility, that the Jews would seek a national homeland in the land of Abraham, Isaac, and Jacob. "What right do these people have," she asked, "to move in on this particular spot in the world and claim it as their own?"

The question was directed to the minister's wife, a woman whose parents supported Carl McIntire's so-called Twentieth Century Reformation, as well as that system of doctrine expounded in the Scofield Bible. Three decades of marriage to a Presbyterian minister have not dampened her faith that God still has great things in store for His ancient covenant people Israel. So it was quite in keeping with convictions held from childhood that she answered Lulane's question with one of her own. "Don't you agree," she asked, "that when we see the Jewish people becoming established in their homeland we are seeing prophecy fulfilled?"

"But when we talk about Jews," Lulane parried, "aren't we talking about a religion?"

Personal involvement in Jewish-Christian activities were about to pay off for this erstwhile daughter of American Fundamentalism turned mistress of the manse. "I think we're saying that

People, Land and Torah go together," she replied. "No matter where Jews have settled, they have been—and often still are—considered outsiders, except in Israel. In prewar Germany, for instance, the Jews considered themselves Germans first and foremost. But the Germans really never accepted them as anything other than Jews."

But some women had a ready response for that one. The town traditionally has remained *Judenfrei*, except for a young expatriate from New York City who is married to a gentile. There are also within the population a few well-hidden *meshumadim* and a couple of *Mischlinge*.[7] However, even so scant a Jewish presence was enough to reveal anti-Semitism virtually without Jews! Jews just didn't assimilate very well because of what these women perceived to be Jewish traits—"shrewdness," "money-makers," "penny-pinchers." Or, as the mayor's sister-in-law put it: "You usually think of Jews making money and owning businesses."

At this point, the minister's wife recalled that her husband had delivered an address on the Holocaust before the local Ministerial Association a week earlier and, in the question-and-answer period which followed, was quizzed, not about anti-Semitism and genocide, but rather about "the economic status of German Jews during the Weimar period." Now, as then, the pastor's spouse recalled that *Kristallnacht* served to show where much of prewar Germany's capital was concentrated.

She told Circle members that the mindless crowds thought they were driving out Jewish merchants when they burned synagogues and smashed plate glass in hundreds of stores operated by Jews. "Only later did top Nazis like Hermann Goering learn that the properties themselves were leased to Jewish businessmen by German owners," she noted. "Goering was infuriated when he learned that good Aryan insurance companies would go bankrupt if they had to pay fellow gentiles for the destruction." Then, she added: "In the end, of course, the Jews themselves were forced to pay for this Night of Broken Glass. Aryan owners and insurance carriers got off scot-free!"[8]

But Circle members weren't all that interested in learning that the bulk of German wealth rested in the hands of those whom William L. Shirer once labeled arrogant and "petty profit-seeking"[9] Junkers and not the Jews. Rather, it was Lulane who again parried: "But why was Israel chosen for the Jewish homeland?"

The minister's wife knew nothing of early suggestions that

European Jewry be resettled in Argentina or Uganda. But her own early religious training had given her that gut reaction that only in the Land of Israel could the Jews ever really feel at home. In her attempt to reinforce this contention, she drew the analogy of Israel among the nations and the problems trans-planted Yankees experience in the South. "No matter how long you live here," she observed, "you're always from somewhere else."

"Then I feel sorry for the Tibetans," declared Lulane. "They built all of their shrines and then ended up as refugees."

Becky, a young teacher, demonstrated less concern about ref-ugees and far greater indignation that American tax dollars will be spent, she said, "to pay for peace in Israel."

"I can only feel," said this writer's wife, "that we have a Presi-dent who realizes the importance of peace in Jerusalem."

"But," pressed Becky, "at our expense?"

I

There is no question that every woman present at this Circle meeting would be highly incensed if accused of anti-Semitism. At the same time, however, Edward H. Flannery has noted the marked similarities of response within Christendom to the Nazi Holocaust and to the re-creation of the State of Israel.[10] These similarities are symptomatic, says Flannery, ". . . of determinative unconscious forces, specifically, of an unrecognized antipathy against the Jewish people."[11] At the same time, Alice and Roy Eckardt have commented:

> The two events (i.e., the Holocaust and national rebirth) are at opposite poles in Jewish experience and as his-tory: the one represents Israel prostrate; the other, Israel triumphant. And yet, while the stimuli are poles apart, the response in our Christian world to the Jew-ish situation has been the same: indifference-hostility, often accompanied by passionate denials that we are anti-semitic.[12]

Moreover, the Eckardts agree with Father Flannery that this similarity of reaction to such different realities ". . . points to the presence of irrational forces within us."[13] Such an explanation helps us understand why a group of basically intelligent women would respond in what can only be described as an irrational way to what was presumed to be rational discourse. For only some type of avoidance-indifference-hostility mechanism can explain the intrusion of Tibet at a point at which logic would have required either a negative or a positive response to that prior comment on the existential need for Israel as a national homeland for the Jewish people. So it is that Father Flannery has observed:

> A certain vague uneasiness attends the idea of Jews restored to Palestine, and to Jerusalem in particular. This uneasiness *may* serve as the subliminal foundation for a Christian anti-Zionism and as the dynamics (behind) the various "reasons" supplied for disfavoring the State of Israel . . . .[14]

In even bolder terms, Father Flannery has contended that Christian indictments of Zionism, particularly during periods of great peril for Israel, may well conceal unrecognized and unconscious motivations.[15] "In anti-Zionism and anti-Israelism," the Eckardts have claimed, "the death wish that far too many Christians have for Jews is carried forward."[16]

It must be conceded, of course, that the attitudes reflected among a small group of Southern Presbyterian women hardly warrant a generalization. However, these attitudes, with variations on the same themes, are found increasingly among Christians of various backgrounds all the way from Scarsdale to Sacramento. Accordingly, Arnold Forster and Benjamin R. Epstein have noted that Jewish communities around the world now are asking the question with increasing frequency: "Is the post-World War II honeymoon with the Jews over?"[17] In reply, these researchers have concluded:

> There is abroad in our land a large measure of indifference to the most profound apprehensions of the Jewish people; a blandness and apathy in dealing with anti-Jewish behavior; a widespread incapacity or unwillingness to comprehend the necessity of the existence of Israel to Jewish safety and survival throughout the world.

> This is the heart of the new anti-Semitism.[18]

After World War II, for example, public knowledge of the enormity of Nazi crimes against the Jews brought swift condemnation to most, but not all, manifestations of anti-Semitism.[19] Although traditional anti-Jewish prejudices prevented some Jews from making it in their chosen professions, many others never had it so good in a society with an expanding civil service and a burgeoning technocracy.[20] Even the churches, which for centuries had maligned the Jews on so-called theological grounds, were obliged to reassess dogma in the afterglow of Auschwitz.[21]

Slowly, however, perceptible changes began to be observed in what might be described as the American gentile-Jewish symbiosis. For example, while many gentiles cheered Israel's lightning victory in the Six Day War of June 1967, most American Jewish leaders were "profoundly alarmed and depressed"[22] by the insensitivity demonstrated by their Christian counterparts before and after this crucial conflict.[23]

If the Six Day War "precipitated a crisis in the Jewish-Christian dialogue,"[24] Christian scholars of the stature of A. Roy Eckardt had become increasingly alarmed by March, 1972, when he addressed the Third Annual Scholars Conference on the German Church Struggle and the Holocaust at Wayne State University in Detroit. In his address, Dr. Eckardt warned of "the highly pervasive, contemporaneous anti-Semitism of the theological left,"[25] which, in intensity, at least equaled that of "the biblicist and theological right."[26] As if strangely prophetic, Eckardt's warning was followed by a virulent anti-Israel attack by the Very Rev. Francis B. Sayre, Jr., Dean of National (Episcopal) Cathedral, Washington, D.C., on Palm Sunday 1972.[27] The Dean fired a second salvo that fall.[28]

Yet Dean Sayre's outbursts reflected but a growing antipathy toward Israel which has at times been marked by insensitivity and/or hostility in several areas of American life, including the government, education, the arts and media, as well as the churches.[29] Still a certain low point in the Jewish-Christian encounter undoubtedly was reached during the 1973 Yom Kippur War when the activist priest, Daniel Berrigan, accused Israel of what he called "domestic repression, deception, cruelty (and) militarism."[30] Ironically, Israel was at that time in no position to defend herself against verbal assaults because she was then engaged in a life-and-death struggle which had been launched by a preemptive Arab strike against her on the most solemn day in the Jewish calendar.

Meanwhile, a "war" of quite a different order was about to

threaten America's own commitment to the survival of the Jewish State. As Robert F. Drinan noted, the oil crisis which emerged initially in late 1973 made the United States ". . . ever more vulnerable to the temptation of preferring a steady flow of oil over the fulfillment of America's commitment to Israel."[31] How many Americans succumbed to that "temptation" was revealed in one of its cruelest forms as Israelis mourned their losses in the Yom Kippur War. In New York's affluent Westchester County, it was reported at that time, gasoline pumps bore the crude legend: "We Need Gas — Not Jews!"

That is one of the reasons why the expressed responses of a small group of Southern Presbyterian women may be of more than passing interest to those professionally engaged in the Jewish-Christian encounter. For others elsewhere may share the belief that a full gasoline tank is more important than a peace treaty sustained by American tax dollars. If so, the escalation of the world's energy crisis may well have introduced a new and ominous dimension of libel and violence against "history's favorite victim."[32] Or, as Forster and Epstein have warned,

> Anti-Semitism is an insidious disease. It can linger in the body politic almost invisibly for years without erupting. Its effects can be long delayed. Moreover, unless expunged it grows. Of all the ills of the world, anti-Semitism is the least likely to die a natural death.[33]

Meanwhile, Gertrude J. Selznick and Stephen Steinberg observed in their brilliant study[34] of a decade ago that there is a ". . . correspondence between belief and behavior, even though, as our data show, the correlation is far from perfect."[35] "Even today many people are puzzled by the fact that pre-Nazi Germany was not characterized by an unusual amount of discrimination," they write. "Had a survey been conducted during that period, there would probably be less grounds for bafflement."[36] Correspondingly, the signs of the times now call for a reassessment of earlier historical, theoretical and descriptive research regarding anti-Jewish and anti-Israel attitudes in light of the Forster-Epstein thesis that a "new anti-Semitism" is abroad in the land.

II

At the same time, however, this paper will not attempt to deal with those extreme forms of pathological Jew-hatred which find

their epitome in a paranoia[37] that can become homicidal[38] as it
seeks a tangible scapegoat[39] within its "single limited delusional
system."[40] In this regard, Jean-Paul Sartre's delineation of the
anti-Semite closely follows the definition offered by Gordon W.
Allport of that paranoid personality who represents the extreme
pathology of prejudice.[41] Sartre has written of the Jew hater:

> He is a man who is afraid. Not of the Jews, to be sure,
> but of himself, of his own consciousness, of his liberty,
> of his instincts, of his responsibilities, of solitariness,
> of change, of society, and of the world — of everything
> except the Jews . . . . The existence of the Jew merely
> permits the anti-Semite to stifle off his anxieties at
> their inception by persuading himself that his place
> in the world has been marked out in advance, that it
> awaits him, and that tradition gives him the right to
> occupy it. Anti-Semitism, in short, is fear of the human
> condition. The anti-Semite is a man who wishes to be
> pitiless stone, a furious torrent, a devastating thunder-
> bolt — anything except a man.[42]

While paranoia may manifest itself in various gradations in
otherwise normal persons,[43] disaster may well result when paranoid tendencies encounter demagoguery.[44] For example, T. W.
Adorno has demonstrated that "the authoritarian personality"
may turn to the demagogue or the dictator because it finds
totalitarian or closed systems congenial, even psychologically
necessary.[45] In addition, says Allport:

> When a true paranoiac becomes a demagogue . . .,
> (his) success will, of course, be greater if he is normal
> and shrewd in all other phases of his leadership. If so,
> his delusional system will seem reasonable, and he
> will attract followers, especially among those who
> themselves have latent paranoid ideas. Combine
> enough paranoiacs, or enough people with paranoid
> tendencies, and a dangerous mob may result.[46]

What is so disturbing is that body of evidence that suggests
that demagogues need only the necessary mix of social conditions to attract large numbers to their cause.[47] In Eric Hoffer's
analysis, the majority of mankind potentially could be swayed
by a fanatical faith in the face of continued frustration of a

political, economic or social nature.[48] The lessons of history would appear to support this thesis.

Whatever one's reaction to Hoffer's profound pessimism,[49] Hannah Arendt has concluded that anti-Semitism is endemic to totalitarian theory and practice.[50] Moreover, Franklin H. Littell has insisted that this is true because ". . . the Jew — whether he is a man of faith or not — is by his very existence a representative of the Author of history whom the totalitarian ideologues deny."[51] As Littell has observed:

> Both Stalin and Hitler were bitter anti-Semitics, and they collaborated, for example, in the destruction of the Warsaw Ghetto. Under temptation and pressure, the gentiles can revert to tribalism and racism. The baptized Catholics and Orthodox of Russia and Eastern Europe go back to pan-Slav mysticism.[52]

According to this scenario, "the grotesque excesses of anti-Semitism"[53] initiated by the Nazis cannot justly be attributed exclusively or even principally to Christianity.[54] "Hitler's extravagant assaults on the Jews were . . . different in a significant way from anything that had preceded them," says Father Drinan. "Hitler's anti-Semitism was transcendental, all-purpose, and final."[55]

Moreover, Father Drinan is among those scholars who have noted the limits imposed by the Nazis on Christian action while, at the same time, readily conceding Christian failure in the hour of testing. On the one hand, Hitler was completely indifferent as to whether certain Jews had been baptized or had renounced Judaism.[56] On the other hand, ". . . the Christian churches had been ousted as the moral leaders of Europe several generations before Hitler came to power."[57] In this regard, Raul Hilberg has sought to put the matter in perspective:

> The anti-Semites of the nineteenth century, who divorced themselves from religious aims, espoused the emigration of the Jews. The anti-Semites hated the Jews with a feeling of righteousness and reason, as though they had acquired the antagonism of the church like speculators buying the rights of a bankrupt corporation.[58]

Surely no reputable Christian scholar today would deny that anti-Jewish teaching has infected the relationship between Church and Synagogue for at least 1,500 years. While Father Drinan is among those who resist the notion of a "unilinear" movement from theological anti-Judaism to Hitler's genocidal policies,[59] he nonetheless speaks for many colleagues when he writes: "Almost no group, Christian or otherwise, can boast of its role in preventing, postponing, or alleviating the Holocaust. The usual way most Christians treat it is to ignore it."[60] At the same time, J. Coert Rylaarsdam has noted that Christians over the centuries have generally operated on the tacit assumption that "a good Jew" is either a dead Jew or a Christian. "So, alternately," says Rylaarsdam, "they have consented to the death of Jews and prayed for their conversion . . . ."[61] Consequently, Hilberg has concluded:

> The Nazi destruction process did not come out of a void . . . . The missionaries of Christianity had said in effect: You have no right to live among us as Jews. The secular rulers who followed had proclaimed: You have no right to live among us. The German Nazis at last decreed: You have no right to live.[62]

Whatever the historical connection, Irving Greenberg has warned that Christianity may be "hopelessly and fatally compromised"[63] if it can be shown that "The Teaching of Contempt"[64] contributed in any way to Hitler's war against the Jews. In terms of traditional Christian teaching, Greenberg has raised the following questions: (1) Did this teaching present stereotypes which brought the Nazis to focus on the Jews as the scapegoat in the first place; (2) Did this teaching create a residue of anti-Semitism in Europe which affected the attitudes of local populations towards the Jews; and, finally, (3) Did this teaching enable some Christians to think they were doing God a service by either collaborating with or consenting to the mass murder of European Jewry?[65] Says Greenberg pointedly:

> The fact is that during the Holocaust the church's protests were primarily on behalf of converted Jews. At the end of the war, the Vatican and circles close to it helped thousands of war criminals to escape . . . . Finally in 1948, the German Evangelical Conference at Darmstadt, meeting in the country which had only

recently carried out this genocide, proclaimed that the terrible Jewish suffering in the Holocaust was a divine visitation and a call to the Jews to cease their rejection and on-going crucifixion of Christ.[66]

Questioning whether a person may "morally be a Christian after this,"[67] Greenberg has contended further that ". . . there is an inverse ratio between the presence of a fundamentalist Christianity and the survival of Jews during the Holocaust period."[68] According to Greenberg, fundamentalist Christianity would include any expression of the Christian faith, Roman Catholic, Orthodox or Protestant, which perpetuates what Jules Isaac termed the "Teaching of Contempt." Isaac's own monumental studies, born of great personal suffering and loss, led him to conclude that three erroneous themes perpetuated by the churches have fanned Jew hatred down through the centuries.[69] Those themes follow: (1) Judaism at the time of Jesus was in a state of moral and spiritual decline; (2) The dispersion of the Jews represented a form of punishment for the crucifixion; and (3) The Jews, and the Jews alone, are guilty for the monstrous crime of "deicide" — that is, guilty of being "Christ killers."[70]

In response to Jules Isaac's entreaty that Christian teaching be purged of "contempt," Pope John XXIII received this eminent French-Jewish historian in audience on June 13, 1960. At the conclusion of their talks, Isaac asked whether there was reason to hope that Catholic teaching would be cleansed of its traditional anti-Jewish bias. With characteristic honesty, the Pope replied: "You have every right to more than hope . . . . But this requires deliberation and study. What you see here is not an absolute monarchy."[71] However, Eugene Fisher has noted:

> In preparing for the Second Vatican Council, John kept his promise to start the wheels of reform in motion. . . . After much discussion, revision, and not a little bargaining, the Council finally promulgated the draft on the Jews as a part of its *Declaration on the Relationship of the Church to Non-Christian Religions.*[72]

Although the document *De Judaeis* hardly met with the enthusiastic approval of many Jewish leaders,[73] there is no question that it helped to initiate "a new age of dialogue between Jews and Catholics."[74] In the early 1960's, for example, Sisters Rose Thering, Rita Mudd and Mary Gleason completed dissertations which provided ". . . the first full studies of Roman Catholic textbooks."[75] Their pioneer work later was supplemented by that of John Pawlikowski,[76] Claire Huchet Bishop,[77] and Eugene Fisher.[78] In his study, completed in 1976 as a dissertation for New York University, Fisher studied 161 student texts and 113 teachers' manuals used in Catholic schools between 1967 and 1975.[79] In general, says Fisher,

> . . . the results of my American study are encouraging, though negative aspects still persist. Using the 1975 Vatican Guidelines and the statements of the American bishops as criteria, I found that American Catholic religion materials are significantly more positive toward Judaism than they were before the Vatican Council. They are also more positive and historically accurate than the earlier European textbooks studied by Bishop.[80]

In keeping with Fisher's research, Father Pawlikowski has made the following assertions regarding American Catholic textbooks in use in 1977: (1) overt denigration of Judaism and the Jewish people has virtually disappeared; (2) The twin notions of Jewish collective guilt and their perpetual punishment for the crucifixion have been largely eliminated; (3) Little that is positive has been added to neutralize the highly negative picture of "the Pharisees" which emerges from the pages of the New Testament; (4) Some attempts have been made to introduce Catholic students to the positive values inherent in contemporary forms of Judaism.[81] In short, denigrating portraits of Jews and Judaism have been largely excised from Roman Catholic textbooks. "Virtually nothing, however," says Father Pawlikowski, "has been included about Zionism, the State of Israel, or the Holocaust, three core elements of the modern Jewish soul."[82]

In the Protestant camp, meanwhile, it would appear that interfaith concerns remain "notoriously ambiguous," a phrase used by the late Bernhard E. Olson to describe conditions when he completed his landmark study of Protestant curricula in 1963.[83] In 1972, for example, Gerald S. Strober was forced to conclude that Dr. Olson's monumental research, known popularly as the Yale Study, ". . . has not had the long-term effect which its initial reception seemed to promise."[84] Except in remote cases, Strober noted, Protestant literature still presents certain key themes "...in ways likely to foster hostility against Jews, their religion and experience."[85] Among the themes singled out by Strober were the nature of Judaism, Jesus' relationship to His Jewish contemporaries, the Pharisees, Judaism's rejection of Jesus as the Messiah, and alleged collective guilt for the crucifixion.[86] At the same time, Strober has contended that his update of the Yale study has uncovered a pattern in Protestant teaching which

> ... begins with a theological anti-Judaism, moves to an inability to come to grips with the Holocaust and the twin tragedies of its effect upon Jewish life and the Christian conditioning which aided its development, and concludes with serious misapprehensions concerning the meaning of the State of Israel to Jewish life.[87]

If anything, certain comparisons can be made between the Olson and Strober studies which point to a regression in some aspects of the interfaith encounter over the last two decades. In one mainline denomination, for example, a 1952 adult lesson writer lamented Christianity's long history of forced conversions and persecution in Europe and America.[88] "The Jew will not be able to forget," he wrote, "until we start remembering."[89] In 1968, however, this same publication carried a lesson by another writer which hinted that the Jews of Jesus' day "... wanted no part of a kingdom such as Jesus had to offer."[90] What was left unsaid was the fact that not too many contemporary Christians appear to be visibly impressed either by Jesus' vision of the peaceable kingdom! In the immediate postwar period, it is at least interesting to note the following rather remarkable warning made to teachers of younger children in another major denominational curriculum:

> Do not use the expression "the wicked soldiers who were ill-treating Jesus," without taking care that the children do not identify "to be a soldier" with "to be wicked" .... One should not speak of wicked soldiers "but of wicked Jews." In the Passion narrative the soldiers should be treated as simply doing what they are ordered to do.[91]

Meanwhile, the notion persists in some quarters that conservative evangelical Protestantism is perpetuating anti-Semitism in its educational materials, while "... liberal Christian leaders have been trying to expunge invidious depictions of the Jews from church teachings."[92] Such at least is one of the conclusions of the widely-touted study by Charles Y. Glock and Rodney Stark.[93] In their findings, they have even gone so far as to write:

> The causal chain that links Christian belief and faith to secular anti-Semitism begins with orthodoxy — commitment to a literal interpretation of traditional Christian dogma. Orthodoxy, in turn, leads to particularism — a disposition to see Christian truth as the *only* religious truth. Particularism produces a two-fold response toward religious outsiders. On the one hand Christian particularism prompts missionary zeal: The faith is open to all mankind if only they will accept it. But when others reject the call to conversion the hostility latent in particularism is activated. This hostility is directed against all religious outsiders whether they are of another faith or of none. Because of their historic link with Christianity, the Jews are singled out for special attention. The specifically religious hostility toward the Jews generated by particularism is not merely a result of blaming the historic Jews for the death of Jesus. Particularistic Christians are not alone in holding such a view; less orthodox and unparticularistic Christians are also likely to implicate the ancient Jews in the Crucifixion. The difference lies in the interpretation given this view of history. In the eyes of most particularists, the Jews *remain* guilty; the Jews provoked God's wrath by crucifying Jesus, and have suffered under divine judgment ever since. Their tribulations will not cease until they extirpate their guilt by accepting salvation through Christ. Less orthodox and less particularistic Christians are unlikely to draw this link between the ancient and modern Jews.
>
> This process — orthodoxy to particularism to religious hostility — culminates in secular anti-Semitism. Almost inexorably, those caught up in this syndrome of religious ideology are led to a general hostility toward the Jews.[94]

Although Glock and Stark concede that their data does not wholly explain how certain orthodox Christians ". . . restrain themselves from taking up a particularistic view of their own religious superiority,"[95] they suggest that, for many, ". . . the answer seems to be their commitment to ideals of religious liberty."[96]

On the whole, however, Glock and Stark insist that anti-Semitism is much less common ". . . in those denominations where orthodoxy has been replaced with a more liberal doctrine."[97] At the same time, these researchers concede:

> Without the reinforcement provided by the deicide tradition, the link between particularism and religious hostility would probably still remain. The simple fact that Jews remain outside the "true" faith would be enough to sustain a degree of hostility. But it seems certain that this hostility could be significantly muted if the deicide issue could be laid to rest once and for all.[98]

Apart from the malignant effects of this horrible deicide calumny, however, a growing body of recent scholarship has demonstrated that liberal anti-Semitism is no less invidious than those strains propagated and nurtured by orthodox Christianity. In America, for example, it was the liberal *Christian Century* that kept up the drumbeat against a Jewish homeland and aiding those victims who survived Hitler's war against the Jews.[99] In Europe itself, the apostates and betrayers more-often-than-not represented those Christians who embraced what Franklin H. Littell has aptly defined as ". . . religion-in-general, without intellectual discipline and ethical content beyond that imposed by the society at large."[100] "In Nazi Germany," says Littell, "the very center of Protestant anti-Semitism was this type of 'liberal' Christianity, for the Jews remained the irreduceable sign of a divinely ordered counterculture after the baptized gentiles had apostatized and become good Teutonic heathen again."[101] It is not surprising, therefore, to discover that Littell believes that the Glock and Stark study leaves something to be desired. He writes:

> The anti-Semitism of liberal Protestants was analyzed in depth in Bernhard Olson's brilliant study, *Faith and Prejudice*, which is still the best study of the religious roots of prejudice although unfortunately overshadowed by the Glock and Stark series. In his study

> of the curricula of four religious groupings, Dr. Olson
> . . . discovered that the most 'liberal' curriculum
> was also the most anti-Semitic. It was anti-Semitic for
> the same reason it was also anti-Catholic and anti-
> Fundamentalist; that is, it was marked by a 'predispo-
> sition toward abstraction' which rejected particularity
> and repudiated the peculiar history of any religious
> community.[102]

This same tendency has been observed by the Eckardts who
certainly are no defenders of biblical literalism and the theological right. They would agree with Glock and Stark that more
liberal Christians *should* develop more positive and more
sympathetic attitudes toward the Jews. "This has happened,"
Roy Eckardt has written. "But it does not necessarily happen.
Orthodox Christian particularists often criticize Jews for their
universalism. But Christian universalists fault Jews for their
particularism."[103]

Apart from such crucial theological concerns, however, several
studies have attempted to deal with the relationship between
education and religion. For example, the American Jewish Committee in 1961 published Charles Herbert Stember's somewhat
limited findings on education and attitude change, a work which
did not deal specifically with religious values.[104] A more recent
survey is that of Gertrude J. Selznick and Stephen Steinberg,
whose research was conducted under a grant from the Anti-
Defamation League of B'nai B'rith.[105] In their survey Selznick
and Steinberg concluded:

1) Lack of education is the most important factor in
   anti-Semitism, but it is not the only one, although
   no other factor has an impact approaching that of
   education.[106]

2) Anti-Semitism among the college educated is generally
   low, but it is far from trivial in its social consequences.[107]

3) Since the working class are most apt to suffer in an
   economic crisis, their present acceptance of anti-
   Semitic beliefs takes on more than incidental significance. In normal times the relative economic deprivation of the working class has little to do with their
   acceptance of anti-Semitic beliefs. In a period of
   crisis, however, it could be crucial.[108]

4) Personal psychopathology may explain the rabid anti-Semite and the few who take an active role in creating and promulgating anti-Semitic propaganda. But, on the whole, initial acceptance of anti-Semitic beliefs is no more distinctively rooted in personal psychopathology than is acceptance of other unenlightened beliefs . . . . A pathology is present, but it is in the beliefs, not necessarily in the individual who accepts them . . . . Lack of cognitive sophistication in the individual rather than the psychic significance of unenlightened beliefs appears to be the crucial factor in their acceptance.[109]

5) Education reduces prejudice, but not any kind of education does so . . . . Not all education is equal in modernity, in quality, or in relevance to prejudice. Even among college graduates, as past studies have shown, commitment to democratic values varies by major concentration in college, with students in the social sciences and humanities scoring as more civil libertarian than those in the physical sciences or business administration.[110]

6) As the education level in the country rises, anti-Semitic prejudice is likely to decrease; however, education is not a cure-all. Prejudice can be combated either by attacking the social institutions that perpetuate prejudice or by strengthening countervailing institutions. The first strategy is attractive because it gets to the root causes of prejudice, but the second is probably the more realistic.[111]

Some will justifiably argue that certain generalizations drawn from the Selznick-Steinberg data fail to take certain other factors into consideration. However, few, if any, would fault their basic conclusion that education plays a significant role in the perpetuation or diminution of prejudice. Moreover, earlier historical, theoretical and descriptive research only serves to buttress their delineation of the problem of dealing with the bigot:

He understands well enough that prejudice has something to do with being irrational and unfair. But he defines irrationality as disliking or hating people for no reason at all. Since he has reasons, he sees himself

as unprejudiced. But what the bigot cites as reasons
the social scientist defines as prejudice.[112]

III

In his own characteristic way, S. I. Hayakawa has called the
word "Jew" ". . . one of the most sloppily constructed abstrac-
tions in the language – that is, one of the most difficult to refer
systematically down the abstraction ladder to lower levels."[113]
According to context, he observes, the word "Jew" may or may
not refer to a race, a religion, a nationality, a physical type, a
state of mind, or a caste. As for himself, Hayakawa finds it difficult to improve upon the *operational definition* that "anyone
who calls himself a 'Jew' is a Jew."[114] At the same time, he points
out that the abstract "Jew" of the anti-Semite ". . . is automatically condemned, no matter who he is or what he does."[115] In
Eastern Europe, one elderly Jew recalled how his people were
viewed by their gentile neighbors:

> If they crept along the wall, they were cowardly. If
> they stepped out of the shadows, they were impudent.
> If they were thrifty with their money, they were miserly.
> If they were generous with it, they were ostentatious.
> If they strove to get on, they were eaten up with am-
> bition. If they behaved modestly, they were lacking
> courage . . . .[116]

Nathan C. Belth has suggested that contemporary perceptions
of anti-Semitism in America have been influenced as much by
the fears as by the facts of history. "The ultimate unease with
which Jews regard the future," he says, "even in these, the best
of times, and in this the most hospitable of societies, lies in
their understanding of history and their long memories."[117] As
Belth says:

> The Jew has been pictured as the archcapitalist and
> arch-Bolshevik and chastised for both, whipsawed by
> contending forces. The Soviet authorities see Jews as
> a threat to the state and Alexander Solzhenitsyn, who
> castigates Bolshevik terror, sees Jews as libertarians
> who brought on socialism, after, of course, rejecting
> Christ. What are Jews to make of such a history? In

what can they place their confidence? Is America different?[118]

This is the towering question for Christians no less than for American Jews.

At the same time, the complex history of anti-Semitism has demonstrated that this virus can not only survive but prosper in virtually any environment. Pagan Rome found Hebraic monotheism intolerable and destroyed Judea. The so-called Christian West afforded either conversion or condemnation when confronted by the Jewish quest for the rights of integrity and self-definition. In the post-Christian era, traditional Jewish liberalism has met with persecution both from the right and the left. It now remains to be seen just how expendable American gentiles will consider Israel and the Diaspora if the energy crunch becomes an energy crisis.

Whatever the case, the convolutions of *centra Judaeus* down through the centuries would indicate the need for a broad range of remedial programs. In this regard, Allport has suggested the following approaches: (1) formal educational methods, (2) contact and acquaintance programs, (3) group retraining methods, (4) mass media, (5) exhortation, and (6) individual therapy.[119]

Formal Educational Methods: Within the Christian context, Father Pawlikowski has contended that, despite peripheral advances, there is little hope for substantial change within the churches until substantial changes are made within the core curricula of Protestant and Roman Catholic seminaries.[120] If new attitudes toward Jews and Judaism are to be developed at the seminary level, however, he contends that ". . . the impetus must come from the seminary professors' own peers and not directly from agencies, whether Christian or Jewish."[121] In addition, says Pawlikowski:

> A further problem at the seminary level is due to the loss of interest in "formal ecumenism" typical of Vatican II among many of the more liberal professors. They have tended to turn to issues such as the church's role and responsibility in the Third World, and its dealings with minorities in this country. In such a perspective Jews are usually included among the "haves"; therefore specifically Jewish questions are met with indifference, and in a few cases even with open hostility.[122]

In his attempt to delineate the radical reorientation required at the seminary level, Father Pawlikowski has observed that more liberal professors also tend to demonstrate a fascination with other world religions — with the exclusion of Judaism within this category. "Could this be due," he asks, "to a lingering belief that Christianity has subsumed whatever there is of value in Judaism?" He writes:

> While there has undeniably been an intensification of interest in, and appreciation of, the Hebrew Bible, the vast majority of Christian Scripture professors . . . tend to rely exclusively on Christian exegetes . . . . Inclusion of Jewish resource material, both primary and secondary, could have a significant impact on core Christian teachings.[123]

That Protestant as well as Roman Catholic theological education should heed Pawlikowski's recommendation is evident when one surveys the dissertations written by clergy studying for doctoral degrees in America's seminaries. For example, a Southern Presbyterian minister with a long and enviable record in fighting bigotry in all forms at great personal cost wrote his Th.D. thesis under a widely-respected Christian Biblical scholar. He wrote on the highly pertinent topic, "Particularism and Universalism in the Restoration of Judah from Exile."[124]

In this case, the student sought to demonstrate that the concepts of universalism and particularism are not mutually exclusive. On the one hand, he can chide Charles Malik for insisting that, while "there is the deepest craving ... for the return of the Jews everywhere to the Cross," Christians may not derive from this "craving (anything) political about the State of Israel or the return of the Jews to Palestine . . . ."[125] On the other hand, this same student rejects what he calls the "Jerusalem particularism" of Isaiah which, he says, inspired ". . . the removal of the capital of Israel from Tel Aviv back to 'the city of the great king' despite protests from the United States, the United Nations and, of course, the Arabs and the Vatican."[126] Indeed, he adds, Isaiah's "Jerusalem particularism" may yet prove to "be a fatal roadblock to the United Nations' plan to internationalize the Holy City."[127]

Whatever one's perspective regarding the use of the Biblical materials in reference to the rebirth of the Jewish State, there is little doubt that this student would have benefited immeasurably had he been directed to other than Christian sources. For example, it becomes evident in reading this dissertation that the researcher's own best efforts constantly are suborned by a Christian triumphalism that pits an allegedly narrow, if not decadent, Judaism against the ultimately victorious true Israel of the New Covenant.[128] What's more, this student later indicated that his doctoral studies did not prepare him fully to isolate one historical event from another in the area of human rights to which he has committed his ministry with a large measure of personal integrity.[129]

Meanwhile, the periodic fulminations of religious leaders of the stature of Dean Sayre and Daniel Berrigan would tend to lend credence to the observation that "the more things change, the more they remain the same." Witness this homily delivered by one of America's greatest Methodist leaders just a decade before Hitler's accession to power:

> The holidays were at hand. The school children were rehearsing for the Christmas festival. A little girl had chosen for her "piece" Longfellow's "The Wreck of the Hesperus." All went well until these lines were reached,

> "She thought of Christ, who stilled
>   the wave
> On the Lake of Galilee."

> At this point the teacher who was a Jewess, said, "Lucy, you may omit that." Those lines were omitted. But that night the teacher sent to that girl's home the report for the term and dated it "December 21, 1923." 1923 what? A.D. She could not cut Christ out of the calendar. No, the world has moved too far. The protest comes too late. No scissors were ever ground sharp enough to cut Christ out of the world's calendar. The stone that the builders rejected has become the head of the corner.[130]

One has only to consider the pulpit offerings of men like Dean Sayre to discover that those molded by America's theological schools haven't changed that much over the last half century. At least as far as their understanding of Jews and Judaism is concerned. No wonder, then, that anti-Semitism has been described as "the most basic and original 'ecumenical' trait."[131]

At the same time, the content analysis of recent Christian education materials should offer no surprises to those acquainted with theological education and the pulpit and professional posture of those molded by it. Even the best efforts of those engaged in the Jewish-Christian encounter can be subverted by an indifferent or hostile cleric or educator. For example, the Roman Catholics have developed a set of guidelines for evaluating the treatment of Jews, Judaism and Israel in catechetical materials.[132] But the question remains as to whether these guidelines are considered by most pastors or by the average lesson writer or editor. The degree of insensitivity still existing within the Christian education enterprise is indicated by a promotional blurb announcing publication of this writer's book, *O Christian! O Jew!* It was described in this promotional item as ". . . an exceptional journey of discovery by an evangelical minister who returned to the Jewish roots to touch true *Christian* love and fellowship." Apparently it was beyond the comprehension of one nurtured on the superseding theory to even imagine that a Christian could discover the depth and richness of *Jewish* love to a stranger without its gates!

On the brighter side, however, efforts have been made by both Jews and Christians to move beyond disputation to dialogue and, in the process, take steps to eradicate the pervasive effects of "The Teaching of Contempt." In this enterprise, the National Conference of Christians and Jews has played a major role. For the NCCJ has served both as a catalyst and a clearinghouse for information and in establishing interfaith contact and dialogue. As a result, there are today Jewish faculty members at a few Christian seminaries. There also are Christian scholars who are continuing research at Jewish institutions often with the aid of stipends from Jewish agencies.

Moreover, both the American Jewish Committee and the Anti-Defamation League of B'nai B'rith have sought to cultivate rapprochement with present and future leaders of various segments of American Christianity. For example, in 1975, the AJC's Interreligious Affairs Department joined the American Institute of Holy Land Studies in co-sponsoring the National Conference of Evangelical Christians and Jews. At the same time, Rabbi Solomon S. Bernards, ADL's national director of interreligious cooperation, has been engaged in an ever-widening circle of contact with Christian scholars. Among his more ambitious undertakings have been annual seminars at Princeton Theological Seminary and Vanderbilt University. At such gatherings, one constantly is reminded of the observation of the late Martin Buber:

> That peoples can no longer carry on authentic dialogue with one another is not only the most acute symptom of the pathology of our time, it is also that which most urgently makes a demand of us. I believe, despite all, that the peoples in this hour can enter into dialogue, into a genuine dialogue with one another. In a genuine dialogue each of the partners, even when he stands in opposition to the other, heeds, affirms, and confirms his opponent as the existing other . . . . Let us release speech from its ban. Let us dare, despite all, to trust.[133]

In keeping with this mandate, Christian theologians of the stature of Franklin H. Littell, Paul van Buren, and Robert McAfee Brown are insisting that Holocaust studies in particular must transcend what Littell has called "the critical/analytical/comparative/abstractive method."[134] Unless such research is balanced by "aesthetic and/or religious awareness," he insists, "it . . . can lead easily to absurdity in the treatment of the mysterious and the sacred."[135] Accordingly, Brown and others, who have been influenced by Elie Wiesel and the Hasidic tale, are attempting to inhibit flights into historical and theological abstraction by introducing the story as a model for theological interaction.[136] For Brown, this may mean not only the juxtaposition of conflicting stories, but also the possibility of the destruction of the story which had been "normative" for the individual.[137] In the process, however, it is to be hoped that the reader or listener occasionally will be able to respond: "That's my story, too."[138]

Meanwhile, Henry Friedlander has gone so far as to charge that, if the interpretation of the Holocaust itself is left to most historians and textbook writers, . . . ignorance and distortion will not only hide but bury it."[139] In the case of American textbook writers, Gerd Korman has noted that the time now has come for textbook historians to ". . . interlace Gentile-Jewish relations in the mainstream of European history and in contemporary American history."[140] In this regard, American writers might take their cue from younger German historians like Karl Dietrich Bracher whose book, *The German Dictatorship*, ". . . places German anti-Semitism and the consequent annihilation of the Jews in the very center of the historical action."[141]

At the same time, however, great strides have been made in Holocaust studies since Friedlander and Korman leveled their reasoned criticisms. For example, the NCCJ annually sponsors the Bernhard E. Olson Scholars' Conference on The Church Struggle and the Holocaust. In addition, the Anti-Defamation League has promoted Holocaust conferences for clergy and public school teachers from Massachusetts to California. As a result of these ongoing efforts, ADL's Center for Studies on the Holocaust recently reported that some 300 public school systems across the country have integrated material on Hitler's genocidal program into their curricula. The league has indicated that statistical projections suggest that more than half of the 15-million students who attend the nation's 30,000 junior and senior high schools eventually will be exposed to Holocaust studies.[142]

However, the growing worldwide crisis would appear to point up the need to accelerate programs designed to acquaint youth with the painful and tragic lessons of the past. This challenge becomes all-the-more pressing when one views with alarm the often sorry spectacle of colleges and universities engaged in a battle for bodies and balanced budgets. Here are just a few of the recent grants made to U.S. institutions by the Arab states:

> $1-million to endow the King Faisal Chair for Arab and Islamic Studies at the University of Southern California, from the Government of Saudi Arabia.

> $1-million to endow a medical chair at St. Luke's Hospital, an affiliate of Columbia University, from the Government of Kuwait.

> $750,000 from the Government of Libya for the al-Mukhtar Chair of Arab Culture at Georgetown University, and $88,000 to help fund an interdisciplinary program on Arab development at the University of Utah.

> $200,000 for a program of Islamic and Arabian development studies at Duke University, from the Government of Saudi Arabia.

> An annually endowed chair at Harvard University, the only chair in the history of Islamic science in the world, from the Government of Kuwait.[143]

Surely the community of scholars cannot help but applaud the stated desire of the Arab states to "support . . . international programs devoted to better cross-cultural communications in a shrinking world."[144] Or, as Dr. Abdulhamid Sabra, incumbent of the Harvard chair of the history of Islamic science, puts it: "The Arab nations know they have a stake in American education. They are not well enough understood, and they know it will benefit them when Americans know more about them than how many barrels of oil are being imported, and what it cost."[145]

Those engaged in Jewish-Christian relations are only concerned that the academic recipients of Arab largesse maintain sufficient oversight so that none of these programs can provide an occasion for anti-Jewish, anti-Israel propaganda. For it would be tragic if students left such studies with a narrowed rather than broadened view of our "shrinking world."

Contact and Acquaintance Programs: Some sociologists have held that disparate groups of human beings pass through successive stages in their relationship with one another before "peaceful progression" is achieved.[146] Allport, however, has noted that this "law of peaceful progression" is anything but universal[147] and appears to depend "on the *nature of the contact* that is established."[148] Says Allport:

> To be maximally effective, contact and acquaintance programs should lead to a sense of equality in social status, should occur in ordinary purposeful pursuits, avoid artificiality, and if possible enjoy the sanction of the community in which they occur. The deeper and more genuine the association, the greater its effect.[149]

Apart from efforts by national Jewish and Christian agencies to establish such contacts, the present writer himself initiated a seven-year teaching-learning experience on Jews and Judaism in 1971 while serving as the pastor of a conservative Presbyterian church on Long Island. This highly-successful encounter has continued to date, even after the writer moved South to serve another parish. Its initial impetus was in no small part derived from the conviction that Jules Isaac was correct in his observation that "Only education can undo what education has done."[150]

At the outset, the present writer and his wife sought to introduce a group of Christians both to people and land at the same time. Accordingly, the Israel Government Tourist Office responded to the spirit of the project by providing both an excellent film program and a sampling of Israeli delicacies. In addition, the Temple Youth of Long Island presented a show-stopping performance of Israeli folk songs and dancing.

But this "Israeli Night" celebration represented only a prelude for the decidedly conservative group of Christians who later journeyed to Israel for a two-week tour that literally took them from Dan to Beersheva and beyond. While many of them fulfilled a lifelong desire to "walk where Jesus walked," none were able to leave the Holy Land without a better appreciation as to why contemporary Jewry considers *eretz Yisrael* as much a national homeland as did the Jews of the Biblical period. In terms of breaking down stereotypes, it was somewhat humorous to hear tour members say of blond, blue-eyed Sabras, "But they don't look Jewish!"

It has been this writer's experience, however, that intercultural contact through travel can, on occasion, arouse prejudice rather than diminish it. For example, it is sad but true that some church-sponsored tours to "the Middle East" or "the Holy *Lands*" often leave participants with broadened appreciation for "the rich diversity of Arabic culture," and, at the same time, hostility for Jews and Zionism.

Meanwhile, the Israel tour hosted by this writer and his wife represented the first in a long series of contact and acquaintance programs at the parish level. For example, pulpit exchanges became a regular tradition over the years as church members became active in the Interfaith Council of Southwest Queens and, to a lesser extent, in the work of the regional affiliate of the National Conference of Christians and Jews. Such contacts provided church members with the opportunity to participate in programs arranged for the Jewish festivals, particularly Passover and Hanukkah. In addition, they met other gentiles, such as the *B'nai Shalom*, who identified themselves with the people Israel and, at the same time, eschewed all talk of proselytism.

However, the most ambitious program attempted by this writer involved a 15-week course on the Holocaust, which was patterned after one taught by Eva Fleischner, a Roman Catholic scholar and a Professor at Montclair State College in New Jersey.[151] What Fleischner reported of herself and her students could also be said of those who met in the writer's living room during the Winter of 1976:

> At the interpersonal level, we became a community
> in the course of those four months, based on a

> deep common concern. Barriers were broken down
> and a level of trust was established which made it
> possible for us to challenge, without threatening, each
> other . . . .[152]

During the Sunday afternoon meetings, the 14 participants considered such topics as the historical matrix that gave birth to Nazism, the course of Jewish life in Europe and elsewhere, the extent of Jewish and Christian resistance to Hitler, and the silence of the nations during the Holocaust. In addition, special attention was given to counteracting the "Teaching of Contempt" which resulted in that "harvest of hate" that culminated in the Final Solution. Yet the most dramatic moment came one Sunday afternoon when the group met personally with a female survivor of Auschwitz. As one participant expressed the feelings of all concerned: "It really was just like it says in the books."

The writer's introduction to life in the South demonstrated that a climate of confidence must be created between pastor and people before such emotion-laden material can be discussed in a mutually satisfactory way. For example, the writer himself was not prepared to deal with a prevailing anti-Semitic mood apart from the presence of any Jews. At the same time, he discovered that his parishioners could not deal emotionally at this point with many of the theological issues raised by the Holocaust. Ironically, however, he was perceived by the community as something of a resident "authority" on all things Jewish! He was asked to speak on such topics before high school groups, civic associations, and ministerial organizations. Even more significantly, several high school students were directed to the manse for assistance on term papers on the Holocaust, World War II, and Jewish-Christian relations.

But such encounters only deepened this writer's concern that adequate support structures be provided for those Christians engaged in Jewish-Christian relations. As one views the present situation, it sometimes appears as though scholars in the field have been playing an elitist game of musical chairs, moving among themselves from one conference to another without providing adequate opportunity for younger colleagues to move into their circle. In addition, there is a pressing need for some kind of *modus vivendi* between certain Christian groups to insure that their common concern for Israel and the Jewish people stimulates unity of purpose rather than divisive competition. Above all, clergy and laity at the so-called grassroots level require sustained emotional support from both Jewish and Christian friends as they carry on their often lonely and discouraging projects to counteract anti-Semitism in their congregations and communities. Suspicion they get, when support is what they need and deserve.

Group Retraining: To some extent, beliefs can be attacked and altered among rational people. Even then, Allport has noted that they usually ". . . have the slippery propensity of accommodating themselves somehow to the negative attitude which is much harder to change."[153] As a case in point, Allport cites the following dialogue:

> Mr. X: The trouble with the Jews is that they only take care of their own group.
>
> Mr. Y: But the record of the Community Chest campaign shows that they gave more generously, in proportion to their numbers, to the general charities of the community than do non-Jews.
>
> Mr. X: That shows they are always trying to buy favor and intrude into Christian affairs. They think of nothing but money; that is why there are so many Jewish bankers.
>
> Mr. Y: But a recent study shows that the percentage of Jews in the banking business is negligible, far smaller than the percentage of non-Jews.
>
> Mr. X: That's just it; they don't go in for respectable business; they are only in the movie business or run night clubs.[154]

While the various retraining programs used by the social psychologist would probably meet with limited success at best in the above case, the dialogue itself might be used in a role-playing setting in which the facilitator is aiming for what Allport has called "forced empathy."[155] As Allport says:

> Unlike the citizen who reads a pamphlet or listens to a sermon, the individual who submits himself to a retraining program is in it up to his eyes. He is required to act out the roles of other people . . ., and he learns through such "psychodrama" what it feels like to be in another's shoes. He also gains in insight regarding

his own motives, his anxieties, his projections . . . .
Along with such personal involvement comes better
conceptualization of the principles of human relations.[156]

This certainly was true for those who participated in the
writer's Holocaust seminar. For the high point of this teaching-
learning experience unquestionably found expression in the
presentation of a *Yom Ha-Shoah* service in the church at the
conclusion of the Sunday afternoon sessions. Each participant
was asked to read a particularly moving passage from the literature covered during the weekly meetings. These stories, poems,
songs and Scriptures were in turn fashioned into "A Midrash on
the Whirlwind," a program which drew the support of the local
Jewish community as well as the attention of the Interreligious
Affairs Department of the Consulate General of Israel. But the
greatest impact undoubtedly occurred in the lives of those who
assumed the roles of the Jewish victims and survivors, and, in
sharing their stories, understood a little better what it is like to
be the object of a blind, irrational hatred. For one woman who
grew up in Hitler's Germany, the experience represented genuine
catharsis. "I only wish," she sobbed, "that I had had this experience twenty years ago."

Her reaction was not unlike an unusually-talented high school
senior who was introduced to the writing of Elie Wiesel. This
lovely young Southern belle had been active both in her school
drama club and in a puppet ministry conducted by the Southern
Baptist Church of which she is a member. But her dramatic
ability was strained to the breaking point when she attempted
to read a particularly poignant passage by Wiesel before a social
studies class. She began to weep, and several of her classmates
wept with her.

Meanwhile, Allport has suggested another "retraining" technique that the writer and his wife have found to be singularly
effective. That technique involves mustering the courage to nip
the anti-Semitic remark in the bud.[157] Our own experience has
borne out research which indicates that a favorable effect can
be attained by countering the prejudicial remark in a calm
voice, marked by sincerity.[158]

Mass Media: Although Joseph Goebbels demonstrated uncanny
ability in using modern propaganda techniques in whipping up
hatred, Allport has noted that grounds exist ". . . for doubting
the effectiveness of mass propaganda as a device for *controlling*

prejudices."[159] What Allport observed in the 1950s is even more the case today:

> People whose ears and eyes are bombarded all day with blandishments of special interests tend to develop a propaganda blindness and deafness. And what chance has a mild message of brotherhood when sandwiched in between layers of news reporting war, intrigue, hatred, and crime? What is more, pro-tolerance propaganda is selectively perceived. Those who do not want to admit it to their systems of belief find no trouble in evading it. Usually those who admit it do not need it.[160]

In terms of the Holocaust itself, one sometimes senses that a whole set of disparate dynamics are at work in the minds of many gentiles. Therefore, the following observations can serve only as springboards for further discussion on what, after all, remains ". . . an event which may have been so unique and unprecedented that language fails to come to terms with it."[161]

1) There is the ever-present danger that audiences can be — and often are — desensitized by reports of the mass suffering of others, particularly when these reports are channeled through the electronic media. As a result, one perceptive TV personality has commented: "Television may have made this a nation of spectators. That's the real danger. All those evenings, weeks, months and years of people sitting there passively staring at screens cannot help but numb the brain."[162]

2) There also remains the need for media specialists to remember that various "target audiences" may react differently to the same message. The same thing holds true for those who are concerned about the so-called "trivialization" of the Holocaust. For example, Elie Wiesel wrote a rather scathing review of the American-made "Holocaust" television series.[163] Yet West Germany's Wickert Institute reported that the films led many West Germans to believe there should be no time limit set on the prosecution of Nazi war criminals.[164]

3) Those concerned with attitudinal change must further come to grips with the ramifications of Leon Festinger's theory of *cognitive dissonance*.[165] For example, there still are those

who deny that the *Protocols of the Elders of Zion* represent a forgery; yet many of these same people will insist that Anne Frank's *Diary* is fake and that the ovens at Auschwitz were used to bake bread rather than to cover up mass murder. It is, therefore, this writer's conviction that the literature of racism must be used with extreme prudence in a classroom setting. For no guarantees exist that a budding sociopathic personality may adopt rather than reject such poison.

4) The media will continue to play a crucial role in the ongoing Jewish-Christian encounter. In an earlier day, public opinion polls demonstrated that outside events such as *Kristallnacht* and the rape of Czechoslovakia helped to harden American attitudes against Hitler.[166] In our own day, however, political events can be used just as easily to turn American gentiles against their Jewish neighbors. One has only to remember that "the principle of pyramiding stimulation"[167] is at work as Arab propagandists remind the energy-starved West that oil can — and will — be used as a political weapon against those nations who favor Israel.[168] The constant repetition of this warning cannot help but have a cumulative effect on those who would place creature comfort and convenience above integrity and commitment.

On a brighter note, this writer has discovered that both the media and even exhortations from the pulpit still can be used to counteract the pernicious "Teaching of Contempt." In his own case, sermon offerings and a weekly newspaper column were used to correct Christian myths concerning "the Jews," the Pharisees, the crucifixion, the so-called displacement theory, Christian triumphalism, and many other interfaith matters. The column itself was published in newspapers from North Carolina to Indiana.

Meanwhile, note with satisfaction that West Germany extended the statute of limitations for major Nazi war criminals. But this good news was somewhat blunted by the report that a former Nazi was inaugurated as the fifth president of the Federal Republic. And then there's that crazy lady up by Columbia University who sends out pornographic anti-Semitic tracts that equal in intensity those that once appeared in *Der Stürmer*. So this somewhat soured Swede must end this inconclusive unscientific postscript with the identical observation made by a dour Dane more than 125 years ago:

It is said to have chanced in England that a man was attacked on the highway by a robber who had made himself unrecognizable by wearing a big wig. He falls upon the traveler, seizes him by the throat and shouts, "Your purse!" He gets the purse and keeps it, but the wig he throws away. A poor man comes along the same road, puts it on and arrives at the next town where the traveler had already denounced the crime, he is arrested, is recognized by the traveler, who takes his oath that he is the man. By chance, the robber is present in the court-room, sees the misunderstanding, turns to the judge and says, "It seems to me that the traveler has regard rather to the wig than to the man," and he asks permission to make a trial. He puts on the wig, seizes the traveler by the throat, crying, "Your purse!"—and the traveler recognizes the robber and offers to swear to it—the only trouble is that already he has taken an oath.

So it is, in one way or another, with every man who has a what and is not attentive to the how: he swears, he takes his oath, he runs errands, he ventures his life and blood, he is executed—all on account of the wig.[169]

Notes

1. *Louise H. Farrior, Courage for Commitment: Studies from the Gospel of Mark,* 1978-79 Bible Study Book. Atlanta: General Assembly Mission Board, Presbyterian Church, U.S., 1978.

2. *Ibid.,* 36.

3. *Ibid.*

4. *Ibid.,* 37.

5. *Ibid.,* 37-38.

6. *Ibid.,* 38.

7. *Meshumadin* (traitors) and *Mischlinge* (persons of mixed blood) were used, after considerable thought by the writer.

8. See Rita Thalmann and Emmanuel Feinermann, *Crystal Night -*

9-10 November, 1938, trans. by Giles Cremonesi. New York: Coward, McCann & Geohegan, Inc., 1974, 97-104, *et passim.*

9. William L. Shirer, *The Rise and Fall of the Third Reich.* New York: Simon and Schuster, 1960, 94.

10. Edward H. Flannery, "Anti-Zionism and the Christian Psyche," *Journal of Ecumenical Studies,* Spring, 1969, 173.

11. *Ibid.*

12. Alice and Roy Eckardt, *Encounter with Israel: A Challenge to Conscience,* New York: Association Press, 1970, 22.

13. *Ibid.*

14. Flannery, "Anti-Zionism and the Christian Psyche."

15. *Ibid.*

16. Alice and Roy Eckhardt, *Encounter with Israel,* 222.

17. Arnold Forster and Benjamin R. Epstein, *The New Anti-Semitism,* New York: McGraw-Hill Book Company, 1974, 1.

18. *Ibid.,* 324.

19. *Ibid.,* 1.

20. *Ibid.,* 2-3.

21. *Ibid.,* 2.

22. Manfred Vogel, "Some Reflections on the Jewish-Christian Dialogue in Light of the Six-Day War," in *The Annals of the American Academy of Political and Social Science,* January, 1970, 98.

23. *Ibid.*

24. *Ibid.,* 97.

25. Cited by Forster and Epstein, *The New Anti-Semitism,* 79.

26. *Ibid.*

27. *Ibid.,* 80-85.

28. *Ibid.*, 83-85.

29. *Ibid.*, 1-18, *et passim.*

30. *Ibid.*, 89.

31. Robert F. Drinan, *Honor the Promise: America's Commitment to Israel*, Garden City, New York: Doubleday & Co., 1977, 209.

32. Forster and Epstein, *The New Anti-Semitism*, 18.

33. *Ibid.*, 4-5.

34. Gertrude J. Selznick and Stephen Steinberg, *The Tenacity of Prejudice*, New York: A Harper Torchbook, 1969.

35. *Ibid.*, "Introduction," xx.

36. *Ibid.*, xxi.

37. Gordon W. Allport, *The Nature of Prejudice*, Garden City, New York: A Doubleday Anchor Book, 1958, 394-396.

38. *Ibid.*, 396.

39. *Ibid.*

40. *Ibid.*, 395.

41. *Ibid.*, 396.

42. Jean-Paul Sartre, *Anti-Semite and Jew*, trans. by George J. Becker, New York: Schocken Books, 1965, 53-54.

43. Allport, 396.

44. *Ibid.*

45. T.W. Adorne, *The Authoritarian Personality*, New York: Harper & Brothers, 1950, *passim.*

46. Allport, 396.

47. Erick Hoffer, *The True Believer: Thoughts on the Nature of Mass Movements*, with an introduction by Sidney Hook, New York: Time Incorporated, 1963, 12-14, *et passim.*

48. *Ibid.*, 14-16, *et passim.*

49. See Sidney Hook, "Introduction," in *True Believer*, xix-xxv.

50. Hannah Arendet, *The Origins of Totalitarianism*, Cleveland: Meridian Books, 1959, 349-350, *et passim.*

51. Franklin H. Littell, *Wild Tongues: A Handbook of Social Pathology*, New York: The Macmillan Company, 1969, 141.

52. *Ibid.*

53. Drinan, 41.

54. *Ibid.*, 41-42.

55. *Ibid.*, 43.

56. Drinan, 43.

57. *Ibid.*, 42.

58. Paul Hilberg, *The Destruction of European Jews*, Chicago: Quadrangle Books, Inc., 1961, 3.

59. Drinan, 43.

60. *Ibid.*, 45.

61. J. Coert Rylaarsdam, letter to the editor of *The Christian Century*, October 26, 1966, LXXXIII:43, 1306.

62. Hilberg, 3-4.

63. Irving Greenberg, "Cloud of Smoke, Pillar of Fire: Judaism, Christianity, and Modernity after the Holocaust," in *Auschwitz: Beginning of a New Era? Reflections on the Holocaust*, ed. by Eva Fleischner, New York: KTAV Publishing House, Inc., 1977, 12.

64. See Jules Isaac, *The Teaching of Contempt: Christian Roots of Anti-Semitism*, trans. by Helen Weaver, New York: Holt, Rinehart and Winston, 1964, *et passim.*

65. Greenberg, 12.

66. *Ibid.*, 12-13.

67. *Ibid.,* 13.

68. *Ibid.,* 12.

69. See Isaac, *The Teaching of Contempt, et. passim.* Cf. Jules Isaac, *Has Anti-Semitism Roots in Christianity?* trans. by Dorothy and James Parkes, New York: National Conference of Christians and Jews, 1961, passim; and Jules Isaac, *Jesus and Israel,* ed. by Claire Huchet Bishop and trans. by Sally Gran, New York: Holt, Rinehart and Winston, 1971.

70. Isaac, *The Teaching of Contempt,* 74-75, *et. passim.*

71. Quoted by Eugene Fisher, *Faith without Prejudice: Rebuilding Christian Attitudes toward Judaism,* New York: A Paulist Press Deus Book, 1977, 5-6.

72. *Ibid.,* 6.

73. See A. Roy Eckhardt, *Elder and Younger Brothers: The Encounter of Jews and Christians,* New York: Charles Scribner's Sons, 1967, 80-81.

74. Fisher, 6.

75. See John T. Pawlikowski, "The Teaching of Contempt: Judaism in Christian Education and Liturgy," in *Auschwitz: Beginning of a New Era?,* 156. Cf. Fisher, 124.

76. John T. Pawlikowski, *Catechetics and Prejudice,* New York: Paulist Press, 1973.

77. Claire Huchet Bishop, *How Catholics Look at Jews,* New York: Paulist Press, 1974.

78. Eugene Fisher, a 1976 NYU doctoral dissertation, published as *Faith Without Prejudice.*

79. *Ibid.,* 125.

80. *Ibid.*

81. Pawlikowski, "Judaism and Christian Education," in *Auschwitz: Beginning of a New Era?,* 161-162.

82. *Ibid.,* 162.

83. Bernhard E. Olson, *Faith and Prejudice: Intergroup Problems in Protestant Curricula,* New Haven: Yale University Press, 1963, xiii.

84. Gerald S. Strober, *Portrait of the Elder Brother: Jews and Judaism in Protestant Teaching Materials*, New York: American Jewish Committee, 1972, 12.

85. *Ibid.*

86. *Ibid.*

87. Quoted by Pawlikowski, "Judaism and Christian Education," in *Auschwitz: Beginning of a New Era?*, 162.

88. Quoted by Olson, *Crossroads*, Presbyterian, U.S.A. Adult Curriculum, April-June, 1952, 34-35.

89. *Ibid.*

90. Quoted by Strober, *Crossroads*, United Presbyterian Church, U.S.A. Adult Curriculum, April-June, 1968, 77.

91. See James Brown, "Christian Teaching and Anti-Semitism: Scrutinizing Religious Texts," *Commentary*, December, 1957, 494-501.

92. Charles Y. Glock and Rodney Stark, *Christian Beliefs and Anti-Semitism*, New York: A Harper Torchbook, xviii.

93. *Ibid.*, 208-212, *et passim.*

94. *Ibid.*, 208-209.

95. *Ibid.*, 209.

96. *Ibid.*

97. *Ibid.*

98. *Ibid.*, 210-211.

99. See Hertzel Fishman, *American Protestantism and the Jewish State*, Detroit: Wayne State University Press, 1973, *et passim.*

100. Franklin H. Littell, *The Crucifixion of the Jews: The Failure of Christians to Understand the Jewish Experience*, New York: Harper & Row, 1975, 35.

101. *Ibid.*

102. *Ibid.*

103. A. Roy Eckhardt, *Your People, My People: The Meeting of Jews and Christians*, New York: Quadrangle, 1974, 108.

104. See Charles Herbert Stember, "The Recent History of Public Attitudes," in Stember *et al.*, *Jews in the Mind of America*, New York: Basic Books, 1966.

105. Gertrude J. Selznick and Stephen Steinberg, *The Tenacity of Prejudice: Anti-Semitism in Contemporary America*, New York: A Harper Torchbook, 1969.

106. *Ibid.*, 185-186.

107. *Ibid.*, 187.

108. *Ibid.*, 188.

109. *Ibid.*, 189-190.

110. *Ibid.*, 191.

111. *Ibid.*, 192.

112. Selznick and Steinberg, "Introduction," xviii.

113. S.I. Hayakawa, *Language in Thought and Action*, New York: Harcourt, Brace and World, Inc., 1964, 203.

114. *Ibid.*, 204.

115. *Ibid.*

116. Cited by Paul R. Carlson, *O Christian! O Jew!*, Elgin, Illinois: David C. Cook Publishing Company, 1974, 37.

117. Natahan C. Belth, *A Promise to Keep: A Narrative of the American Encounter with Anti-Semitism*, New York: Times Books, 1979.

118. *Ibid.*

119. Allport, *The Nature of Prejudice*, 445, *passim*.

120. Pawlikowski, "Judaism and Christian Education," in *Auschwitz: Beginning of a New Era?* 170-171.

121. *Ibid.*, 171.

122. *Ibid.*

123. *Ibid.,* 171-172.

124. Harold L. White, "Particularism and Universalism in the Restoration of Judah from Exile," unpublished dissertation for the Th.D., Union Theological Seminary of Virginia, 1955.

125. *Ibid.,* 539.

126. *Ibid.,* 534.

127. *Ibid.*

128. Harold L. White, "An Outline of Problems to be Discussed" in his Th.D. Thesis, n.d., unpaginated.

129. Letter from Harold L. White to Manford G. Gutzke, Columbia Theological Seminary, Decatur, Georgia, December 13, 1961.

130. Elmer Ellsworth Helms, *Forgotten Stories,* New York: The Abingdon Press, 1924, 200-201.

131. Dietrich Pfisterer, "America and the Holy Land," *American Jewish Historical Quarterly,* September, 1972, LXII:1, 40.

132. See Fisher, *Faith without Prejudice,* "Appendix A," 141-151.

133. Martin Buber, "Genuine Dialogue and the Possibilities of Peace," in *Men of Dialogue: Martin Buber and Albrecht Goes,* E. William Rollins and Harry Zohn, eds., New York: Funk and Wagnalls, 1969, 26-27.

134. Littell, *The Crucifixion of the Jews,* 12.

135. *Ibid.*

136. See Robert McAfee Brown, "My Story and 'The Story'," *Theology Today,* July, 1975, XXXII:2, *passim.*

137. *Ibid.,* 167, *et passim.*

138. *Ibid.,* 168.

139. Henry Friedlander, *On the Holocaust: A Critique of the Treatment of the Holocaust in History Textbooks Accompanied by an Annotated Bibliography,* New York: Anti-Defamation League, 1973, 8.

140. Gerd Korman, "Silence in the American Textbooks," *Yad Vashem Studies*, ed. by Livia Rothkirchen, Jerusalem: Yad Vashem, 1970, VIII, 184.

141. Lucy S. Dawidowicz, "The Holocaust as Historical Record," in *Dimensions of the Holocaust*, Evanston: Northwestern University, 1977, 32.

142. Associated Press dispatch, April 25, 1979.

143. *Aramco World Magazine*, May-June, 1979, 30:3, 9.

144. *Ibid.*

145. *Ibid.*

146. Allport, *The Nature of Prejudice*, 250.

147. *Ibid.*

148. *Ibid.*, 251.

149. *Ibid.*, 454.

150. Isaac, *Has Anti-Semitism Roots in Christianity?*, 71.

151. See Eva Fleischner, "Holocaust Seminar at Montclair State College, Spring, 1973," *Journal of Ecumenical Studies*, Spring, 1974, 11:2, 321-328.

152. *Ibid.*, 328.

153. Allport, *The Nature of Prejudice*, 13.

154. *Ibid.*, 13-14.

155. *Ibid.*, 455.

156. *Ibid.*

157. *Ibid.*, 456.

158. *Ibid.*

159. *Ibid.*, 456. The italics were inserted by this writer.

160. *Ibid.*, 456-457.

161. "Scholars Ponder a Dilemma: Can Holocaust Be Understood?" *Religious Service News Service*, March 6, 1975, Domestic Service, 20-21.

162. See "Cavett's Cure for Commercial Television: Start All Over," *U.S. News and World Report*, June 4, 1979, LXXXVI:22, 54.

163. Elie Wiesel, "Trivializing the Holocaust: Semi-Fact and Semi-Fiction," *The New York Times*, April 16, 1978, 2:1, 29.

164. Associated Press dispatch, Bonn, West Germany, May 16, 1979.

165. Leon Festinger, *A Theory of Cognitive Dissonance*, Stanford: Stanford University Press, 1957, *passim*.

166. Hadley Cantrill, *The Psychology of Social Movements*, New York: John Wiley and Sons, Inc., 1941, 13.

167. Allport, 457.

168. Associated Press dispatch, Cairo, July 4, 1979.

169. Soren Kierkegaard, "Concluding Unscientific Postscript to the Philosophical Fragments," in *A Kierkegaard Anthology*, ed. by Robert Bretall, New York: The Modern Library, 1946, 258.

ADDENDUM®

ON MATTHEW 5:17 AND ANTI-SEMITISM

Hays H. Rockwell
Rector, St. James Episcopal Church,
New York City

Among the nastier truths about our present precarious time is that it is marked by a reawakening of the ancient demon of anti-Semitism. The nauseating evidences are everywhere around us, from the bizarre parading of neo-Nazis through the streets of mid-western cities and towns, to the growing membership in the Ku Klux Klan, to the arrogant claims of a Southern Baptist preacher that God does not hear the prayers of a Jew. Last week, another preacher, an organizer for the so-called Moral Majority in the New York area, gratuitously proclaimed that he loved "the Jewish people deeply" and went on to observe that God had given the Jews special gifts, among them "an almost supernatural ability to make money." (*New York Times*, 2/5/81.) That kind of slur is increasingly in the open along with the usual ugly store of anti-Semitic jokes. All of that is compounded by the darker fact that episodes of violence against Jews in this country increased by nearly 200% from 1979 to 1980, and included bombings and burnings, as well as the vulgar daubing of swastikas and insulting graffiti. Disturbingly, for us, the highest incidence of this hostility is in our State of New York, and the most typical offenders, when they have been apprehended, turn out

---

*This sermon was preached by the Rev. Hays H. Rockwell on Sunday, February 8, 1981, at St. James Episcopal Church, New York, N.Y. It is a fitting conclusion to this book of essays on "The Future of Jewish-Christian Relations."

to be white, middle-class adolescents. (cf B'nai B'rith Anti-Defamation League materials.)

The causes of anti-Semitism, like the causes of most irrational destructive behavior, are not easy to locate. It has been suggested that when there is a weakening in the fabric of the culture, especially when it is accompanied by economic distress, the scapegoating of the Jews is commonplace. But whatever the sources of this sordidness, the deeper question for us who mean to be Christ-followers is the question: "How are we meant to relate to Jews, to Judaism?" The answer we give to that question will have everything to do with the way in which we respond to the presence of anti-Semitism in our world. I don't mean to say that it is an answer easily given. From the beginning of the history of the church, Christian people have been perplexed about their relationship to Judaism. On the one hand, the Christ in whose name we gather is, as St. Paul said of him, a "Jew of the Jews." On the other hand, by his teaching, by his life, he seemed to break with much of the life and teaching of first century Judaism. The first Christians were all Jews, of course, but it wasn't long after they began proclaiming Jesus as Lord that they felt distinctly ill at ease in the synagogue. The addition of non-Jews to the church made the condition sharper. Some bogus versions of the Christian faith—certain gnostic sects—broke entirely with the Jewish heritage and abandoned the use of the Old Testament altogether. The New Testament itself reflects something of this conflict, affirming the law of Moses and the prophetic tradition in one place, criticizing the limitations of Mosaic law in another. At no point is the faithful Christian urged to *hate* Jews, but there are things in the literature of the New Testament that require only a little twisting in order to be put into the service of anti-Semitism. So the question, "How are we meant to relate to Jews?" is complicated and perplexing.

The way into the heart of that question, I think, is in the claim of Jesus which comes at the beginning of that luminous collection of his teachings known as the Sermon on the Mount. "Do not suppose," Matthew's gospel has Jesus say, "that I come to abolish the law and the prophets?" - which is a reference to the whole tradition. "I did not come to abolish, but to fulfill, to complete." In that singular claim we are given the clue we need to the meaning of our relationship to Judaism. The Jesus who drew men and women to himself, who draws us still by the gentle power of his holy spirit, draws us also to the eternal claims of the scripture and tradition of Israel. They are, he says, claims upon the inheritors of the new promises, no less than upon the children of the old. The law by which Jews are meant to live is also *our* law, delivered to us by Moses through Christ. The prophetic judgments are applicable to our lives; the prophetic call to justice and mercy is a call to us. The gospels do not give us an iconoclast, bent upon annulling the tradition. Not at all. The gospels describe one who, by his coming, embraces the tradition and then goes on to seek its deepest meaning. "The tradition prohibits murder," he says. Well, it means to point beyond that prohibition to a deeper truth: that God means for us to forego every murderous thought, every impulse to harm. There are rules about the marriage bond, and the meaning beneath those rules is that husband and wife are meant to know and to love one another with their whole hearts, and to live by forgiveness. And so it goes. Jesus takes the great tradition of Israel, the Judaism of the time and place of his earthly being, and he fulfills it, draws out its richness, applies it to life so that it becomes not just a set of regulations but the charter of compassion, the definition of loving justice. "Do not suppose that I come to abolish the law and the prophets;" "I come to complete them, to fill them up with the authority of the love of God, to charge them with the energy of decisive selflessness. I come to bring you the astonishing power of grace so that you *can* fulfill the ancient claims in your life."

All of that comes down to us across the two-score centuries in a time when people are again hating Jews. Knowing what we know, that by the life and teaching of Jesus of Nazareth we are of a piece with Judaism, can we tolerate the abuse of even one Jew? Believing what we believe, that the God who speaks with the voice of Moses and Amos and Isaiah and all the rest, is the very God who utters his definitive word in Christ, can we abide any attack upon the descendents of Moses? Can we go on reading from the Hebrew scriptures week by week, nourishing our spirits by their richness, and keep silent while acts of persecution, large and small, are carried out against the community of believers that is nourished by that same richness?

I don't think so. I think that of all people, the company of Jesus' followers are meant to stand by the Jews. I think that it is a part of our calling to be willing to speak up, loud and clear, against every evidence of hostility to Jews. If we tolerate anti-Semitism, by our silence, by our more open complicity, we contradict entirely the Lord we claim to follow, whose name we take for our own, and we render our worship, our life together, a shallow folly.

Bonhoeffer saw the point clearly back in the Germany of the 30's: "Only he who cries out for the Jews," he said, "has the right to sing Gregorian chant." (Quoted by R.M. Brown, *Theology Today*, 1/67.)